# OUT BACK

**Also by Andrew Stevenson:**

*Annapurna Circuit: Himalayan Journey*
(Constable and Robinson)

*A Nepalese Journey: On Foot Around the Annapurnas*
(Constable and Robinson)

*Kiwi tracks: A New Zealand Journey*
(Lonely Planet)

*Summer Light: A Walk Across Norway*
(Lonely Planet)

Andrew's photography may be viewed on his personal website www.awstevenson.com and readers may contact him by e-mail at stevenson_andrew@ibl.com

# OUT BACK

## ADVENTURES OF AN INTREPID INTERLOPER IN AUSTRALIA

Andrew Stevenson

ALLEN&UNWIN

First published by Travellers Eye in 2003

First published by Allen & Unwin in 2003

Allen & Unwin
83 Alexander Street
Crows Nest NSW 2065
Australia
Phone:  (61 2) 8425 0100
Fax:      (61 2) 9906 2218
Email:   info@allenandunwin.com
Web:     www.allenandunwin.com

National Library of Australia
Cataloguing-in-Publication entry:

Stevenson, Andrew
    Out back adventures of an intrepid interloper in
    Australia.

    ISBN 1 7411 4165 6.

    1. Stevenson, Andrew - Journeys - Australia. 2. Australian
    aboriginies. 3. Australia - Description and travel. I. Title.

919.4047

Set in 10.5/13 pt Garamond by Bookhouse, Sydney
Printed by McPherson's Printing Group, Maryborough, Victoria

10  9  8  7  6  5  4  3  2  1

*To Mum*

# Contents

# Acknowledgements

I'd like to thank Annabel Carter, Belinda Carter, Wenche Fosslien, Ann Mello, Rosemary Rayfuse, Sally Simons, Caroline Stockdale and Ingrid Zondervan for their helpful comments in putting together this description of my trip around Australia.

# Introduction

For a peripatetic cultural nomad such as myself, not having visited Australia seemed a conspicuous oversight, especially given the size of the continent and the relative ease with which I could both get there and travel once I'd arrived. So, a year after spending four months tramping the length and breadth of New Zealand, still single (not by design) and relatively unburdened with responsibilities (read: virtually unemployable), I decided to visit this illusive, ochre land. My original intention, full of extravagant ideas hatched while safely ensconced in an armchair half a world away, was to buy a small plane and fly myself around.

Visitors who had travelled to Australia with the goal of possibly settling there told me that the biggest drawback was its isolation. I disagreed. While this might strike some as naïve, to an erstwhile North American such as myself Australasia seemed remote enough to be a relatively safe haven from much of the turmoil of the world. And while Australia's recent involvement in the war in Iraq and events such as the Bali bombing may have dampened this view it still seems to me an attractive spot to bury one's head in the sand while letting the world hurdle by.

I am as rootless as you will find anyone. Born in Canada, one of four children of a British foreign correspondent, as youngsters we were ferried by cargo ship from posting to posting around the world. Speaking several languages, (some would describe this affliction more succinctly as speaking in tongues) and carrying multiple dog-eared passports, but resident in tiny Bermuda (population 60,000), Australia was not only a place to visit, but potentially a country I might definitely one day call home, assuming of course they'd have me. As an island, albeit a heck of lot bigger than Bermuda's 21 square miles, Australia boasts communities reputed to be the most isolated in the world. And that was something as a resident of a tiny speck of rock in the middle of the Atlantic, 900 miles off the North Carolina coastline, I could relate to.

I have spent almost equal amounts of time in Africa, Asia, North America and Europe, some as a child growing up, some as an adult, still growing up. I loved Africa, and Africans, but recently I find myself increasingly drawn to Asia, which happens to be just a hop-skip-and-a-jump away from Oz. I can list a dozen Asian countries I'd love to explore, and that's not including the allure of the Pacific Isles, which I have yet to discover.

Europe, with its rich history and culture, is of course inherently attractive. Scandinavia in summer is paradise on earth, but then you have to hibernate through the winters. Western Europe provides endless cultural opportunities and inspiration, but more and more I'm drawn to emptier horizons. North America? Well, it definitely has its appealing states and provinces . . . and yes, the more I travel around South America the more intrigued I am by it. But Australia isn't just a place to celebrate summers, or play tourist. This is a place I might just want to put down, dare I say, roots.

So with a suitcase packed, and a flying jacket thrown flamboyantly if temporarily over my shoulder, I set off for the only country that is a continent, as far from tiny Bermuda as I could get. Never good at just taking time off, I decided to write about my adventure. I was undeterred by the perception that Australia might not be the most original premise for a travel book, nor by the fact that I knew very little about the country, its people or its politics. Ignorance can be bliss, or at the very least it can lead down less beaten paths. I still make no claims to be an expert on this fascinating, incongruous land, but I hope I've successfully captured a foreigner's raw yet honest first impressions. I had no axe to grind, and not being Australian I was accepted by Aussies for who I was: a candidly ignorant, sartorially challenged, accident-prone, but by and large inoffensive, guest in their country.

And the flying? Well . . . I had first obtained my pilot's licence when I quit the United Nations and had flown in East Africa for five years during my mid-twenties while incompetently attempting to run my own safari business in the Selous Game Reserve. The quixotic memories of bush flying and the wonderful freedom it entailed are still ingrained in my mind, despite the Tanzanian government's tedious insistence that I was a CIA spy (Austin Powers, maybe . . . Mr Bean, more likely). Australia, at least from the photographs I'd seen, reminded me so much of Africa, and flying about the empty interior of the continent struck me as the best way to see it. But after two weeks comfortably ensconced in Sydney, without doubt the most liveable large city I've ever visited, and having been confronted with the practicalities of finding and buying a plane and then selling it again, I realised this nostalgic flight of fancy would be more time-consuming and far more expensive than I'd anticipated.

Reluctantly, I dropped the idea, along with my authentic retrograde flying jacket (although given my unfortunate flying record, these were probably prudent actions . . . ), boarded a backpacker's bus to Cairns, sat back and relaxed. It was all too easy and too tempting to refuse. I didn't even have to make my own way to the bus station, the 'Alternative Coach Network for the Like Minded Independent Traveller' mollycoddled me right from the start, picking me up from my friend's front door. It lacked the sweeping romance of flying to inaccessible corners of Australia in a light aircraft, but it did entice me out of cosmopolitan Sydney with minimal effort.

So, along with a busload of testosterone-charged Europeans and North Americans, most in their late teens and early twenties, I was spoon-fed quintessential Aussie experiences at archetypal backpacker enclaves all the way up the East Coast—over-nighting at cattle stations, sheep farms, derelict gold mines and beach resorts. Two weeks later, dog-tired by the nocturnal antics of the 'Like Minded', I arrived in Cairns, the end of the line.

While the backpacker's bus would now turn around and haul another newly arrived crew of excitable 'Like Minded Independent Travellers' back down to Sydney, it wasn't until after I had left the East Coast behind me that I felt as if I'd finally arrived in the Australia I'd imagined. And once I had arrived, I wasn't disappointed. It was all that I had expected, and a lot more. The down to earth sense of humour of the Aussies appealed to me, as did their effusive gregariousness, generosity and hospitality despite my less than prepossessing attire: standard backpacker's dress for my entire journey consisting of a pair of increasingly smelly thongs and one set of clothes, indelibly and darkly stained with the fatty drippings of greasy roadhouse food.

Over the next two and a half months I executed a figure of eight around the continent, and the unfolding panoramas I witnessed were as heartbreakingly beautiful as they were diverse. But it was the overriding emptiness that stirred me most. There's something immensely satisfying about being small and insignificant in the midst of a landscape that hasn't changed for millions of years, and where human intrusion is still the exception, not the norm.

It didn't take three months roving around Australia to be fully convinced that this secluded part of the world was the place of the future. Ironically enough, returning to my tiny island in the middle of the Atlantic I met and fell in love with a resident New Zealander. Now, just some years after my big OE in Oz, we're married, with a baby daughter, and I'm champing at the bit to move back to Australasia. Being wedded to a Kiwi you can guess which side of the Tasman Sea that will be . . . but hey, that's close enough to Australia for me, although now, like the T-shirt says, 'I support the Kiwis and whoever's playing the Aussies!'

# 1  Queensland

A beer-soaked poster outside a Cairns bar:

Party Hard!
Free Entry if dressed in board shorts.
Soggy box and wet T-shirt competition
$500 to be won
Titillating games

Avoiding the ubiquitous tourist hangouts, I seek out a regular working man's bar-hotel distinct with lattice ironwork overhanging a wide wooden veranda. The bartender asks, 'Howya goin?' His hair is cut short on the top and sides, but is long and permed at the back. With fingers splayed like a comb, he flicks long curls off his shoulders and asks, 'What'll you have, mate?'

I order a floater, a meat pie drifting in a sea of pea mash, with a beer to wash it down. Waiting for the meal, I ruminate. For the first occasion in a long time, I don't have any commitments, least of all romantic. I've given myself three months off to journey around Australia. Unlike tripping around Africa or Asia, traipsing around this continent has a tantalising extra dimension: for the rootless Western traveller still casting about for a place to call home, this continent is a valid option.

'Good eye, mate,' an Aussie says as he wobbles onto the adjacent bar stool.

'Good eye,' I answer. 'How'ya going?' I ask in the local patois, having picked up the lingo in two weeks travelling up the East Coast from Sydney.

'No worries,' he replies confidently despite the few drinks too many he has on board. He retains rugged good looks despite the likelihood of years of alcohol abuse. His square shoulders, lean frame, blue eyes and tatty, sweat-stained bush hat give him a decidedly authentic Ocker appearance. 'Name is Smithy,' he says, while reaching out a callused hand. 'Done everything in my time: ringer, stockman and jackaroo. Do just about anything I put my hand to.'

'Where're you from?'

'Nowhere. Just keep moving.' He sees me making notes. 'You a writer?'

'I keep detailed diaries of my trips,' I reply. 'Especially conversations.'

'I'm a poet.' He may be able to do just about anything, but he certainly doesn't look like the average poet with his broken nose and tattooed forearms.

'Recite one of your poems,' I challenge.

'Buy me a beer and I will.' He sees me considering the option. 'A Guinness,' he says with the flair of a businessman on an expense account.

I order him a Guinness.

'What kind of poem do you want to hear?' he asks when the Guinness arrives and is securely wrapped within the protective confines of both fists.

'Anything,' I reply.

'How about a love poem?' he asks.

'Sure.'

'OK. This one is called 'For Love'. He leans over the bar and puts his lips down to the glass and sips the Guinness. He stares into the middle distance with his rheumy blue eyes, and concentrates on recalling the poem. He sits upright again and looks at one of the women in the bar as if for inspiration and then recites from memory:

## For Love

I would climb the highest mountain,
I would swim a raging sea,
I would gladly go through the fires of hell,
If you would just say you love me.

'That's really good. Any more?'

'Buy me another beer and I'll tell you a longer one, even better. About the Aborigines.'

I order another.

He finishes the first Guinness and recites easily enough when the second is firmly ensconced within his scarred hands:

## The Australian

In a land unique and shared by all,
They led a simple life,
Hunting to live instead of sport
With rarely a trace of strife.
And then one day big boats came
And were welcomed by these gentle folk.
These beautiful people were herded like cattle
And forced to wear the white man's yoke.
Now living in missions not fit for dogs
Infested with sickness and bugs
These once proud people living in squalor
Dying from alcohol and drugs.
So don't laugh and sneer and put them down;
Long ago their bubble was burst
While the white man gets richer the black man suffers.
Just ask yourself: Who was here first?

'Well put,' I tell him, genuinely impressed.

He assails the second Guinness with a vengeance, downing half the glass at a single go as if he were afraid someone might swipe it away from him.

'Who wrote those?' I ask. This could be just a scam he has perfected to wangle beers out of tourists.

'Me. Who else?' This tough wrangler with the soul of a poet smiles and laughs at my obvious doubt. 'Used to have heaps of them in my head.'

On the scraps of paper on which I have transcribed the poems, he signs his name: *Smithy*. 'Be worth a fortune some day,' he says with apparent conviction.

Studying the ads outside a real estate office so that the automatic sliding doors stay open, I feign oblivion to the satisfying cool current of air spilling by me into Cairn's tropical heat and humidity. With a diligence instigated more by the artificial change in climate than any immediate need for housing, I read:

> You can own your own home in Surfers Paradise
> with no deposit and only $2/week.

Sounds good. Even I could afford two dollars a week. I examine the newspaper clippings pasted on the front window for further details. The caption of each article is highlighted in fluorescent yellow:

> The Gold Coast population will rise by more than 50% in the next fifteen years.
> 58% of new jobs created in Australia were created in Queensland.

We need 94 new houses each week.

Queensland has the best investment scenario.

A middle-aged man steps out of the air-conditioned office and instead of chastising me for emptying his office of the cool air he says, 'Give me ten minutes of your time and I'll show you how you can own your own property here for next to nothing.' Despite my grease-stained shorts, crumpled T-shirt and seasoned sandals, he enthusiastically lures me into his spider's web. 'The Gold Coast is Australia's number one tourist destination,' he says quickly. 'They've got Warner Brothers Movie World, Dreamworld, Tiger Island, Sea World, Wet'n'Wild Park, White Water Mountain, Cable Ski World. You can go scuba diving or bungee jumping.' Ushered inside, the automated doors close behind us. 'You can do anything there and it's just an hour south of Brisbane's international airport and . . .'

Enticing me with the offer of a free coffee, he deftly manoeuvres me to a computer and proceeds to dazzle me by completely changing the financial boundaries of my life situation.

'OK, let's say you're earning 50,000 taxable dollars a year and buy a property worth 200,000.' He pulls a chair beside me and taps numbers into the computer. 'Now, we can create wealth for you by property investment and what we call negative gearing . . .' He quickly glosses through his front-loaded commission and monthly finance charges. Then we meticulously detail the total income, which includes the tenants' monthly rental and annual tax savings from deductions allowed by the government. By pushing a few keys on the computer, pre-calculated figures compute total weekly outgoings of only two dollars weekly. 'How's that?' he says as proudly as a magician pulling a rabbit out of a hat. 'Two dollars a week.'

'I wouldn't mind putting ten bucks aside each week and owning five of these places,' I confess truthfully to the enthusiastic realtor. 'But I'm not earning a taxable living in Australia, so negative gearing doesn't help,' I tell him politely. When he argues back, I give him a reality check, 'Look, honestly, I hate to disappoint you, but I'm just a backpacker, OK, and I'm returning to a crappy old backpacker's lodge which costs a measly $11 a night but that includes a free big dinner.' I shrug helplessly. 'I'm hardly in a position to negative gear my way to the top of the material world when I don't even have a job never mind a taxable income.' I push the chair back and reluctantly accept his business card with a bundle of brochures.

'Imagine, in the same day you could enjoy surfing on golden beaches, bushwhacking in subtropical rainforests, cruising down ocean boulevards in a fun convertible, or a dinner cruise aboard a luxury yacht,' he says, following me outside into the tropical heat, side-stepping crab-like beside me on the sidewalk. 'The Queensland economy has grown by over twenty per cent, matching the economic growth of the Asian Tiger economies. Regional job creation increases are up seventeen-and-a-half per cent and Government projections predict this regional growth will continue to record levels.' He stops walking but continues to spout off his marketing patter, yelling after me, 'By 2041, Queensland is expected to have more people than the state of Victoria and a quarter of Australia's population! Real estate prices are going to *have* to increase so it's a safe investment with a *high* rate of return . . .'

Victoria was populated by the gold rush.

'You're missing your chance for an investment of a lifetime . . .' he yells threateningly after me.

The gold boom ended with a crash too.

I continue along the Esplanade past cafés, ice cream parlours, tour operators and just as I stop in front of an art shop, I hear a scream and then see a woman fleeing two policemen on bicycles. She doesn't stand a chance of out-pacing them. They jump off their bikes, give chase on foot, and catch up to her. They grab her and she kicks out at them with her bare feet, shrieking, 'I didn't do anything you fucking cunts.' They handcuff her. She is frail and skinny and they are big and bulky but she keeps kicking. One of the cops grabs her ankle from behind and pulls, tripping her up. With her hands cuffed behind her back she is unable to break her fall and lands with a loud crack on her cheekbone. They pin her down with their knees. She looks at me with deep-set, frightened eyes, blood pouring from her nose. 'You fucking cunts, I'm going to rip your balls off and take them to heaven.'

'How tight do you want these cuffs?' the younger of the two policemen says to her. He is impatient and angry but conscious of the crowd of onlookers. The other policeman is older but seems more resigned. Young kids in baseball caps and skateboards tucked under their arms smirk at the spectacle. Four shocked tourists stand with mouths open as we witness the woman struggling under the weight of the two policemen's knees pressed hard on her back between her handcuffed arms. One of them reaches for the radio on his belt and calls for support.

Within minutes a paddy wagon arrives and four more policemen emerge. They are so huge their inflated biceps are busting out of their shirtsleeves. I wouldn't want to be in the position of messing around with any one of them, let alone all six. They pick up the woman and dump her kicking and screaming in the cage at the back of the vehicle. Then they drive off and the whole frightening episode is over and the streets of Cairns are sanitised for the tourists again.

She might be an axe murderer for all I know, but my sensibilities are offended by the obvious display of over-whelming force.

I ask the sales assistant who has stepped out from the Aboriginal art store, 'What was that all about?'

'Ah, the Abos in Cans,' she pronounces Cairns 'Cans' with a nasal twang as if her nostrils were welded shut. 'They beg from the tourists and if they don't get a cigarette or money they can get abusive so the police take them away in a divvy van.'

Although they represent less than one per cent of the Australian population, Australia's indigenous people loom disproportionately large in my perspective of this continent. I don't believe I am alone. For many of us visitors to this continent, Australia and its Aborginal people are almost synonymous. Not only neatly packaged and extensively marketed abroad through their art and music, they are advertised as the oldest living culture in the world, isolated for some forty, fifty, or maybe even sixty thousand years. That fact alone would be enough to attract me to Australia, to witness first-hand a people whose culture goes so far into pre-history it makes the origins of Christianity seem contemporary. But with almost a month under my belt in Australia, albeit only in Sydney and the East Coast, I've yet to meet an Aboriginal. It's almost as if the Australia I imagined didn't exist.

I am in awe of the original Australians, an ancient and dignified race in my imagination. My preconceptions about the original inhabitants of Australia derive from the marketing myths portrayed by the tourism industry and the few books, documentaries and films I've seen. To witness a woman treated this way is a rude introduction to the reality of modern Aboriginal life.

My original intention, full of extravagant ideas hatched safely at home, was to buy a small plane and fly around Australia, a continent that has captivated me ever since reading Bruce Chatwin's book *Songlines* about the weird Australian wildlife and how its native people survived in their harsh environment. I had flown my own aircraft in East Africa for five years during my mid-twenties. The memories of flying, the freedom it entailed, are still ingrained in my mind. Australia, from the photographs I'd seen, reminds me so much of Africa, and flying about the empty interior of the continent seemed the best way to see it. But two weeks comfortably ensconced in Sydney, clearly the most liveable large city I've ever visited, and pursuing the practicalities of finding and buying a plane and then selling it again, demonstrated that the notion would be both time-consuming and expensive. Reluctantly, I dropped the idea.

Instead, I took the opposite tack, the course of least resistance. I took the backpacker's bus from Sydney to Cairns and sat back and relaxed. It was too easy and too tempting to refuse. I didn't even have to make my own way to the bus station in Sydney; the Alternative Coach Network for the Like Minded Independent Traveller would mollycoddle me right from the beginning and pick me up. It was hardly the romantic ambition of flying into isolated corners of Australia in a small plane, but it did entice me out of cosmopolitan Sydney with minimal effort.

With a busload of Europeans and North Americans, most in their late teens and early twenties, we were spoon-fed Aussie experiences at backpacker enclaves, overnighting at cattle stations, sheep farms, derelict gold mines and beach resorts, all the way up the East Coast. Two weeks later, Cairns was the end of the line. The backpacker's bus would take an excited, newly arrived crew of Like Minded Independent Travellers back down the coast to Sydney.

Not good at group travel at the best of times, and looking for a way to slip out of the backpacker world, I flip through the newspaper's accommodation section and find a house advertised for rent on a weekly basis. A short phone call later, I check out of the backpacker's. Trevor, my host, is so eager to rent a room that he generously offers to pluck me out of the backpacker's enclave before I change my mind.

Ten minutes later, sitting in his van, we stop at the intersection of a wide back street in the old residential section of Cairns to let an Aboriginal woman cross the road. 'I've been in Australia almost four weeks now,' I observe, 'and that's almost the second Aborigine I've come across. The first was yesterday being chased by a couple of cops down the Esplanade.'

'Aboriginal people, not Aborigines,' Trevor corrects. 'And even the term Aboriginal is contentious. It's the same thing as calling your Sioux, Cherokee and Navaho "Indians".'

'I'm not American.'

'Well, same thing applies to the Canadian Natives then. What were they, Iroquois, Mohawks?'

'I, um, don't know.'

'Exactly.' We accelerate out of the intersection.

'So, what do I say if I don't know the names of an individual Aboriginal clan?' I ask.

'Don't worry, neither do I. Most of us don't.'

'OK, so I haven't seen any Aboriginal people,' I correct myself.

'You didn't see any on the way up here?' he asks.

'Not really; you know, I think I might have seen them in the distance kind of thing, through the bus window, but not really close up.'

'Never went to Redfern in Sydney?'

'Nope.'

'Lots of them live in the ghettos in Sydney and most cities. But you're right in the sense that it shows how effectively the British settlers wiped them out. How long are you going to be in Australia?'

'Two more months.'

'Plenty of time,' Trevor tells me, stopping at traffic lights. 'But if you want to meet them nowadays, you've got to go beyond the black stump.'

'Beyond the black stump?' I repeat, looking around. The streets here are so wide and so empty.

'Yeah. Back of Bourke. Into the Never Never. Back of Beyond . . . You know, the Outback.'

'Ah right, the Outback.'

'If you want to meet some Aboriginals easily, right now, take the train up to Kuranda for the day and come back this evening. It's not far, and certainly not beyond the black stump as anyone from Cairns will tell you, but it's different from what you've experienced so far.' He looks at his watch. 'In fact, if we hurry, you could catch the train.' He drops me off at his home to quickly unload my pack. As he drives to the nearby station he continues on the theme. Once he's on a roll, Trevor doesn't stop.

A human rights lawyer, he is also a born orator. He gives me a quick background of Australia's population. 'Two hundred years ago convicts were considered genetically predisposed to be law-breakers and there was no way to rehabilitate them. Prisons were so full they used hulks of ships to hold the overflow. It wasn't a leap of faith figuring out that the best thing to do was send these genetic deviants to an uninhabited corner of the world and be rid of them permanently. Some prisoners they sent to the colonies in America. More of them, as we all know, were sent here. When the criminals, the scum of Britain, arrived here, they beat up on the original Australians, viewed as being even lower down the chain of human development, and maybe not even human. Some Australian Aboriginals were killed as specimens and their skulls sent back to England to be studied by curious scientists.'

A little old lady scurries across the road. 'When the settlers and squatters first arrived,' Trevor continues, giving the old woman a wide berth but not bothering to stop, 'the Aboriginal warriors had the upper hand. They could escape easily into the bush; they were so good at evading the settlers they even used to bare their bums at the whites to taunt them, until European diseases, poisoning, firearms and probably most effectively, the Native Police killed 'em off.'

'Native Police?'

'Aboriginal troops mounted on horseback, led by white officers; they knew their own people's ways and were lethal in tracking them down in the bush.' His dissertation is interrupted by our arrival at the station. Trevor pulls into the massive building and asks, 'You dive?'

'Yeah.'

'Take you out diving on the Great Barrier Reef tomorrow if you want. I'll book us a couple of places on one of the better dive boats.'

'Great.' Australians have this extraordinary propensity to make friends instantly. I wave at him and quickly buy a ticket and board the train. Despite the huge size of the train station built into the back side of a modern shopping mall, there are only a handful of train arrivals and departures a week, a reminder that Cairns is still at the outer reaches of mainstream Australia.

The historic old Kuranda train threads though rainforest and skirts steep-sided hills and cliffs. It's a dramatic ride. Deliberately not wearing a timepiece, I guess it must be about an hour before I disembark at Kuranda. Trevor was right. Unlike Cairns, so many of Australia's original people wander around the sidewalks that they easily outnumber the whites. These circumstances might seem irrelevant to a white Australian given the dwindling minority of the Aboriginal population, but as a foreigner, it's as if at long last I'm in the Australia I had unrealistically imagined but wanted to see. I wander in and out of the numerous Aboriginal art shops, chatting to the Aboriginals running them.

Today is Thursday, payday. Trevor told me if I wanted to get an idea of what it is like here, the best place to go is the bar.

The gloomy bar at the top end of the settlement is full of equally dark men and women. I walk in, not at all sure about what I am doing. Apart from the bartenders, I am the only white. Many of the clients are clearly already drunk. Despite finding myself thoroughly intimidated, there is a convivial atmosphere. I walk as coolly as I can to the bar counter and stand next to a heavy-set man.

Three thin-lipped unsmiling white female bartenders work efficiently enough, taking money, handing over drinks. The man next to me catches their attention and orders a round of beers for the two of us. We clink glasses together; he doesn't take his eyes off me as we drink, then he thumps his mug on the table. 'Ralph,' he says, offering me his hand.

'Andrew.' We shake hands. His grip is firm.

'Where you from?' he asks, raising his half-emptied glass. His face is partially hidden by a well-worn Aussie hat pressing down a halo of frizzy hair. A thick moustache dripping beer suds reaches down to the bottom of his chin. He tilts his hat back so that he can look me directly in the eye when he speaks.

'Canada,' I reply to keep things simple, although I don't feel Canadian at all and haven't lived there for over a decade. It isn't so simple nowadays to reply honestly and simply to the question, 'Where you from?' You mean, where was I born or where do I live now or where do I consider my home?

'I've been to Canada three times,' Ralph informs me, putting his beer down on the bar and wiping the froth off his moustache. 'With the Tjapukai dance group.' He takes a shine to me, perhaps because I am Canadian.

I ask questions about his people and he politely answers my interminable queries. 'Tell me a story about the mob in your country,' he asks eventually, sipping his beer.

I tell him, 'Well, as you know, Canada is similar to Australia being a big country colonised by white settlers from Britain, and the indigenous people, the North American Natives, were robbed of their land much the same way the Australian Aboriginals have been here.'

He ignores my rhetoric and cuts to the heart of the matter. 'Do you have Native Indian friends in Canada?'

I come here earnestly seeking out Aboriginal friends in Australia, but in my own country, I never bothered doing that with Canadian Natives. I reply, 'It isn't easy. They live on reservations and don't live in white areas so much.' But it's a good point Ralph makes, and in a way he has seen right through me. My excuses for not having any Indian friends aren't any different for many urban whites living here in Australia.

'You know what's strange in Canada?' he asks. I shake my head. 'The streets; even in big cities like Vancouver, the streets are narrower than in Cans.' He says Cairns, 'Cans', like everyone else in Cairns. If everyone in Sydney can say 'Seed-knee' instead of Sydney, there's no reason why people in Cairns can't say 'Cans'.

'You know what I find strange here?' I ask, thankful he's let me off the hook, and changed the topic of conversation.

He shakes his head.

'Your streets; they're so wide.'

He laughs and raises his beer and we clunk glasses again. 'Cultural differences,' he says.

'You still work for Tjapukai?' I ask, pulling a folded brochure of the Aboriginal theme park out of my pocket. My pockets are full of brochures. A whole rainforest must be decimated every day to provide the pulp for all the tourist brochures available.

'I don't dance so much now, I train the others, but that's me on the brochure. I teach tourists how to throw boomerangs, or throw a spear with a *woomera*.'

'A *woomera*?'

'Yeah. It's like a rocket launcher. Gives you more power when you throw the spear by giving extra leverage. We were pretty smart, eh.' On a napkin he draws a diagram for me showing how the *woomera* is held in the same hand with the spear. As the shaft of the spear is thrown, the end, fitted into a notch in the *woomera* stick, is catapulted with even more power, as the *woomera* is swung in an arch after the spear.

Someone comes up to him and asks him for money. He hands over a banknote. 'That's my son.' He points out the door with his chin to a woman lying passed out on the pavement using an empty wine carton as a pillow. 'And that's his mother. He's going to take her home,' he says, matter-of-fact.

We watch as the son helps his mother to her feet and guides her away.

'My ancestors knew the aerodynamics of a helicopter thousands of years ago. It's a rotating wing, same principle as the boomerang.' He points his forefinger into the air and spins it around like a helicopter blade as he makes a whooshing sound. 'Know what we call a boomerang that won't fly?' I shake my head. 'A stick.' He laughs at his own joke although he must repeat it a dozen times a day. 'Used to be a stockman. Tough life that, but it taught me a lot. Sorry my kids won't get a chance to work as stockmen and get out into the bush and toughen up a bit.'

Apparently well respected by his peers, Ralph stands at the bar very sure of himself. We alternate buying each other a round. Several men and women help themselves to a packet of cigarettes in his pocket, as if these are not his so much as a communal resource to which they are entitled. Now that I am in the bar, and after a couple of beers, it doesn't seem nearly as intimidating as it did from the outside looking in. Everyone is friendly. A couple of times a glass of beer is generously offered with an outstretched hand from someone that I have yet to meet. The hospitality and friendliness is remarkable and I feel ashamed I had considered giving the bar a miss just because it was full of people whose skin colour was darker than mine.

Two tourists peer inside the dim bar and are dissuaded from entering.

Ralph says, 'See those two tourists come in and go out again? They have no idea what we are all about. They just see black faces. Even our government officials see us just as black faces. Once we had some Government of Queensland people come up from Brisbane.' He puts his mug down again and wipes his moustache with his shirtsleeve. 'Big *corroboree*.'

'What's that?'

'Meeting. Wanted to discuss land issues with us. All our top blokes were at the meeting, same as all the Queensland Government people. The Minister talked for two hours. Then he says, "Well, I've been talking for a while; you people probably want some time to discuss the issues I've raised." We didn't need to do that. We had been discussing the issues as they were brought up. We communicate with our eyes, our faces, and movements of our hands, fingers and thumbs. We already knew our answers to issues he brought up because we decided each question as he raised them.' He laughs at the memory. 'White people think we're telepathic. Maybe we are.' He shrugs and looks at his watch. 'If I really was telepathic, I'd be rich, but I can never figure out which horse is going to win . . .' He laughs. 'But us Aussies will bet on anything,' Ralph informs me, buying us yet another round. 'National pastime is betting, eh. Bet on two flies on the wall to see which one stays there longest.'

White Australians say that the Aboriginals cannot hold their liquor; that they never had alcohol before the white men came, and that they have not had the time for their genes to adapt so their bodies can process alcohol the same way whites can. Alcohol goes straight to their heads and can very quickly destroy them. I have no idea if that is true, but sitting on the other side of me is an empirical case in point. Although probably quite young, she is also so drunk she is barely able to sit upright. The older man adjacent has to support her although he could very well go down for the count first.

By contrast, on the other side of Ralph is a woman standing alone, waiting to buy a drink. I met her briefly at a community-owned art shop. She impressed me with how ambitious she is for their art business to succeed and her eloquence on Aboriginality. Ralph excuses himself to place a bet on the horses. The woman turns around and recognises me, and we are discussing the merits of their art when a man approaches her from behind.

'Hello stranger,' he says to her aggressively. 'Haven't seen you for a while.' She does not turn around to face him. 'You bloody whore,' he adds with a vengeance. Her face reflects her embarrassment. He is clearly wound up for a fight and hurls more verbal abuse at her, raising his voice, gesticulating violently. 'You think you're fucking smart don't ya? Fucking smart ass.' The two white bartenders come over to keep watch over him. He continues to swear at her, raising his voice. 'Think you're too fucking good for me don't ya?' His eyes are bloodshot, full of anger as he stands behind her, looking as if he is about to punch her. Everyone in the bar turns to see what the commotion is about. I wonder if I have precipitated this tirade by talking to her.

The pub manager tells him. 'That's it. You're cut off from any more alcohol. You're drunk.'

Ralph returns and calmly says to me, 'That's her husband. You'll be right, I'll look after you.' During the ugly scene, which I feel somehow responsible for, Ralph's reassurances are welcome. The woman moves away from her husband to avoid his tirade. He follows her, yelling abuse, and it seems as if everyone in the bar, while resuming whatever they were doing, is ready to step in if he hits her.

A few minutes' later two policemen walk in, immaculate in their starched and ironed uniforms. They are so big they look like over-blown caricatures of themselves. Compared to the ragtag clientele, they are formidable, and armed. Two more policemen stand outside the door keeping an eye on the entrance. The bar is noticeably quieter; half the clientele seem to have melted into the floorboards or walls.

Ralph says angrily, 'They wouldn't mess with me.'

'Why would they?' I ask, surprised. We haven't done anything wrong.

'Because I'd make too much fuss; they can take me if they got a reason but not otherwise. Nobody messes with me, no one makes me out to be a mug.' He relaxes again when the two cops leave empty-handed.

The whole episode is too much for the unfortunate looking woman on the other side of me. She slides off the barstool and lies on the floor in a crumpled heap, no one having noticed. Not even the older man next to her with whom she spent most of the evening bothers to shift her.

For every beer I buy Ralph, he insists on buying a round back. I'm feeling the effects of this largess when I realise it's time to leave if I want to catch the train back to Cairns.

Ralph escorts me outside. He seems genuinely sorry to see me go. 'Next time you come back, come over to my place. Got my own house now,' he says proudly. He yells after me as I walk unsteadily down the street. 'Look me up next time you're here. My last name is O'Reilly.' He holds his forearm up to show me the dark colour of his skin and laughs. 'Someone must have left us O'Reillys out in the sun too long. Someday we'll go back to Ireland and meet our white family.'

Taking the day off to go diving, Trevor listens as I tell him about seeing the woman chased down the Esplanade by the police on bicycles. He turns down the music in the van as he sets off from his typical Queenslander home raised on posts so that air can circulate and cool the house.

He reminisces, 'When I was a student I bought a camper van and drove around Australia. Painted a map of Australia on the side of the van, and marked the dates as I progressed around the country. In the middle of the map I painted an Aboriginal flag. I got so many damn dents in my van, especially on the flag, that I finally gave up and painted out the flag. It was a nice gesture of solidarity on my behalf, but the van was too valuable to get the shit kicked out of it.' He parks his new van in a huge parking lot and we walk through the glittering new shopping complex beside the marina.

The interior of the shopping mall could be anywhere in the Western world. A band, its musicians dressed in identical cowboy outfits: plaid shirts, pointy boots and Stetsons, croon Country and Western songs. We stop to listen. Trevor snorts,

'After two centuries of being stuffed by the British, Australian Aboriginal society has been replaced by the culture of Western cowboys.'

We listen to the end of the cowboy song before I ask, 'So what's the answer to the problems the Aboriginal people face?' As advised, I'm careful to use 'Aboriginal people' instead of 'Aborigines'. Seems a bit of a mouthful. I didn't think there was anything pejorative about the word Aborigine. In fact, the connotation, if anything, for me at least, had been something positive.

'A lot of them will tell you it's a matter of land rights.' An Aboriginal man stops in front of us to watch the cowboy singers. Barefoot, he looks out of place in this white, middle-class setting. A clown hands out balloons filled with helium to the kids. 'Just to give you an example,' Trevor pursues, 'the local mob around here had a network of pathways through the rainforest interior that you saw yesterday when you took the train to Kuranda. They didn't fence off their land; there was no need to. They migrated with the seasons, taking advantage of what was plentiful. After he'd sailed up the East Coast and reached the tip of the York Peninsula in 1770, Captain Cook declared Australia a British territory. Took possession of the continent, just like that. Stands there and says, "I declare this British territory!" There was no treaty with Australia's indigenous people. It didn't matter that there were people already living here.'

The band takes a break.

'I imagine most white Australians have a different perspective of their history.' We head outside.

'Of course they do,' Trevor replies, shielding his eyes from the bright sun, and repeating himself, 'But the fact of the matter is, the Aboriginals *were* the prior owners of Australia and were deprived of their land by European settlement.'

We continue walking along the boardwalk where dozens of boats are about to leave for the Barrier Reef. 'Wasn't that illegal?' I ask naïvely. 'I mean, if there were people here already . . .'

'Of course it was illegal.' Trevor explains, 'European powers expanded their empires three ways: by conquest, cession, or occupation of land that was deemed *terra nullius. Terra nullius* literally means land of no one, and there wasn't much uninhabited land left anywhere in the world two centuries ago. Because Australia's original inhabitants appeared to have no apparent form of social organisation or system of law or "ownership" of land, the continent was conveniently deemed *terra nullius.*'

'Why'd they even bother with that formality?'

'Because, had the British recognised any indigenous population, contemporary English law at that time would have awkwardly provided for the continuation of native law; a lot less advantageous to the white squatters who moved inland and took whatever land they wanted.'

'But it wasn't *terra nullius.*'

'Of course not.' We continue walking, Trevor passionate about the issues he raises. The riverfront is lined with an assortment of tour boats, many of them huge catamarans, about to take thousands of tourists out to the Great Barrier Reef. He stops to look at the water and digresses. 'They caught a salty here not so long ago.'

'You mean a sea crocodile?' I ask incredulously.

'Yeah.'

Shit. In the middle of Cairns.

Excited as I am to dive, I am equally fascinated by the history behind Australia's habitation. I tell Trevor, 'I've started reading up on all this land issue stuff and it's complicated. Sometimes I think I understand it, and then I realise I don't.'

'Look, even us lawyers have trouble trying to figure out who has the right to land in Australia,' he tells me. 'In fact, it's next to impossible, the legalities are so complex I bet less than ten per cent of the Australian population could tell you what it's all about.' He adds, 'Unfortunately, there's no evidence that granting land title has improved the living conditions and lifestyles of the Aboriginal people.'

'But I thought you said it was all about land issues.'

'They've got to raise their self-esteem too, got to have a sense of pride in their identity.'

I follow him to the gangplank of a dive boat. 'But how?'

He stops and shrugs. 'I don't know. One idea would be to take the Union Jack out of the Australian flag and put the Aboriginal one there, instead. A gesture like that would help.'

Almost half of my life I have spent either growing up in developing countries, or working in developing countries for the United Nations, bilateral aid agencies, or non-governmental aid organisations, a career I found at the same time fascinating, fulfilling and frustrating. In the end I quit working trying to help others and started doing things for myself. It didn't seem to me there was any easy solution to helping people to help themselves. There was an inherent contradiction to the paradigm anyway. Foreign aid to assist Third World nations become self-reliant inevitably had the opposite effect. The same problem exists with the Aboriginal people and it's difficult to know what is the best policy for them but to me, their history seems particularly tragic. First hunted down like vermin, then forced onto missions and reservations to protect them from the settlers, and then this century coerced to assimilate into white society. Now with the rise in awareness of indigenous people's rights all over the world, there is an Aboriginal-inspired movement towards self-determination and even the spectre of a separate nation, of two Australias.

But the possibility of self-determination becomes clouded when defining who is an Aboriginal person. Before arriving here I had thought of them as being a homogeneous group. I realise now that they are as disparate as African tribes, the First Nations Americans, or European nations, with different languages, customs and personality traits. Many are no longer full-blooded and statistics show more than fifty per cent of Aboriginal Australians marry people with no Aboriginal ancestors. If the trend continues, or more likely accelerates, within a few generations most Australians will have Aboriginal forebears somewhere in their family tree, which would make nonsense of a separate nation.

A crewmember looking suspiciously like Mel Gibson yells at us from the deck. 'You two coming on board or not? We're waiting for you.'

Trevor turns to me. 'You don't have to talk about this on the boat, but I'll give you some books to read when we get back.'

We are the last clients to board. The mood instigated by our heavy conversation dissipates with the irrepressible humour of the boat crew.

'Any Americans here?' the captain asks as we set out. Someone raises his hand. 'Well it's obvious you've never dived in Australia before and we might not let you now either.'

'What do you mean? I've got my diving certificate,' the American replies defensively.

'Get the bungee chord and tie it to his ankles,' the captain tells his crew.

'Bungee cord?' he asks. 'On a dive boat?' The American doesn't get the joke.

One thing I have learnt already: Aussies love to take the piss out of everyone and everything, including themselves.

The captain explains. 'Ever since that dive boat lost those two Americans during a dive in 1997, we make sure if we have any Americans on board, we secure them to a bungee cord, just in case they get any ideas about abandoning us.' The crew and dive instructors laugh more than we do. 'Just joking folks. Now that we have the introductions over with, our safety course.' The boat leaves the dock in the company of dozens of other boats of varying size and description, all commuting into the Great Barrier Reef. It looks like rush-hour traffic.

A crewmember puts a life jacket over his head and ties it around his waist and tells us formally: 'Three warnings if there is something wrong with this vessel. First warning, if you find water up to your knees, be suspicious. Second warning, if you hear the captain yell, "Get off!" you should be more suspicious. Third and final warning: if you see the seven crew members in the dinghy 300 metres behind you, be highly suspicious that the Queensland Government is about to reclassify this vessel as a submarine with the floating qualities of a mooring block. In other words, abandon ship.' He looks around. 'Clear?' He takes the life vest off. 'Good. Now on to more important things, like, if you want a drink, just put a tick beside your name on this list. Whatever you want, drinks, food, underwater camera, sunscreen, boyfriend for the night, just tick it off. We've also got an underwater video filmmaker on board, and if you want a video of yourselves diving off the Great Barrier Reef, tick him off now so he knows who to make a star and who not to. And by the way, when that bottle of sunscreen says it's waterproof, they mean the container, not the sunscreen. After you've been diving, put the sunscreen back on again.'

Behind us on shore, two white-breasted sea eagles sit conspicuously in a tree. 'Those birds mate for life,' one of the crew says after pointing them out. 'Bit unusual for us Australians.'

Within minutes of setting out we see some two dozen river dolphins, then two green turtles and the dark shadow of a manta ray. The captain informs us, 'Our first stop will be a shallow dive off a mid-shelf reef. Then we'll head further out to a ribbon reef, or outer reef.' He gives his daily spiel. 'The reason we're lucky enough to have the Great Barrier Reef is because we have perfect conditions of salinity, temperature and sunshine. Only three places on the planet have fringe reefs: here, Thailand and Columbia. The living reefs are protected from the sunshine by mucus, which acts as a sunscreen. Yep, that's right, just like you, reefs are living animals. If the conditions are not perfect, the coral can get sunburned too. It's called bleaching. Speaking of which, when you see coral in souvenir shops, don't buy it. They're animals that have been soaked in chlorine to make them white, and then painted to make them look pretty. Dead coral without the bleaching or the tinting looks brown and yucky. Bit like us when we are dead and left hanging around for a while. Buying coral that has been dyed a pretty colour is like . . . like buying a stuffed puppy.'

'Ah, dunno about that,' one of the crew comments, 'If it was painted a nice colour it would be pretty good, eh?'

I reckon they've got this banter carefully rehearsed.

Trevor briefs me on what we are about to see as we sip hot tea to wash down complimentary pastries from the galley. 'The Great Barrier Reef Maritime Park is bigger than Britain in area. The sea itself is pretty well lifeless but the reefs contain more marine life and plants than anywhere in the world; you'll see so many fish you'd never think you'd be able to categorise them. But it's not that difficult if you divide all those colourful reef fish into several different groups. Once you have those divisions under your weight belt, it's a lot more interesting as you get to recognise the fish and differentiate amongst them.'

There are twenty divers on our boat including the crew. 'Doesn't this tourism disturb the coral?' I whisper to Trevor.

'Two million tourists a year are bound to have a negative effect, but the real threat comes from the runoff of fertilisers and muck from the farms and cattle stations and from over-fishing the reef. Sixty years ago the coral reefs were being destroyed faster than the rainforest and most people didn't know or care. With so many people snorkelling and diving nowadays, there's a greater awareness of the economic basis for protecting the reefs and the animals that live there. In that respect, tourism has helped preserve the reefs because there's a greater perception by the public of what is going on.' Trevor gets us both a refill of tea and Danish pastries. 'Comes with the cost of the trip, might as well stock up,' he says as he piles the pastries onto his plate again. Not only are the pastries free, but the dive boats are so competitive that Trevor has been given a complimentary pass just for bringing me along.

An hour or so later the boat anchors off a patch reef and we suit up and flip backwards into another world.

Sandy patches between the coral are full of pelagic or predatory travelling fish, streamlined and darting about like so many flashing knives thrown by a circus juggler. Almost as soon as we enter the water, batfish swim around us, hoping to be fed. They brush against our bodies and swim past my mask so close and fast they make me dizzy. Shaped roughly like pet angel-fish, but the size of a bicycle wheel, they are intimidating even if they are harmless. They broil the water like gargantuan piranhas in a feeding frenzy as they fight for bread thrown in by our skipper. A huge Maori wrasse the size of a bathtub floats by. Within minutes of diving down to the lower part of the coral reef, I find myself nose to nose with a white-tipped reef shark resting in a cave. I can see the details of its eyes. I had glibly accepted conventional wisdom that white-tipped reef sharks are harmless, when I was safely out of the water. But the homily is decidedly debatable in the present circumstances. I stare, the shark stares back, and nothing happens. Surviving this encounter, several minutes later Trevor places his hand over his head like a fin and points at another reef shark approaching us, its tail swishing lazily sideways. There's not a hell of a lot I can do about it. I can't out-swim it, certainly couldn't beat it up.

Like their colourful airborne namesakes, tiny butterfly-fish flit in and out of coral crevices. Trevor points out several tiny wrasse picking at a cod at what he describes as a cleaner station. A unicornfish is obviously named even if I haven't been briefed on it beforehand. So is the double-horned cowfish. The dive of forty-five minutes goes by quickly. I am tempted to stay down and finish my tank, but Trevor signals for me to come to the surface. He asks, 'How'd you like it?'

I take off my mask and tread water. 'It was great . . . but . . .'

'Great but . . ?'

'I thought it was better diving in the Whitsunday Islands at the lower end of the Great Barrier Reef National Park.'

'It is.'

'Why's that?'

'Protected waters down there so it's not over-fished, and there's less runoff from farms.'

'Why don't more people dive there?' I ask, taking the goggle and snorkel off my face.

'The international airport is here, the infrastructure, the marketing.'

'But it was definitely a lot better diving in the Whitsundays.' That was the highlight of my trip up the East Coast. Three days sailing and diving off the Whitsunday Islands was paradise, the islands largely untouched by human development and the waters teeming with fish. By comparison, the diving around Cairns is overrated. I'm hesitant to admit this, like the fairytale of the little urchin in the street telling the townspeople the emperor isn't wearing any clothes. We swim towards the back of the dive boat.

When we board, the dive master asks us what we saw. 'Heaps of parrot fish,' an Australian woman says excitedly as she sits on the side of the boat and pulls off her flippers. 'We could even hear them munch on the coral like cows grazing.'

'Did you know,' a dive instructor says as he sidles up to her, 'That parrot fish are females until they come to their senses and become males?' he winks conspiratorially at his mates and subconsciously flexes his swollen pectoral muscles. His biceps are so large he can't keep his arms down by his sides; he has to walk around with his arms up, like a crab. Funny how guys will do that: build up their pectoral muscles so much because that is what they see in the mirror, and then neglect their back muscles, so that the overdeveloped pectoral muscles pull their shoulders forward, giving them that awkward crab-like stance. They are almost all nut-brown, freckled, muscular, covered in bleached blonde body hair and overconfident. They seem maddeningly self-satisfied, but that interpretation could just be jealously on my behalf.

'Shows you what little they know,' the Aussie woman from Sydney replies sarcastically, handing her flippers to the dive instructor. 'I don't know about you mate, but I definitely wouldn't model my future career, or sex, on the basis of what a simple-minded parrot fish does.'

Clearly out of intellectual depth, the dive instructor involuntarily flexes his pectorals again, not giving up his chances of a date. 'Did you see any crown-of-thorns starfish?' he asks her conversationally.

'What are those?' she replies sceptically, moving away from him as he insinuates himself closer to her.

'Biggest threat to our coral reefs are thick-skinned starfish; they eat hard coral, spit it out, and eat it again. Mouth and anus are the same hole.' He pulls a face. 'So, if it has bad breath, it's not its fault. Latin name is *crapus crapus*.' He obviously has this routine well rehearsed. 'Imagine going into a pub, having dinner and spewing it out, and then eating the vomit up again. You'd probably be called something like *crapus crapus* too.'

'Wouldn't surprise me at all to see that happen in a pub in Queensland,' she throws back at him, unimpressed.

The dive instructor tries to amaze the street-smart Sydney woman with even more information, indiscreetly eyeing her figure. 'Did you know the sea cucumber throws its lungs out its anus when annoyed?'

'Annoyed by you, mate, even I'd consider that an option too,' she warns without a trace of a smile.

Although there are more crew and dive instructors on the boat than clients, the professionals leave the Sydney woman to her own devices. Her quick wit and urbane tongue is too much for them.

It takes some hours to reach the fringe reefs. Once there we do one shallow dive and then move to the outer reef where we do a drift dive of more than twenty metres depth. The drift dive is less relaxing. Strong currents, like underwater storms, sweep us between coral heads to meet up with the boat further down the reef. It doesn't surprise me that two diving tourists could have disappeared. As we climb back into the boat the dive master checks our names meticulously against a manifest.

'What do you think happened to the two Americans who disappeared during a dive?' I ask earnestly, still high on the underwater experience. Now that I've survived my own drift dive I'm cocky enough to ask what happened to the others.

'It was staged. Americans are trying to ruin our tourism,' the captain replies, dismissing my question.

'Strange way to sabotage your diving industry,' I comment, not unfairly in my opinion.

'What?' he asks, as if he had just noticed me for the first time.

'Sending out two sacrificial Americans to sabotage your reputation? Anyway, that isn't the point is it?'

'What's the point?' he asks.

'Whether they staged their own death, a suicide pact, nutters, or two spies, the point is, the skipper and crew of the boat didn't know they were missing until the dive boat was docked and they noticed the unclaimed clothes and shoes on board' I reply. 'And by then it was too late.'

That evening I return to the working man's bar. A burly man with bulging, tattooed biceps, flowing red hair and manicured beard saunters over and stands at the bar next to me, interrupting my metaphysical musings. He orders a drink. His hair is short on the top and sides and long and curly at the back, same as the bartender. 'Howya goin, mate?' he says to me.

'By bus,' I reply literally.

'Ah yeah, where you been?' he asks, not put off by my reply.

'Up the East Coast on the Alternative Coach Network for Like Minded Independent Travellers,' I expand. 'I still happen to have the brochure describing the trip.' I pull the brochure out of my back pocket and hand it to him.

He studiously examines the brochure, including the small print at the bottom of the folded pamphlet:

> This paper is recycled, non gloss,
> and unbleached—good for the
> environment, easy on the bum.

'Whad'ya drinking, mate?' he asks, giving me back the brochure. I've barely sucked the suds off my beer but he buys us both a round anyway with the open hospitality Australians are celebrated for.

The bartender serves us beers and resumes his habit of combing his permed locks with his fingers and then flicking his hair over his shoulders.

My new friend waxes lyrical, overwhelming me with Australian affability. 'We got a good life here in Oz, mate.' He raises his glass to that and winks at me. 'You're not an Aussie unless you drink, fight and fish,' he says after he finishes the contents in one go and thumps the mug on the bar. 'We got heaps of beer, tons of beaches and plenty of sheilas. Perve the sheilas, do what you have to do. She goes or she don't. Spread her legs, suck face for a dollar, maybe go halves in a baby. I'm no oil painting, but my little girl, she goes great.' He wears a sleeveless tank top, which looks as though his mother might have bought it for him when he was a child and it subsequently shrunk in the wash; as if he swallowed a soccer ball, his furry red beer belly protrudes from under the bib-sized top. His diminutive stubby shorts are too tight to slip a coin into never mind the sum extent of his family jewels. 'My wife and I split up, mate.'

'Ah yeah,' I drawl in the vernacular.

Satisfied with my answer, he orders another round of beers.

'She got the house and the kids but I got my bike and my sheila,' he continues. 'Going to retire when I'm forty and buy a place down in Surfers Paradise; ride around on the Harley, take it easy. It's a good life, eh?'

He's a truckie, driving road trains up and down Australia.

I shout another round as a pair of Irish dentists, who were on the Alternative Coach Network coming up from Sydney, recognise me and join us at the bar. While my Australian mate has been loquacious with me, he is strangely reticent with the two Irishwomen present, like a bashful teenager. Despite his bravado about perving the girls and taking them for rides to motels on his Harley and doing what a guy has got to do, this trucker is painfully shy when it comes to actually conversing with members of the opposite sex. Their quick chatter is too much for him, and intimidated by their conversation, he takes his leave.

After spending the morning at the Australian Flying Doctor Service, the local manager generously obtains approval for me to fly on one of their routine flights out of Cairns to the interior of Cape York. It's the only way I can get there. Beyond Cape Tribulation, the roads are still inundated after the Wet, and the regular mail plane is fully booked with residents trying to get back to their homes or farms.

At dawn the next day I wait on the tarmac talking to Dr Cathwell Ross. Jarrod, the charter pilot on loan today while the regular Flying Doctor aircraft is being serviced, does his preliminary exterior checks. The lingering smell of aviation fuel and the sound of turbo-props coughing into life are reminders of how I had hoped to travel around the continent. 'This is one of our routine flights to the interior of Cape York,' Dr Ross tells me with evident pride, 'to provide medical care to an area larger than Western Europe, roughly the size of continental United States, excluding Alaska.

Average forty-six emergency retrievals a day, mostly from vehicle accidents.'

We board the aircraft and I take the co-pilot's seat up front with Jarrod. Dr Ross and a nurse are more comfortable sitting behind, reading their newspapers. Six months ago, Jarrod had to belly-flop a twin-engine aircraft here with its landing gear jammed in the 'up' position and half of Australia watching on television.

Within minutes of taking off, we leave the coastline bordering the azure waters of the Great Barrier Reef and fly over the rolling green landscape of the Atherton Tablelands. We head directly West, beyond the green belt of coastal vegetation, into the dry red bush of the Outback. For most of the flight, there is no sign of human habitation or infrastructure.

Half an hour later, a splattering of white buildings marks the old gold-mining settlement of Chillagoe: total population 300. Thankfully, the landing gear drops into position and three green lights indicate we won't be making a belly-flop onto the runway. A car pulls onto the empty airstrip as the twin props shudder to a stop. Although it is early in the morning, and dry, it is already hot. The air smells parched and dusty. The resident nurse greets us affably and drives us the short distance to the immaculate sixty-year-old community hospital, an old low-slung wooden building with a surrounding covered porch. The atmosphere in Chillagoe perfectly fits my preconceived notion of an Australian Outback settlement.

Nola, a stocky no-nonsense woman doubling as the hospital caretaker, welcomes us to a table covered in fresh white linen and loaded with pancakes, tea, jam and thickened cream, or as they call it here, Malanda Dollop. Dressed in work overalls, she hospitably pours everyone tea and loads our plates with pancakes.

Although there are no patients lying in the empty hospital beds, already waiting for the doctor is Wayne, wearing stubby shorts, an open sleeveless shirt without buttons and a coiffure which has been untouched by comb for months, if not years. Barefoot, his feet are as worn as old leather boots. Although he is probably around my age, he is prematurely wrinkled from exposure to the sun. His right forearm and wrist are swollen to twice their normal size and he's reluctant to admit how it got that way.

Dr Ross inspects his injury while I wander around the museum-like hospital. A poster on the wall advises:

Eat good tucker. Be strong for yourself.
Too much sugar, butter, oil, margarine,
soda pop, cigarettes and lager leads to diabetes,
heart problems, stroke, kidney damage.

There's also a poster advertising the upcoming 'Chillagoe Big Weekend':

Friday—meeting of the sportsmen and dance
Saturday—Chillagoe turf club annual race day
Saturday night—country music spectacular
Sunday—annual rodeo

Wayne refuses the doctor's advice to go to the nearest town to have his arm X-rayed. There isn't much she can do in the circumstances. He leaves and Nola sits down to have a cup of tea with me and a bit of gossip. 'We had a visiting nurse here once,' she says, casting her eyes about to make sure no one is listening. 'Wayne asked her out. I warned the nurse, but oh no, she wouldn't listen to me. Said "He wouldn't dare touch me". That evening, the nurse came back disgusted. Her shirt was all crumpled and her hair was out of place. "Never go out with him again. He doesn't bother asking either." Boy, she was mad something wicked.'

Even without hearing about Wayne's reputation with women, it's hard to imagine a nurse willing enough to go out with him. Nola whispers to me, 'He threw his first wife off the second-floor balcony. Dragged his second wife up the front steps of the pub by the hair.' She pours another cup of tea and loads more pancakes on my plate before adding, 'Wayne's a builder and he's flattened three building inspectors in his time.' She raises her eyebrows to emphasise that bit of scandal. 'He can be pretty handy to have around but you don't want to mess with him.'

To kill time, Nola asks cordially, 'You wanna see the town?'

'Sure.'

She leads me out into the blazing heat and we climb into the hospital ambulance, a 1950s model resembling an American pickup converted to an ambulance. 'Never been further than Cans in my life,' she tells me as we rattle away at ten kilometres an hour in the big old emergency vehicle. 'Born and bred here.'

This is the real Australia, I reflect, as we drive through Chillagoe, which doesn't stretch more than 100 metres from the crossroad in any direction. The centre of town is the Black Cockatoo Pub. A sign outside, 'Ice cold beer, friendly service', has been defaced; the words 'beer' and 'friendly' have been crossed out. She points out a building. 'There's the town hall where we have dances and there's the general store and that's the coffee shop. The post office is in the hotel, there's a butcher, and there's a bakery and a Laundromat. Good, eh?' There's not a car in sight, not even parked, never mind no traffic. The generous width and long length of the road emphasise the eerie emptiness of this settlement. It looks like a ghost town. You could land a Boeing on its main street and no one would be the wiser. 'Goldmine's been closed down for a while but people are coming back.'

'Why's that?' I ask, not sure from the tone of her voice whether Chillagoe's re-population is a good thing or not.

'Ah look; it's people on the dole. They come out here because housing is cheap and 'cos they know they won't get a job so they can stay on the dole.' She stops the ambulance at what looks like a huge block of concrete. 'That's marble,' Nola says proudly, pointing at the grey slab. 'And that there is the souvenir shop. You can get anything in there.' We walk in and she's right, you can get anything in there as long as what you want is kitsch knick-knacks made from marble. 'Beautiful things here, eh,' Nola comments, picking up a marble ashtray and passing it on for me to cherish.

'Don't smoke,' I say when I have admired it sufficiently to hand it back to her graciously.

'That's OK; you don't have to buy it. You can just look,' Nola confirms, glancing at the owner, 'Owns the Laundromat too. Good, eh?' she says enthusiastically.

What does Nola's friend do in this shop all day? Wait, hope and pray someone will come by? Who would come by, besides visitors Nola brings over in the ambulance? Maybe during the Chillagoe Big Weekend . . .

Nola stands there like a tough guy, thumbs hooked in the pockets of her work pants, with dirty sneakers and a worn green work shirt. I'd bet she'd be pretty handy to have around too and I bet you wouldn't want to mess with her either. She catches me staring at her and I smile innocently, trying to disguise my thoughts.

Not needing any marble knick-knacks, we climb back into the ambulance. 'I'll take you to the church.' Nola insists I do up my safety belt, despite the fact that we haven't seen another vehicle yet. We drive over to the other side of the road. It takes more time to get in the ambulance, buckle up, start the engine, unbuckle and get out, than if we had just strolled across. 'Church is beautiful, eh?' Nola asks as we stand in front of a structure made entirely of corrugated tin, sides, roof and all. 'It's painted white all over.'

'Do you come to his church?' I ask as we enter the corrugated tin church painted white all over.

'Nah, I'm not churchified.' Nola's enthusiastically delivered tour of the interior is interrupted when a man walks in with a crab-like gait and a small girl in the crook of a colossal arm. 'This is our police officer,' she says when she notices him.

Are all Queensland policemen built like body-builders on steroids?

'Everything OK?' he asks, no doubt concerned at the inauspicious sight of the town ambulance, the only vehicle around, parked in front of the church.

'Yeah, except we have heaps of lamingtons in our freezer,' Nola replies, happy to report the latest municipal emergency to the authorities. 'Electricity went off at the school and the cakes are going off; only two dollars fifty per dozen. Come over now and I'll give you some for free.' We walk out into the blinding sunlight and blazing heat. 'I'll put the billy on for ya,' she adds as an additional incentive.

Apart from the police Landcruiser, we still haven't seen a single other vehicle. Even Wayne walked to the hospital because he's off the road for drunken driving. An elderly Aboriginal couple with a small child in hand asks Nola for a lift to the hospital. It's only 200 metres or so but she agreeably offers them a ride. They cram all together in the front seat with Nola while I climb into the back of the ambulance. I overhear their conversation about the relative merits of four-gear transmission boxes versus a three-gear box as we rattle down the road to the hospital where Nola immediately heads around the back to fetch lamingtons, sponge cake covered in chocolate icing and topped with a layer of coconut. I join the two Aboriginals waiting on wooden benches on the front portion of the hospital porch. They seem a nice older couple. 'Is this your child?' I ask to break the barriers of shyness as their cute little boy comes around the corner with a deteriorating lamington held proudly in his tiny hands.

'No, he's my cousin's son,' the woman replies. 'We adopted him because my cousin is an alcoholic.'

Dr Ross calls the boy in and the aunt gets up to accompany her adopted son.

The man tells me in a quiet voice, 'Used to be a ringer; worked with cattle all my life. Retired now. We like it here,' he says. 'It's peaceful.' He is reserved but once he warms up, is talkative enough, but he becomes uncomfortable when I ask too many direct questions and he excuses himself, 'I better go in with them.'

Around the back porch a tea party is in full swing with Nola pulling an unending supply of lamingtons out of the freezer. Mynah birds fly cheekily onto the table to steal crumbs from under our noses. Despite her rotten teeth and a smoker's cough, an emaciated woman radiates old-fashioned elegance, as if she had been a lithe ballet dancer half a century ago. Her grey hair is pulled back tightly and tied neatly with a ribbon. She says to no one in particular, 'See the big lightning on the weekend?' She shakes her head at the memory. 'Four or five flashes at once; cat went crazy. But no rain.' She pulls out of her trance and asks me directly, 'Where you from?'

'Canada,' I reply, keeping my story simple.

'Ah, never been there. Next time you're back, think of me will ya? I'd love to sit in front of a fireplace and feel the cold. Never seen snow.' She drifts off into her own world again, obviously happy to have the social occasion to sit and chat with others.

'Had to pull a king brown out of a house the other day,' the policeman says, making conversation.

'True?' the frail ballet dancer shudders. 'You'd have to be crazy to do that. Hate snakes, especially king browns.' When no one follows up on her conversational gambit, she asks Jarrod the pilot, studiously reading the newspaper from cover to cover, 'How's Cans?'

'Still there,' he replies without looking up. 'No dramas.' The front page of the *Cairns Post* has a photo of a teenager under the headlines 'Bicycle theft leaves dream in tatters'.

'Went to Cans once,' she comments.

An unkempt older man climbs the wooden steps onto the porch out of the heat and sunlight. Like Wayne, he is barefoot although he looks like he might have tried to dress up for the occasion; he wears clothes that once were white, but are now covered in grime and red dirt.

'How's it here in Chillagoe?' the pilot asks without taking his eyes off the newspaper as the old man brushes by.

'Fire a cannon down the main street during rush hour and still not hit anything,' the newcomer replies. Like the aged ballet dancer, he doesn't really seem to care if anyone is listening to him or not. A road map of purple capillaries shows through layers of greasy white sunblock slopped messily over his nose and face. He removes his wide-brimmed Aussie hat revealing a bald head, glistening with perspiration. His trousers are held up with a belt tied around the tops of his trousers outside the belt loops. Like Wayne, his shirt is devoid of a single button. The back of his neck and hands are deeply creased by years of exposure to the sun.

The frail ballet lady mumbles, 'Saw sex on the TV last night. It was something awful. What if kids were watching?'

'Went to Cans once,' the old guy mutters to himself more than the rest of us. 'Now it's over-run, over-crowded, over-rated and they all have a motor car.' He shakes his head and helps himself to a lamington. 'It was OK in 1930 when I was there.' He swallows the cake quickly then replaces his hat, permanently sweat-stained around the brim. 'Well, I might as well burn off into the sunset.' With that, he gets up slowly, helps himself to another lamington for the road, and walks into the glaring sunlight.

'He's just going to the dunny,' Nola says dismissively.

'He doesn't take any medication except for his Four-X,' the frail one admonishes while lighting another in an endless chain of cigarettes. 'His bedroom is full of empty beer bottles and meat pie wrappers.'

How does she know?

'Used to come over and cut my lawn. Doesn't any more,' she adds as if she could read my thoughts.

'Anything exciting ever happen here?' I ask the doctor when no one else seems to have anything to add.

'Had a dog brought in with snakebite last trip,' she amplifies. 'And before that we had a wallaby that was in pretty bad shape. Put its name down as Wallaby Smith for the paper work. The wallaby recovered but he was just wild about women and would attack the nurses' legs and really go at it. Had to catch him and de-sex him. Tried to bush it too, but it just followed us home, no problem.'

Dr Ross shows me around the hospital. 'What's the biggest health problem here?' I ask.

'Alcohol. And the problem is about evenly divided between the Aboriginal community and the white community. Probably have as many, if not more, alcoholics amongst the whites.'

'And the patients? What percentage is white compared to Aboriginal?' I ask.

'About ten to fifteen per cent of our patients are Aboriginal, in a community where they are almost half the population,' she replies without hesitation.

'So, why aren't the figures higher?'

'Probably a hangover from the days when Aboriginal patients, if they were treated at all, tended to be treated on the hospital veranda because they were considered more of a burden than as people entitled to receive health care.'

We have a final cup of tea and a last lamington before flying on to the next clinic. Just as we are about to go, an Aboriginal woman arrives to see the doctor. Nola tells her, thumbs in her pockets, 'Visiting hours are until one, and it's five past one. You're late. You'll have to come back in two weeks when the doctor is here again.'

The Aboriginal world and the Western world clash once again. As we drive out to the airstrip, we pass the woman trudging barefoot along the edge of the road in the heat of the day.

Not able to get a seat on the post plane flying up to the York Peninsula, Cape Tribulation is as far north of Cairns as I can get, by road. The air-conditioned minibus follows the winding coastal road that must be one of the most scenic I have seen anywhere, and hours later drops me off at a tented resort hidden in the depths of the coastal rain forest. I book myself on the nocturnal guided walk, find my tent on the outer edges of the resort, and collapse on the bed, the heat and humidity conspicuous after the air-conditioned bus ride.

When night falls, terrifying primeval sounds echo in the steaming, dark, tropical lowland rainforest.

The guide for our nocturnal walk resembles Hollywood's WC Fields. He has the same large purple nose, the same beer gut. 'Everyone ready?' he asks impatiently.

A desperate cry emanates scarily from the forest we are about to enter. WC's portly figure doesn't inspire confidence. We need a straight-talking Harrison Ford to lead us through this jungle, not a wisecracking WC Fields. Twelve tourists assemble around him: Dutch parents with two children, a young American, several British backpackers, a German couple and myself.

I glance at them and recognise the same worried looks on their faces.

He equips each of us with a head-torch connected to a heavy battery, which we attach around our waists with a belt. 'When I show you something, you must all stop and watch me carefully. There are lots of dangerous things in this tropical lowland rainforest and you don't know about them, but I do.'

We crowd around him a little tighter than before, glancing over our shoulders into the spooky darkness of the rainforest.

'For example, this is the gympie-gympie or the stinging tree.' His beam of light is directed at a nearby bush. 'The leaves are covered in minute stiff hollow hairs each with a swollen base containing an irritant comprised of formic and acetic acids, histamine and at least one other unidentified pain-producing chemical,' WC rattles off by rote. 'When you brush against these leaves, the hairs, like slivers of glass, enter the skin and break off, injecting some of the irritant. At first,' he looks at the kids, 'you'll just feel an itching sensation. Then huge *blisters* will form, and then,' he opens his beady eyes wide at them and leans towards them, '*intense* stabbing pain which can last several hours, days, weeks and even *months.* Affects *kids* much more than adults.' Not only does he look like WC Fields, he seems to have an aversion to kids as well. He bends over even further so that his red nose is almost level with their little faces. 'You're not as big as I am, and your little bodies can't absorb the poison and mine can. You'll be lucky not to *die.* So keep an eye out, and do *exactly* what I say.'

We watch our footsteps carefully as we tread down a well-used path. No one says anything.

'Within a hectare we have over 120 different tree species, more than you will find on the entire European continent,' he says as he leads us into the dense Daintree rainforest. His torch beam cuts into the tangle of vegetation above us and with a theatrical wave of his shaft of light, he illuminates a long vine looping from one tree to another. 'That is a liana.' He shines the light beam up and down the trunk of a tree. 'Around the tree you can see a *strangler* fig.' He wipes the perspiration off his face with a soggy handkerchief.

Despite the tropical heat, I wear jeans tucked into my boots. Others wear shorts and open sandals. Shining their torches up and down their legs, they search for scorpions or giant centipedes crawling up their bare limbs. As we continue along a path, light beams probe the darkness to spot jungle creatures before they see us. Unidentified cries resonate in every direction. While we look out for the really big dangerous creatures, WC seems to have a peculiar fascination for 'crickets'. He identifies five different kinds of cricket and details their ho-hum genealogy and then just as we are being lulled by his commentary into a false sense of security, all of a sudden he stops in his tracks and yells *'Look out!'* He bends down and grabs a snake close by his feet and shakes it violently in our faces.

'Ha ha,' he laughs, having scared us out of our wits. 'It's only a rubber one.' He hides it beside the tree trunk, coiled and ready for the next unsuspecting group.

A lot more alert than before, when WC points out a cassowary plum tree, we bunch together for protection against his schoolboy wit. He says to the kids, 'The cassowary plum tree is *poisonous* to us, but not to the cassowary. Keep your eye out for those cassowaries, because this is one of the places they definitely still inhabit. If you see one, they can be *aggressive*. They are bigger than any of us and the best thing to do is raise your hand above your head with something in it, like a camera, and make yourself look as tall and intimidating as possible.' The woman next to me removes her camera strap from around her neck and holds the camera in her hand, ready to raise above her head in case we come across Australia's version of Big Bird. We wait for WC to reach behind the cassowary plum tree to pull out a giant rubber cassowary to shake it at us, but he doesn't.

Further down the path I see something about a metre in length, clinging to a vertical vine. It looks like a brown iguana. 'Er, WC, there seems to be some kind of large lizard here,' I say, unsure what it is I am looking at. It could be made of rubber too.

WC comments, 'Ah yes, that's a Boyd's forest *dragon*.' We shine our torches into its eyes, transfixed by the odd reptile. We have empirical evidence now of how easily creatures can camouflage themselves, even dragons.

The American teenager is so enthusiastic about this nocturnal walk in the rainforest that he cannot restrain himself from asking a succession of questions. 'I'll tell you later,' WC replies so often the disappointed American remarks, 'That's an awful lot of things you are going to tell us later.'

WC steps off the path again to lean against a small tree. As he explains some esoteric aspect of the rainforest, a giant spider the size of WC's head drops out of the forest canopy and bounces up and down in front of the two children. They recoil in terror. 'Ha ha,' WC laughs joyfully as the children scream, grabbing onto their parents' legs for protection. 'That's a bird-eating spider except it's made of rubber, like the snake. Ha ha.' He pulls on a string attached to the tree and hoists the rubber spider back up into the overhead branches, out of sight. 'Been giving these tours for *years*. Got to keep myself amused somehow. Ha ha.'

The guy is a certified lunatic.

Walking through the forest with this guide is like walking through a chamber of horrors. He was awarded some kind of eco-tourism award some years ago, apparently before he lost his marbles. He stops and puts a finger to his lips. 'Shhh.' We listen attentively to what sounds like a bird. '*Where's* that sound come from?' he asks. We all point in different directions of the forest before he pulls out a little gadget from his pocket. 'Ha ha, it comes from my *pocket. Fooled* ya.'

A hundred metres further down the path, he spots a slender green tree snake in a bush above our heads. It's actually moving its head, so we can conclude it's real, unless it's a wind-up rubber one. 'That is a common tree snake. Actually, *spotting* these snakes is quite easy,' WC tells us. 'It's *tying* them up there that is bloody difficult.' He wipes his brow. He looks like he tied one on himself. 'Got stuck into some red wine last night and I'm feeling the effects now,' he confirms.

Continuing on the path, he informs us, 'Scientists have only identified ten per cent of this rainforest flora. Maybe there are three million different plants and some of them are as rare as rocking-horse manure. You see all these vines growing around the tree trunks? Notice anything about them?'

The American boy replies, 'Yeah, all the vines grow anti-clockwise, unlike in the Northern Hemisphere where they all grow clockwise.'

'Why?' WC asks, ignoring the American who is clearly getting on his nerves.

The American explains with a Brooklyn accent, before WC can answer his own question. 'It's called the Coriolus effect. Water spiralling down the drain in the Northern Hemisphere goes down clockwise. Here it goes down anti-clockwise. It's caused by the rotation of the Earth.'

'How'd you know that?' I whisper to the American.

'I like reading about nature,' he replies.

We head back to the tented resort. It's touch and go whether WC will make it, he looks terminally hung over. Walking at the back of the group, I think I see the tail of a snake disappearing into the undergrowth; it isn't more than a couple of metres away from the path and the others must have walked right by it.

'Er, WC, I think I see a snake here,' I call out, not sure if I'm imagining this or not. Doesn't look like rubber and it's definitely progressing along the ground so it isn't tied up.

The others freeze as if they had bumped into a glass wall. WC returns to the back of the line. 'Where?' he says, disbelievingly.

I step off the path and into the undergrowth. The snake has disappeared but I know where it went. WC follows me. 'There!' I grab at his shirt and point at a middle section of the brown and yellow body with a filmy rainbow sheen, as it continues to slither away, not terribly fast.

'Ah yes,' he proclaims, 'that will be an amethystine *python*. And it's a *bloody* big one too.' The snake slides into the bush until its head emerges into a clearing. To his credit, WC intercepts the snake, getting down on his hands and knees and makes as if he might be thinking of grabbing the reptile but doesn't quite manage to manoeuvre his corpulent body into just the right position. 'That must be a *five, five-and-a-half* metre snake,' WC emphasises as he leapfrogs the snake and ambushes the front end again as if to pluck it from the undergrowth. Still kneeling and breathing heavily, he tells us, 'Got to be careful. Even if it isn't *venomous*, it will bite if *antagonised*.' Seems to me that WC is both antagonising the slow moving python and that he has lots of time to seize it. 'Keep the kids back. Snake like this could swallow them *whole*.' The kids grab onto their parents' legs. Meanwhile WC finds several excuses for not plucking the python up each time he catches up with it. 'Too muddy here, might slip.' Or, 'Oops, it's disappeared into the bush again.' Or, 'Oh-oh, wait-a-bit thorn, don't want to get tangled in *that* with a five-and-a-half metre python wrapped around me.'

It's an impressive sight even if the rotund WC doesn't manage to get the nerve up to actually grapple with the giant reptile. Don't blame him.

Our encounter with this python is only thirty metres away from my tent, on the outer edges of the resort compound. In just several times its length, this impressive snake could poke its head into my tent and stick his tongue out at me. Being in a tent on a raised platform a metre above the ground doesn't help either. If I can climb up the stairs, a five and-a-half metres python can too. 'The amethystine python is Australia's largest snake, often frequenting areas inhabited by humans in search of *food*,' WC tells us, confirming my paranoia.

An alarming yodelling, I imagine a cassowary being strangled with piano wire, rings through the forest. 'Ah, the orange-footed scrub fowl have woken up. We must have disturbed them,' WC tells us, wiping his brow once again. He can hardly wait to get back to camp and sit down and have a bite of the dog that bit him.

Although I had shut my canvas tent tight against the mosaic-tailed rat, I've also gone against the advice of the manager and left half-a-dozen bananas in there. When I return, I see the bananas have been gnawed at, and the tube of mint-flavoured toothpaste is a gooey mess. Fortunately, I don't have any cherry-flavoured lipstick, apple-scented shampoo, or strawberry-flavoured condoms as the little rats scurry around searching through the plastic bags of my backpack. Slumping into my swag, exhausted by the evening walk, I try to ignore the undeniable fact that if the rats got into my tent from the rainforest, so could the python. As I fall asleep, my hand flops over the edge of the bed, dangling like bait.

The Alternative Coach Network for Like Minded Independent Travellers doesn't head beyond the black stump into the Outback from Cairns. Not enough party places to stop in at. In fact, there's virtually nothing to stop in at.

The silver bus with the blue greyhound logo stretched across the side rumbles impressively into the allotted bay at the Cairns coach terminal. A dramatic hiss of air brakes as the hydraulic door opens and the bus driver disembarks with the panache of an airline pilot. Apart from the fact that he wears tight little shorts and knee-high white socks, he looks like a professional aviator with his pressed white shirt, black tie, gold epaulettes and polished black shoes. He whisks his Ray Ban pilot's sunglasses off his face and squints with a far-off stare as if he were out in the bright sunlight and not in the shade of the bus terminal building. This Greyhound Coach Captain is quite the opposite of the Alternative Coach Network driver. The only difference between the shabbily-underdressed Alternative Coach Network driver, and his Independent Like Minded Traveller passengers uniformly clad in sandals and stained T-shirts, was a bus licence and maybe a couple of years.

Completing the airline analogy, the Greyhound staff weighs my backpack on scales at the check-in counter and a computerised airline-like label is attached to it before it is whisked from sight. Very impressive. What a difference from the Alternative Coach Network where we had spent part of a day retracing our route recovering backpacks that had spilled out of the unlocked luggage compartment. A couple of days later a hatch on the roof had blown off without any of the Like Minded passengers, or the driver, noticing. The driver was too hung over and the Like Minded passengers were fast asleep. For the rest of the trip up the coast, whenever it rained, the Like Minded in the back got soaked.

We board the Greyhound bus that will take us back down the coast to Townsville, where I will change buses for the Outback. I have deliberately booked myself onto seat 1A at the front of the bus, beside the window, so I have a full view of what's coming up ahead, I can hear the bus driver, and I can prop my head against the window should I want to sleep.

Right on schedule, with the whine of the powerful engine, the coach backs out and we are off. This will be my mode of transportation covering the rest of the continent. According to the Greyhound timetable, the total distance on this particular leg is 4,000 kilometres, with an approximate journey time of 54 hours. I will be on the bus for some 35 hours to Alice.

I check out my fellow adventurers. Two Danish girls on the other side of the aisle read an article in *Cosmopolitan* magazine on genital makeovers. Captivating reading, illustrated with some remarkably personal photos. I crane to get a better look while pretending not to. The Aussie next to me reads a rugby magazine. Not so personal photos, and nowhere as near appealing reading.

I stop squinting askance at the black and white photos of surgically customised female genitals when our Coach Captain announces, 'Good afternoon ladies and gents, welcome aboard Greyhound's 438 coach to Adelaide via Alice Springs. My name is Greg and I am your Coach Captain. Law prohibits smoking or the use of alcohol and recreational drugs on board this coach.' That's a big change from the Alternative Coach Network. 'Health department regulations prohibit the consumption of hot or dairy foods on board,' our Coach Captain continues. 'Please ensure you have your shoes on at all times. If you exit the coach with bare feet and cut yourself, you will not be permitted back on board. A top must always be worn. What you wear or don't wear between your feet and your top is not covered by regulations and is up to you.' He sounds like a schoolmaster laying down the arcane rules of conduct for the duration of the school term. 'Please refrain from closing the ducts to the air-conditioning above you. This will cause the air-conditioning to back-up, creating condensation.' Even with the air-conditioning on, it is warm in the bus. 'You will notice that there is a toilet at the back. This is for emergency use only.' At least we have one. He goes through a list of things we can and cannot do. 'In a few minutes we will be stopping at the papaya fruit fly inspection post. There is quarantine on fruit outside of this area to keep out the papaya fruit fly. If you have any fresh fruits on board, please eat them now or get rid of them. If you refuse to open your baggage the inspectors can throw you off the bus, fine you, or put you in jail and believe me, folks, they have done it.'

'Just for carrying fruit?' one of the Danish women says, putting down the magazine.

The driver overhears her remark. 'Well, it's as big a threat to orchards as foot-and-mouth disease is to cattle and pork. It might seem silly and stupid to you, but to farmers it's bloody serious.'

'Australian papaya fruit flies can't fly over state borders,' the Australian next to me whispers after a suitable period when he thinks the Coach Captain isn't listening.

Those of us who thought we were very clever in bringing plenty of fresh fruit so as to minimise the greasy roadhouse tucker now have to stuff ourselves immediately or waste all that effort trying to be healthy. We pull up to the quarantine station beside a car full of retirees similarly gorging themselves silly on a tray of mangoes that they don't want to throw out. 'Boy, that'll change the way they walk,' our Coach Captain comments. He shouldn't be so smug. The way we scoffed our fruit, we'll have significantly altered the way we walk to the back of his bus for a prohibited bowel-loosened emergency.

Clear of the quarantine station, our driver, Coach Captain, starts the video at the front of the bus above the centre isle. Driving through monotonous bush countryside there is little else to divert one's attention except road signs.

Two action-packed Mel Gibson characters later we pull into the Townsville coach terminal. Those passengers, who ingested stashes of fruit at the papaya fruit fly inspection post, make a beeline for the non-emergency use public toilets. I anxiously wait my turn outside a noisy cubicle and study two adjacent vending machines containing condoms. 'Savage Bliss' offers 'ribbed sides for greater stimulation'. The alternative to being a tumescent, blissful savage is 'Slim Fits', I assume for men with wee members. How does one hold one's head high while placing a coin into the machine offering Slim Fit condoms? Sneak into the Mens, pretend to put the coin in the Savage Bliss machine, check about for voyeurs, and then surreptitiously move one's fingers over a fraction and quickly needle the dollar into the adjacent more appropriate Slim Fit slot?

# 2   The Centre

We are a motley group heading out into the wide-open empty spaces of the Outback. The Like Minded Independent Travellers on the Alternative Coach Network were uniformed in the cool baggy rags and sandals of the international backpacker. The Greyhound passengers, on the other hand, include bona fide Australians heading into the Outback to go home or look for work. Curiously enough, although it is sweltering hot, the Aussies all carry woollies: woollen hats, gloves, sweaters and thick sleeping bags.

It is tropically hot and sticky when we board the bus in Townsville. We hurtle into the desert as if we had been shot into the empty void of outer space. Gone are the tourist resorts of Cairns and the Gold and Sunshine Coasts. As the sun sets in an enormous sky, our Coach Captain turns on the video at the front of the bus. I ignore the flickering screen. The dry savannah and the trees silhouetted dark against the massive sweeping strokes of the ignited clouds remind me of East Africa. When the sun drops below the horizon it quickly becomes dark. The jagged line of an advancing bush fire on a distant hillside, like the molten lava of a volcano, is the only visible reference point. The few isolated, fluorescent-lit settlements we hurdle through are made all the more desolate by the surrounding inky blackness. This feeling of emptiness is infrequently broken by the whoosh of a huge truck pulling multiple trailers in the opposite direction. They look exactly like what they are: road trains. It's starting to feel more like the Australia I'd imagined.

There isn't much to see; a vast blackness pierced insignificantly and temporarily by the bus headlights as we roll into the void towards the centre of the continent. A kangaroo hops onto the road and stops, blinded by the headlights. The driver doesn't brake or swerve and there is a dull thud as the animal is struck down by the heavy 'roo bar mounted on the front fenders. Our Coach Captain doesn't blink an eye, as if it was merely an insect that had splattered on the windscreen. 'Too dangerous to try braking or swerving to avoid hitting Skippy,' he tells the two Danes behind him when they moan audibly as we witness the poor creature get creamed.

It becomes cold with the air-conditioning on full blast and the cooler night temperatures of the desert. One of the Coach Captain's Ten Commandments is not to close the air-conditioning ducts above our heads. Not thinking ahead in tropically-hot Townsville, I am barely clad in sandals, T-shirt and shorts, and now I am freezing. The Aussie passengers boarding in steaming Townsville with pillows and blankets and sleeping bags and woollen sweaters knew what they were doing. The Aussie next to me puts on a woollen hat and snuggles under a blanket after putting on a heavy wool sweater. I fall asleep, despite the close-to-freezing temperatures and the distinct impression that I'm sitting upright in a fridge.

When I awake everything is quiet. The bus engine is shut off. We have stopped behind a line of road trains in the middle of nowhere. The Coach Captain talks on the mobile telephone, presumably to Greyhound headquarters, 'There's been an accident. Road train has gone off the range. They're retrieving the truck. Looks like we'll be some hours behind schedule.' He opens the door to the bus so we can stretch our legs. 'Might as well take a ciggie break.'

I disembark and with permission from the Coach Captain extract my backpack from the luggage compartment below to retrieve a sweater, jeans, boots and my sleeping bag. Dressed warmly, I stroll away from the coach and circle of chatting passengers taking a smoko break.

Above, a fragment of a silvery moon hangs brightly in a black sky. Although it is only a thin sliver of a moon, the light it casts in this black desert air is enough to see in front of me the shadowy outlines of twenty or more stationary road trains. I breathe deeply and smell the dryness of the air and the dustiness of the earth. The sound of insects amplifies the silence. I'm tempted to think they are crickets, but with some 100,000 species of insects in Australia and fewer than 2,000 of them are crickets, the sounds could be from anything; whatever insect is making the incessant noise, the impression is vivid. Much more than the wet tropical rainforest, or even the Great Barrier Reef, this uninhabited Outback desert is how I had imagined Australia, the driest continent on earth.

This impromptu nocturnal stroll in the middle of the desert is an unexpected bonus. I walk along the line of giant mechanical dinosaurs silhouetted against the black starry sky. Many of the road trains, three trailers long, are lit up like Christmas trees with colourful running lights shining brightly. Some are dark silent hulks. Others have engines idling to provide power for refrigeration units. While many trucks are square-fronted, others have the curvaceous aerodynamics of a sleek sedan. All have massive 'roo bars mounted on the front fenders and wire cages over the bottom portion of the windscreen to protect against bouncing stones. Overhanging visors at the top of windscreens shield from the glaring sun, leaving a relatively narrow slit for the driver to see out of, like looking out the helmet and visor of a knight's armour. Single side-band radios cackle, keeping the truckers informed of progress at the front of the blocked line of trucks where a hive of activity is floodlit by tow trucks with pulsating yellow lights and police cars with flashing blue lights. The rescuers have already retrieved the three empty cattle trailers out of the ditch and are busy pulling out the tractor engine. A man watches, presumably the driver, bloody bandages wrapped around his head. There is a slight, just a very slight bend in the road here. Anywhere else in the world you wouldn't even designate it a bend. It might be off by a couple of degrees, but here, where the road is straight as a latitudinal line for hundreds, even thousands of kilometres, a slight bend is enough to send an overtired driver and his road train into the ditch.

Powerful truck engines rumble and I have to run back in the moonlight, reaching the bus just as the road train in front moves off with a hiss of air brakes and the grinding of dozens of gears. What would have happened if I hadn't reached the bus in time? Would I have been an international headline, like the two Americans forgotten off the dive-boat in the Great Barrier Reef? 'Canadian left in Outback desert as unsuspecting Coach Captain drives off.' With the daytime temperatures here, I would probably have less chance of surviving than the two Americans did, as they drifted in the ocean off the Eastern Coast of Australia. On the other hand, I could always stand beside the road with my thumb stuck out and hitchhike to safety. Somebody would have driven by during the course of the day.

It's a strange sensation, this long trip on a straight road with no terms of reference. Like plunging into unconsciousness. I imagine that's what it's like when you die as your soul is transported from one world to another. Our Coach Captain sits immobile, guiding us to our destination, omnipotent and God-like at the front of the bus, silhouetted against the funnel of light illuminating the road. I wonder what he is thinking. He's got all night to think about it, whatever it is.

A rippled pink desert sunrise ignites bastion citadels of termite hills as if red-hot coals burned fiercely within them. Road signs warn of road trains fifty metres long, or of places where the road is subject to flooding during the Wet. It is impossible to imagine how this area could ever flood. Where does the water come from? Where does it go? Could this immaculate sky be anything but cobalt blue?

Our Coach Captain stares dully through a windscreen, a kaleidoscope of ruptured insect abdomens, thoraxes, heads, legs, wings and guts. A dead bird lies tangled and broken in the giant windscreen wiper. Our heroic Coach Captain has been driving for twelve hours when we finally disembark fuzzyheaded in the mining town of Mount Isa. A mechanic drives the bus away to be cleaned and serviced and the Coach Captain presumably dives into bed to be replaced by another.

With daybreak, millions of flies swarm over us. They settle on our faces, up our nostrils, in our ears and eyes. We perform the Australian wave, that constant sideways brushing motion of the hand in front of the face that could pass for a royal greeting. A road train thunders by and hundreds of disturbed pink galahs rise up, as ubiquitous as the flies. Anywhere else, a horde of pink species of cockatoo would attract attention. I cannot help smiling at the sight, excited as a kid.

Our next major stop at six in the evening will be Tennant Creek, another mining town just south of the intersection where the east–west road from the East Coast meets the north–south road cutting through the Centre. A sign warns 'No fuel for 278 kilometres'. The landscape becomes flat savannah, the road a bumpy single sealed track with red dirt on the shoulders. When a road train approaches, our Coach Captain sensibly moves to the shoulder in advance of the opposing vehicle thundering by. Signs warn 'Unfenced road, beware of stock'. An endless flat expanse of grass is unbroken by mountains, rocky outcrops, or even trees.

As we pass a signpost marking the border with the Northern Territories, our Coach Captain tells us, 'Put your watches back half-an-hour and your minds back half-a-century, we're entering the Northern Territories. In 1976 the Aboriginal Land Rights Act handed all reserves and mission lands in the Territories to Aboriginal ownership.'

'What do you mean?' I ask, leaning forward in my seat.

The Coach Captain looks over his shoulder. 'Unlike the other Australian states, mate, here in the Northern Territories, any land the Aborigines could show traditional ties to, unless already owned, leased, in a town, or set aside for other purposes, was declared open to Aboriginal claims of ownership. Although they're only a quarter of the Territories population, they have fifty per cent of the land.'

Our Coach Captain informs us of all this in a voice devoid of emotion. It's impossible to tell if he is sympathetic to the Aboriginal claims of land ownership or not. Driving a coach half-full of liberal backpackers, and half-full of Australians heading into the Outback to go home for a break or looking for work, he couldn't win whichever side he expressed sympathy for.

On a road that gets increasingly ragged, another sign:

Don't move
insects and diseases
on plants

Is this a warning not to move because there are insects and diseases on plants, or don't move the plants, because they have insects and diseases on them? Unable to read books on the bus without getting motion sickness, there's not a lot to occupy my thoughts on a long coach trip like this. Interpreting road signs looms large on my list of things to think about besides figuring out the plot to *Dumb and Dumber* being shown on the video.

A cyclist so loaded with gear she probably has more baggage tucked into her panniers than I do in the baggage compartment under the bus, is buffeted off the ragged shoulder as we thunder past her. I can't imagine cycling through a stretch like this in the heat of the day while transporting a bathtub equivalent of water so as not to dehydrate.

We stop for lunch at a roadhouse. The passengers enter the restaurant where they sit sleepy-headed while waiting for their meals. I sit at the bar and look at the menu; just five Australian dollars for a huge steak, salad, fried onions and potatoes. They're giving the food away. 'What'll you have mate?' the woman behind the bar asks.

'I'll take your steak.'

'Good on yer, mate,' she says, as if I had made a wise but difficult decision. 'And a beer?'

'Yeah,' I reply, not wanting to disappoint her with a bad choice. She pours me a beer and disappears into the kitchen.

A barefoot man so tall he has to duck under the doorframe walks into the bar and up to the counter and when the barmaid reappears he asks her for a 'slab'. She pulls a carton of twenty-four beers out of the cooler and hefts it onto the counter. He pays her, pulls a corner of the box open and drinks down a tinnie, then pulls out another for the road, tucks the slab effortlessly under his arm, walks out to his pickup, and drives off with a squeal of tyres.

She turns her bloodshot eyes to me when she comes back out with a plate heaped with red meat and chips and fried onion rings. 'South African?' she asks, not placing my accent. I shake my head as I pop a chip into my mouth and wipe my greasy fingers on my shorts. 'Too bad,' she says. 'I usually tell South African visitors they chose the wrong continent.' She grins lop-sidedly. 'Here we got rid of our blacks.' The comment comes out of nowhere. I wouldn't believe it unless I had heard it myself. I blink in disbelief, a chip poised at my mouth. 'And in case you can't tell, I'm a racist.' I quietly hacksaw my way into a section of beef that I haven't a snowball's chance in hell of consuming.

The friendly bartender continues to pour out beer and prejudices with equal generosity, as if they were perfectly acceptable forms of social behaviour.

I bite my tongue and choke down the food as Dolly Parton sings *Stand By Your Man*.

When she disappears in to the kitchen again I take a look around me. Posters advertise beer and reflect the drinking culture of Australia: 'Drink it and stay in charge', or 'Drink it when you have to go back to work', or a photo of a happy guy holding out a six-pack with the caption 'Stay a little longer'.

Drink and stay in *charge*? Drink when you have to go back to *work*? *Staying* power enhanced by the insensibility of an alcoholic haze? Drinking is not just a part of the leisure culture here; apparently it's part of the work ethic, and a preferred sexual stimulant on a par with Viagra.

I study the rack of tapes for sale. Besides Dolly Parton's complete rendition of Country and Western jingles, there's *Twenty Cowboy Favourites, More Songs of the Wild West, Love and Romance* and *Country Selection*.

'Got a little out'a hand one night,' the bartender comments succinctly when she sees me studying the wooden floor of the pub where the skid marks of a motorbike tyre form a figure of eight.

She describes a guy on a motorbike squealing his tyres inside a pub as a matter of things getting a *little* out of hand? What happens when things get *really* out of hand?

'Travelling around Australia are ya?' I nod agreement. I'm tempted to comment on her acute perceptiveness, but I keep my big mouth shut. I've a bad record with stroppy barmaids and she doesn't look as if she would need much of an opening to bring me down to size. 'Travelled as far as Brisbane myself, once, ten years ago,' she admits. 'Far as I've ever been. Don't like cities. Smaller the place, nicer the people, I reckon. Kids have a good healthy life out here, not like in the cities. No drugs here, and no Abos either.'

'What do you do for fun?' I query timidly. Apart from a huge sandpit in which to wrestle some cattle to the ground, or exterminating the indigenous population, it seems a pretty empty place devoid of things to do.

'Drive around. Go fishing. Camp-overs. Only problem is, we might have a drink or two too much.' She finishes her beer and wipes her sweaty brow with the back of her forearm before pouring herself another. Her being a bartender must be the equivalent of putting a gambling addict in charge of servicing one-armed bandits. Maybe it's one of the perks of the job.

She downs the second beer before I have finished my first. Rather than engage in more conversation and run the risk of putting both feet in my mouth, I stand outside in the shade where I am not so easily affronted by her continued racist comments. The cyclist rolls in, removes her helmet, and props her heavy bike against a wall. Her dark brown tan reveals the white lines of her helmet chinstrap. When she takes off her cycling glasses she looks the opposite of a racoon, with white circles around her eyes instead of black.

We talk. She tells me self-deprecatingly, 'I'm half Iraqi and half white trash from New Jersey. I want to write a book about my cycling experience. Trouble is, don't know what to write about. You can't write a hell of a lot when you're cycling all by yourself for weeks on end. After a couple of days, you don't think a lot either. At least, nothing worth writing down.'

Here's an individualist pushing the comfort envelope of her existence and lots of people, especially women, would be interested in her experiences. 'You must have had strange encounters, funny conversations. Tell me the funniest story you can think of,' I prompt.

She thinks for a while, polishing off a whole litre bottle of water taken off her bike, before she continues. 'Well, there was this English girl I met once. She said she was from London. "Whereabouts in London?" I asked. Then she said, "What do you mean?" I said, "Like north, south, east, west London." She looked at me blankly and says, "I don't know."' She shakes her head remembering that story. 'That was pretty weird,' she concludes, pulling a face as if the Londoner must have come from outer space. 'I mean, she lived in London and didn't know if she lived in north, south, west or east London?'

She's spent days cycling in the heat thinking about that weird event.

'Isn't it dangerous cycling on your own?' I ask on a more practical level.

'Uh-uh. Most of the time I take the back roads and the farmers and their families keep an eye out for me. They must radio each other because they all seem to know all about me before I get there. Really friendly and hospitable people.'

'No problems?'

'Nope. Although they keep telling me to watch out for Aboriginals, I haven't had any problems from anyone and I've been cycling through reserves too. Every evening I camp out beside the road and occasionally sleep at a farm if I'm invited.'

'Do you ever wonder how these farmers defend occupation of farmland their ancestors justified grabbing because the indigenous people of Australia in their view had never been 'in possession' of it?' I ask her. I've been thinking a lot about what Trevor said in Cairns. 'They reckoned if you didn't delineate the property, you didn't 'occupy' it,' I expand. 'If you didn't 'occupy' it, you obviously didn't own it. Given the sophisticated use of the land by original inhabitants, it seems extraordinary that the settlers could genuinely construe the land as being 'unoccupied'.

She doesn't say anything.

'Do the farmers talk about Aboriginals' claims to land when you stay at their farms?' I probe provocatively.

'Uh-uh, and I don't want to ruin the nice impression I have of my hosts by asking. They reckon the pastoral leases they've had in the family for generations are theirs to keep. They're threatened by Aboriginal land claims.'

'And you never talk to them about it?'

'Why ruin a nice evening by asking them about their Aboriginal neighbours?' she replies. 'Trouble is, I can see both sides. If I were an Aboriginal, I sure would want to have my ancestral land back. And if I were a farmer whose great-grandfather had built up a farm out of the wilderness three generations ago, I'd be upset at losing it too.'

'But I'm not even talking about farmland that was bought. I'm talking about pastoral leases. The farmers leased it from the Government, they never actually *owned* it.' I've been reading up on the material Trevor gave me.

'Even if they only leased it, they built their farms up on those leases. Anyway, I don't want to get involved in a discussion on it,' she says wisely. 'It just seems to be one of those situations with no solution. Bit like being an Iraqi Jew.'

'Yeah, but the problem won't go away either,' I answer.

She has some two-dozen empty water bottles tied to different sections of her bike. She sees me counting the bottles. 'Bummer carrying twenty-four litres of water with me.' She switches topics to a less loaded conversation, one she is more of an expert in. 'Wouldn't have to worry about carrying drinking water back home, there'd be plenty of water points. Some of these roadhouses though, they want me to pay for it.'

'Where's home?' I ask.

'My bike, these days. Cycled up the States to Alaska, across Europe and the Middle East and now I'm doing Australia and someday I'd like to cycle across Africa.'

The Coach Captain beeps the horn of the bus. I wish her luck before I climb on board where I recline my seat all the way backward. I watch her straddle her bike and jealously admire her well-developed calf muscles bulge with the effort of pedalling into the shimmering vastness of the empty Outback. With the air-conditioning on full blast, I surreptitiously turn down the air-conditioning nozzle, pull a sweatshirt over me to keep warm, and lazily half-watching the video, without moving a muscle besides my eyeballs, cast a dull look out the window. How could anyone even *think* of cycling around Australia?

A couple of hours later, what would take me some days of exhausting pedalling, the road meets another at a T-junction and the bus turns left.

Imagine yourself a roadhouse owner living literally in the middle of the Outback. Now what would you call your roadhouse at a T-junction, a day's drive from Darwin to the north, a couple of days driving from Townsville to the east, and a couple of days driving from Adelaide to the south?

Three Ways Roadhouse.

We stagger stiff-legged off the coach for a non-emergency toilet break. After sitting still for several hours our bums feel as detached from the rest of us as our sense of humour.

We head south now and as the sun drops in the west, I watch the bus shadow lengthen until it resembles the outline of a London double-decker bouncing against the ochre earth. Rocky outcrops deepen red as high clouds tinge pink. There is something innately appealing about being tiny and insignificant and mortal in the middle of this enormous, empty, enduring continent that has changed so little over the millennia since the time of the dinosaurs.

Just after the sun disappears we arrive in Tennant Creek where we have a five-hour wait for the delayed southbound Greyhound from Darwin. Inside the fluorescent-lit bus terminal, backpackers sleep on the floor or watch a television suspended from the ceiling. A man approaches me, 'Excuse me, do you know the time?'

I tell him the time, then, in an attempt to continue communication ask, 'Are you waiting for a bus too?'

He nods and smiles. He is neatly dressed and he seems different. For one thing, he is inside the terminal with a bunch of whites and not outside on the sidewalk with the other Aboriginal passengers. 'Nice shirt,' I comment to him. It's a shirt with a flowery pattern; not one you'd expect to see in the Outback.

He shuffles his feet shyly and studies the shirt. 'I bought it second-hand.'

'It looks good on you,' I flatter. He smiles self-consciously and holds both hands up to the sides of his face, his eyes wide. He tells me he is twenty-eight years old. He is more like a shy teenager. 'Where are you from?' I ask.

'I'm from the hospital 200 kilometres from here,' he replies, pointing east.

'You come from a hospital?' I ask and regret my insensitivity immediately the words come out of my mouth.

'The doctors adopted me.'

'You speak your own language?'

He shakes his head but proudly volunteers, 'I don't drink or smoke.'

'That's good. I don't drink or smoke either,' I tell him a white lie to encourage his abstinence. 'Where are you going?'

He becomes flustered again, the palms of his hands pressed to his face. 'I'm going to Katherine to play music in a band.' When we run out of small talk, he hovers about inside the terminal, clearly not comfortable with his own people outside in the street, but apparently not entirely at ease with us white strangers either. His own people would cynically call him a 'coconut': brown on the outside and white on the inside.

Some time during the middle of the night we board the bus for Alice. The problem with the 1A seat is you can put your seat back but you can't stretch your legs under the seat in front. The metal partition separating the stairwell from my space means my legs are scrunched up all the time. I sleep fitfully, if at all, until we arrive at Alice Springs, another Australian icon, at sunrise. Despite the early hour, competing minibus drivers wait to channel us into an assortment of backpacker's accommodation. I pick a minibus at random and am driven to a backpacker's lodge where I lock my pack in a room. Tired as I am, I want to see Alice Springs, this place that has also captured my imagination, so I cross the dry sand bed of the Todd River, perhaps 200 metres wide, into town. A dozen groups of Aboriginals have collected in the riverbed. Some bands appear composed entirely of men and some are mixed. Some have children with them. Many of the men have

Aussie or Western cowboy hats. Crumpled cardboard wine caskets and their silver lining bags litter the riverbed.

Todd Mall is the heart of Alice Springs. It is lined with fashionable cafés, restaurants, and Aboriginal art shops. Here there are as many Aboriginal pedestrians as there are whites. But the two worlds, the black world of the Aboriginal and the white Australian world, seem to be disjointed. There is little to link the everyday world of whites to the everyday world of blacks. Aboriginals do not work in any of the shops, or sit in the cafés, although they buy food at take-aways to sit in parks to eat. An impression is forming of Australia being two different worlds that exist in the same place and time, but don't overlap. Each race studiously avoids eye contact with the other.

Throughout colonial Africa, even South Africa, the Africans always outnumbered the whites; their own culture and people surrounded the Africans, giving them a sense of belonging and pride. The original Australians are barely one per cent of the total population in their own continent, surrounded by a recent investiture of a totally foreign culture, and totally outnumbered by another race. Australian Aboriginals have become fringe dwellers, living literally and figuratively on the edges of the white world, barely hanging on, not only to their culture but to life itself. In Alice Springs, the clash between the two worlds could not be more obvious.

As an outsider coming to Australia, perhaps I'm more observant to what's going on around me, based on ignorance. I have no political agenda and certainly no desire to judge, and yet it's difficult to ignore a situation that seems appalling. It's not as if I've become impervious to the condition of the Aboriginals by a gradual process of habituation. But as a white North American, I can hardly point my wagging finger at white Australians. What ultimately happened to the original inhabitants in North America is comparable on a scale of inhumanity, treaty or no treaty.

In the middle of Todd Mall a woman sits at a table in front of a book displayed open for people to sign. According to the overhead banner strung between light posts, it is the Sorry Book. I sit nearby and watch. Apart from them all being white, there is no pattern to those endorsing the book. Young and old, male and female, come to the table with a deliberation indicating that they have thought about what they are about to do. These are not casual passers-by. The only segments of the population not querying the Sorry Book are the Aboriginal people themselves.

A bulky farmer-type, with leathery skin and red, creased neck, signs the book. The white-haired woman beside him, I presume his wife, writes her name. Neither says anything; their faces and body language indicate this is an emotional occasion, as it seems to be for all those who sign. In the two hours that I patiently people-watch, there are a couple of dozen individuals or couples who deliberately walk up to the table and add their names in the Sorry Book.

I wander over to read what it says:

The Stolen Generation Sorry Book Project.

The Sorry Book Apology:

By signing my name in this book, I record my deep regret for the injustices suffered by Indigenous Australians as a result of European settlement, and in particular, I offer my personal apology for the hurt and harm caused by the forced removal of children from their families and the effect of government policy on the human dignity and spirit of Indigenous Australians.

I would also like to record my desire for Reconciliation and for a better future for all our peoples. I make a commitment to a united Australia which respects this land of ours, values

Aboriginal and Torres Strait Islander heritage, and provides justice and equity for all.

I sign my name in the book. 'How you going?' I ask the light-skinned Aboriginal woman sitting on the other side of the table.

'Fine,' she replies with a smile. 'How about you?'

'Good,' I reply.

She reaches out a hand. 'Elaine.' I sit on an extra chair at the table. 'I'm one of the lost generation this book is all about,' she tells me.

'What's the lost generation?'

'I was taken from my mother before I was an hour old. The authorities lied to my mother; they told her I had died after childbirth. The authorities will tell you it was because they wanted to protect me from an alcoholic mother. But the real reason was so that I would assimilate into a white society and not an Aboriginal one because, in 1947, the Western Australian Commissioner of Native Affairs said he had proof our dark skin pigmentation could be bred out of us within two or three generations. He reckoned Australians could solve the Aboriginal problem by breeding our blackness out of us.'

'Weren't young girls taken away from single mothers because their part-coloured teenage daughters became pregnant at an early age and not being Aboriginal or white, they didn't have the protection of either culture?' Being an outsider, I can be provocative without the appearance of having an axe to grind. But I am only repeating what I have been told.

'I was taken up to Melville Island, to a mission there. From the age of five, Catholic brothers sexually assaulted me until I was ten. Please don't tell me this was for my own good.' Even if I was being deliberately provocative, I regret my ploy. She continues angrily, 'Being raped by a Father in a mission is worse than just about anything you can think of.' She is furious, and I am sorry for being so naïve. 'The mission was closed down eventually and I was sent down to Tennant Creek to stay with an 'aunt', except it wasn't an aunt at all. It was my mother. Only when I was given back to her did she know I was actually her daughter and that I hadn't died at childbirth, as she had been told. She was warned not to tell anyone, otherwise she would lose her other children as well.'

'I'm sorry.'

She laughs ironically and indicates the book with her eyes. 'That's what this book is all about, saying sorry.' Her sense of humour makes me feel less ashamed for my callous comment. She points at a family of dishevelled pedestrians walking along the Mall. 'For us, family is one of the most important aspects of our society. To take our children destroys the very heart of what we are all about. I've never been offered counselling for the sexual abuse at the mission, although I have reported it to the authorities. One of the Fathers who abused me is alive and still working as a priest. Now I'm taking him to court. The church wants to settle out of court, but they don't understand it's not a question of money. That's not important. It's a question of the church facing up to what its priests, in their positions of authority, have done. I used to be alcoholic and self-abusive.' She shows me the telltale signs of cigarette burns over her forearms. 'I've pulled myself out of all that, and reckon I'm normal now. But the one thing I still cannot handle is when adult men are close to my granddaughters. Then I get real nervous again.'

Several stumble by, apparently having had too much to drink. 'Creekies,' Elaine comments as they pass.

'What are creekies?'

'Aborigines hanging out in the Todd River creek.'

Apparently there is a hierarchy within their own community. I ask, 'Why do they hang out there?'

'They've come from all around,' Elaine explains. 'Clans from this area were nomadic. The Centre didn't provide much food so to survive they had to move around huge areas, hunting and gathering. That's why lots of us go Walkabout.

We need to pick up and go because it's in our genes. We've been doing it for tens of thousands of years. That's how we survived. It's hard for us to remain in one place for too long.' I can identify with that too. 'Many of the creekies come here for meetings, to socialise, catch up on the news and gossip or visit relatives in the hospital or in prison. They may camp out for weeks, sometimes months at a time, waiting.' She laughs ironically again. 'You know, there used to be a two-kilometre limit around the town and we weren't allowed within the town limit?'

'I didn't know that.'

'In 1953 all Aboriginal people in the Northern Territory were declared 'wards', which gave the Government legal rights over our movement, employment, residence, wages, and even who we married.' She has rehearsed her stuff.

'Didn't know that either,' I admit.

'We didn't even get Australian citizenship until 1967 after a national referendum when ninety per cent of Australians voted to let us become citizens of our own country.'

'You're kidding?'

'We weren't even citizens of our own country.'

I've deliberately tried to thwart my sense of Aussie-bashing by reminding myself that what happened in Australia wasn't that different from the United States or Canada at that time. It's not so long ago, after all, that black and white students were bussed to separate schools in the United States. But bussing kids to separate schools is quite different from forcibly taking children from their parents and putting them into missions. Even going back to the capture and abduction of Africans and their subsequent life of servitude as slaves in the United States, heinous as it was, was not the equivalent of what has gone on here in Australia. Here there was an official policy of genocide, to wipe out the Australian Aboriginal. Even the North American Natives got to sign treaties, although that hardly ameliorates what happened to them either. I have no axe to grind, and I try to observe what has happened here with the naïve objectivity that being a foreigner allows, but the brutal colonisation of Australia and the subjugation of its indigenous people, unknown to me before I came here, come as a shock.

Wandering around Alice I find myself drawn by the cheering of crowds to the sports grounds. It's an Aussie Rules Football League game, or footy. Again, I'm confronted by the two worlds of white and black, where the white spectators sit together in their groups in front and the blacks, for the most part, at the back. Even the two opposing sides are almost split white and black, but not entirely. There is a mix. Like other parts of the world, it is in the arena of sports that integration often makes its debut. The white team has a few blacks playing on their side, and the black team has a couple of whites.

I ask the animated spectator sitting beside me in the stands, 'Where're the teams from?'

'It's the South versus the West,' he replies. 'Both teams are from Alice.' He's the manager of the white team. He's talkative and friendly and he explains the game. 'As you can see, the field is round, not rectangular. The ball is shaped like a rugby ball and the goal posts resemble rugby or American football posts, but there is no cross bar, and there are two more shorter posts outside the inner ones.' The players run around the field as if playing a hybrid game of soccer, basketball and rugby. Tight short shorts and sleeveless shirts reveal maximum flesh and muscle. There are almost as many women watching the game as men, which makes me wonder if the women are there to admire the physiques of the men more than any genuine interest in the game itself. The players are for the most part tall and lean, more like basketball players than any other sportsman stereotype. There does seem to be physical contact but it's more like soccer than the outright brutal violence of rugby or American football. 'You get six points for kicking the ball between the two taller inner posts, and a single point for kicking it within the outer posts,' the manager explains to me amiably. 'Aside from that, there's few rules. You can run with the ball as long as you bounce it on the ground. You can pass the ball forward as long as you punch it or kick it. And that's about it.'

He asks me where I am from. When he discovers I am Canadian, he tells me that he and his wife plan to visit Canada next year.

I watch as a short and solidly-built white player with a shaved head punches a downed player on the mouth with his fist. The Aboriginal player doesn't get up after the blow, and his team-mates call for help from the sidelines. A trainer runs onto the field and with the assistance of other players help the injured man off the field, his face contorted with pain as blood streams from his mouth or nose.

'He was hit when he was already on the ground and he didn't even have the ball,' I comment angrily to the manager of the white team. He doesn't reply. He doesn't say anything to me for the rest of the game, and when it is over, he gets up and leaves without saying goodbye.

Late afternoon, I walk to the western outskirts of Alice and climb up the nearby rocky range overlooking the town. At the highest point I sit on a boulder. From the top of the hill I have a perfect panoramic view 360° around to a brazen, three-dimensional sky extending to the horizon with cloud formations arrayed in each quarter. The sun is low, casting its familiar orange-red glow over ochre rocks. It's a dramatic landscape with a profound appeal. Some settings have an allure that seems to reach deep inside, instilling a sense of familiarity as if a previous life had been lived there. I must have lived a few disparate lives; such places include Canadian lakes bordered by pine trees, Himalayan mountains, African plains, windswept Norwegian shores lashed by the sea, and this empty Outback. Or maybe it's just the big wilderness areas of the world that I hold such an affinity for, but there is something particularly magical about the red centre of Australia.

Far to the south, the sky is laden with lead-grey anvil-headed cumulonimbus thunderclouds towering tens of thousands of feet into the sky. To the east subdued pastel colours subtly tint billowing white clouds. To the northwest the sun sets, splintered oblique shafts of light penetrating gaps between the layered clouds and the flat earth. When the sun dips below the horizon, the clouds flush orange as if injected with a dye, and then bleed a deeper red. The blotting-paper earth sops up the celestial colour as if the ground itself were blushing.

A kangaroo scares me when I hear it shuffling on the stony ground behind me. A few minutes later a smaller grey wallaby approaches, adding to the sense of timelessness. Neither animal is frightened.

This is where I want to be, the experience I hoped for, sitting by myself on a rocky outcrop in the centre of the Outback, watching the sun set with a kangaroo and a wallaby and no tourists for company. Oblivious of the passing of time I sit quietly until the first planets, and then the stars, emerge sharp in a steely-blue sky. It's tempting to stay up here and sleep out. I would, if I had brought my sleeping bag with me. With the sun gone, it is already cold and the temperature is likely to dip down to almost freezing.

Illuminated by the light of a starry sky, I descend the steep escarpment and walk back into Alice. As I reach the Todd River, a man and woman approach me. He has a solid sheet of plywood under his arms. They stop to show me the plywood, covered with a beautiful dot painting. Even in the dark I can see how detailed the artistic work is. He offers to sell it.

'I'm sorry, I'm travelling all around Australia for another two months and wouldn't be able to carry it with me.'

'It's only forty dollars,' he says.

I shake my head. I don't want to seem ungracious, but it would be totally impractical.

'I'm hungry,' he pleads. 'Please.'

'Really, I can't carry it. It's very good, but I can't lug something that size around with me.' I suppose I could always send it to Sydney and then pick it up on my way out of the country. I consider the option but it just seems too much of a logistical problem.

Walking further along the Todd River I hear a squabble amongst a group of Aboriginal people somewhere out on the sandy riverbed. Voices are raised, a woman screams. Not sure what to do, I watch. A man sitting hunched over on a tree stump warns me, 'Don't interfere, it's their business.'

'Are you sure?' I ask.

'Yeah. They get upset if you go there.' Having my attention he adds, 'Have you got a dollar so I can get home? It's too cold to sleep out and I've got to get back to my community.'

I give him a dollar. 'How would you get home if you didn't have someone to ask for money?'

'We have night patrols. They take us back to our communities. Maybe they lock us up there if they think we are drunk, but it's better than being picked up by the police.'

I'm not sure how my dollar is going to help get him home although it might help him buy another drink. 'Are the police bad?' I ask as if to galvanise some negative opinion from him.

'No,' he says, pronouncing it 'now'. 'Some are bad, some are OK; depends on if they know you, and how smart you are with them.' He tells me his age, three years younger than me although I would treat him as someone my father's age, he looks so worn out. 'I was born in the Telegraph Station up there. Done all kinds of work, mostly ringer. You don't know where I could get yakka do you?'

'I'm just a tourist. Can't help you there.' Besides, I haven't a clue what he's asking for.

He seems a tragic figure, and although he is probably drunk, he is polite and friendly.

As we watch, a minibus pulls up under a nearby streetlight, and three whites get out and walk towards the squabbling group in the middle of the moonlit sandy river. A fourth white doesn't join the mêlée on the riverbed; he sits on a bench beside the vehicle and watches. I leave my friend with his dollar and walk over to the park bench and sit next to the white man.

'Know him?' he asks me without looking in my direction.

'You mean the Aboriginal I was just talking to?'

'Yeah.'

'No, he just asked me if I knew where he could find yakka. What's yakka anyway?'

'Work.'

'What's happening out there?' I ask, curious to know who would walk into the midst of a quarrelling group of people.

'We're recruiting for a concert tonight.'

'What concert?' I ask.

'Evangelicals from Papua New Guinea.'

'Are you one?' I query.

'An evangelical or a Papua New Guinean?' he asks without any sense of irony.

'An evangelical.'

'Yeah, but we're not from Papua New Guinea. My friends and I are from Melbourne. What are you doing here?' he inquires.

'Travelling around Australia.'

'How do you like it?' He turns to look at me for the first time.

'It's very beautiful. Been a bit of a shock seeing the state of the Aboriginal people though,' I reply.

'I've been in Alice a couple of years and I'm still in shock,' he says.

'From what?' I ask.

'Everything. I used to work in Papua New Guinea. My wife is black. It was pretty hard working there, but I've never seen anything so hopeless as this.'

'What do you mean?'

'They just don't seem to want to help themselves. They drink themselves stupid, they fight, the men abuse and beat up their wives and children. They have money thrown at them by the Government and nothing good seems to ever come out of it.'

'Where's all the money go?'

'Into an inefficient bureaucracy, or into the hands of powerful half-castes. And alcohol. The bottle store behind us is open at ten in the morning. You see them lined up outside. It closes at two in the afternoon. They call it the Animal Bar. At two in the afternoon the white bar opens. They do that on purpose so that the patrons don't interfere with each other. The Aboriginal patrons go in to the bar, hand over money, and get short-changed. You see them afterwards taking a taxi home to one of their camps. Three days later their dole money for the next two weeks is gone and their children are starving. The bottle stores and pubs make money out of them, the government consultants, the taxi drivers, the hospital, their own people at the top.'

'You make it sound desperate.'

'It is. They throw all kinds of money at them. Everyone makes money off the Aboriginal, but their situation gets worse and they don't do anything about it themselves. They're their own worst enemy. The mayor of Alice Springs wants to move the bottle stores out to the Aboriginal dry communities, and who can blame him. The they come into Alice from their dry areas; they get drunk, make a mess of things in town, and if they haven't passed out in the river, they take a taxi or get picked up by their night patrol and are brought back to their communities. There they dry out again until the next binge on pay-day when they come back into Alice.'

'It's really that bad?' I ask. We watch his colleagues making friends with the Aboriginals in the middle of the sand riverbed. One of them takes her sweater off and gives it to a woman.

'Believe me, Alice is a powder keg. I hear there are 300 potential white vigilantes willing to walk through town and clean things up. People are fed up.' He watches his colleagues as they mix in with the quarrelling group. Whatever disagreement there was has ceased and it seems a convivial atmosphere out there now.

My friend on the bench reaches his hand across to me. 'My name is Mark.' He looks back out at the scene being played out on the Todd River. 'I can't take living here any more. The whites are racist and the blacks are hopeless.'

The rest of the white evangelists from Melbourne return to their vehicle with several recruits in tow. Mark introduces me to them and seems to know them all by name, despite his cynicism. In the process, one of the older Aboriginals takes over the introductions and calls each of the others over to shake my hand, explaining, "Im Christian.' This seems to be a magic password that breaks down the barriers of mistrust. As a Christian, it is assumed that I am a good bloke.

Mark invites me to attend the concert too.

The Papua New Guinea evangelists play gospel music at the sports ground, their music an audible beacon. Mark's wife and kids are already there. So are some hundred Aboriginals, already ferried over from the Todd River by the Melbourne evangelists. Most of them sit back on the grass and enjoy the free tucker and soft drinks. Others stand at the front, for the most part barefoot, in rags, and still happily drunk on whatever they had already consumed before the evangelists got hold of them. Some are led onto the stage to be 'saved'. Cynical as I want to be about this quick-fix spiritual 'saving' process, I cannot help but be moved by the mixture of whites and blacks and the brotherly atmosphere between the few whites who are here and the Aboriginals. At least they can see each other.

It is still dark when the alarm goes off and I drag myself sleepily out onto the street where the shuttle bus for the

Ngurratjuta Air mail plane collects me. At a nearby motel we pick up an Australian couple. Gregariously chatty despite the early hour, they tell me, 'We're from Perth and this is our third trip driving around Australia in a caravan. Grey Nomads they call us.' From their motel we drive to two of the seventeen Aboriginal camps scattered around Alice to pick up more passengers. In the first camp, which is within the town boundaries, we enter a fenced-in compound dominated by signs warning trespassers to stay out. It is still before dawn. A man sits outside, huddled under a blanket by an open fire. Another sleeps beneath a tree buried under several layers of blankets on a mattress. Although this is the Aboriginal equivalent of white suburbia, there is a distinct 'bush' feel to the place, with outdoor fires and people sleeping or sitting outside, waiting patiently for daybreak.

Some of the houses are tidy with manicured flowerbeds, others are derelict, with broken windows, missing doors and mattresses scattered about. An Aboriginal wearing a cowboy hat, plaid cowboy shirt, and very worn cowboy boots exits one of the houses and climbs into the bus and goes to the back. At the second camp, two barefoot women join us. They, too, go to the rearmost seat.

As we reach the airport building the sun rises. Another passenger, the white town clerk in one of the communities we will fly into, introduces himself and expands on his life situation as we wait for the aircraft to be fuelled. 'This is the third outstation I've worked at. My wife lives in Alice with our children, and I fly in and out as often as I can. It pays well, and it's a good way to save money and feather your nest. Only trouble is, as the town clerk, it's a 24-hour job. You have to be all things to everyone and if they need me in the middle of the night, they'll come and get me.' He stuffs his pipe full of tobacco. His whiskers and moustache are stained yellow with nicotine.

'What kind of qualifications do you need?' I ask.

'If they like you, and think you can do the job, then they hire you.' He carefully lights the tobacco.

'"They"?'

'The outstation.' He takes a mouthful of tobacco smoke and holds it before exhaling.

'What's the difference between an outstation, a community, a reserve and a mission?' I've been dying to ask someone this.

He takes another pull of his pipe, exhales, and explains, 'The British government back home couldn't prevent massacres of Aborigines by white settlers so reserves were set up to protect the Aborigines, as much as the whites, although the Aborigines got the short end of the stick. Aborigines killed about 270 whites settlers but something like a quarter of a million Aborigines were killed by whites in the same period.' He takes the pipe out of his mouth and exhales another cloud of smoke. It's hard to tell from his facial expression whether he is sympathetic to the Aboriginal people's plight, or is just recounting it dispassionately. 'Mission stations were given the status of reserves and missionaries were appointed 'protectors'. Many of the missions were eventually handed to the government and since then returned to Aboriginal communities. They still call them missions although they are also called reserves or communities.' He sucks on his pipe again and lets the smoke out of a corner of his mouth. The morning air is so still the smoke envelops his beard and face. 'An Aboriginal township is a larger community with a majority of the population Aborigine and almost all townships are located on Aborigine land or pastoral stations.' His explanation is interrupted by the call to board the aircraft.

Each passenger is weighed and ushered onto the waiting Cessna Caravan. I take the co-pilot's seat; no one else seems to want it. The Grey Nomad couple from Perth sits behind and when the three Aboriginal passengers board and take the rear seats, the Perth woman conspicuously sprays the air with a can of air freshener.

Ngurratjuta Air, 100 per cent Aboriginal owned, has served as a mail service to their remote communities since 1987. Sightseeing seats on the aircraft are sold to tourists willing to pay the cost of a round trip, on an availability basis. It is one of the ways, albeit relatively expensive, in which I can get into remote Aboriginal areas which are off limits without a permit from the Land Council or the community itself.

Gil Butler, our pilot, welcomes us on board. As he goes through his pre-flight checks he tells me, in answer to my numerous questions, 'I've been a pilot for Mission Aviation Fellowship for the last couple of decades. Served in Papua New Guinea and Arnhem Land in the far north of Australia before coming here.'

I ask, 'How can an Aboriginal community afford a plane like this?' It must have cost a fortune.

'Mining rights,' he answers. 'Although the Aboriginal people do not actually own the minerals in their communities, they can veto mining exploration. So, to get around that, the mining companies pay them for the right to explore. Mission Aviation Fellowship got involved in this air charter company when the leaders came to us fifteen years ago and asked us to manage and fly the operation for them on the basis of what we had done in Arnhem Land.' Gil ensures we are all buckled up, and starts the single-engine turbo-powered Cessna.

'And it's working out?' I ask as we taxi slowly down to the end of the Alice Springs runway, long enough to take jet airliners full of tourists.

'This aircraft cost two million dollars. Now we have another aircraft on order that will cost four million dollars. So, you could say it's working.'

I admire the state-of-the-art communications and navigation equipment in the cockpit. 'What about training pilots from the community?'

'We had a couple, but they've moved on. They didn't have a commitment to their own people.' He flicks on the intercom and asks for clearance to line up and take off. Cleared, we expedite a rolling start and within a fraction of the runway length the Cessna Caravan is airborne.

'How did you like living in Arnhem Land?' I have to raise my voice so that he can hear me. I'd like to go there, but it seems next to impossible from all I have heard.

Reaching our cruising height Gil switches to automatic pilot and sits there with his hands folded across his chest. 'Although I was working there, it took me years to get to know them. They adopted my family and myself but I can tell you, often I didn't think having Aboriginal rellies was so great. They would show up on our doorstep in Darwin in the middle of the night or some other inconvenient time. Sometimes they ruined a weekend planned weeks in advance. They got up my nose in a big way and I found I could be indifferent to them and their world, but I thought, "No, I'm going to be serious about this and I've got to work at it." And I did, and now I am glad that we did. They are a wonderfully gentle people, with a great sense of humour. I have two children and we would go out and visit them, go hunting, with guns of course; they're ineffective with their spears nowadays. They taught my children their dances and my kids—they're adults now—remember those days as some of the best in their lives. I'm proud to say that my children are not the least bit racists. They've lived with the Aboriginal people, they know them, for good and bad.'

The aircraft bumps in the turbulence and Gil places his hands on the steering column, disengaging the automatic pilot as he changes our altitude in an attempt to avoid the turbulent air. A few hundred feet higher he switches the automatic pilot on again and removes his hands from the steering column.

We fly directly west from Alice, north of the MacDonnell Ranges. In the early morning light, the eastern facing slopes of the range catch the light from the sun, their western edges still in shadow. They are spectacular, but even more wonderful, the sense that this is, as far as we can see, virtually empty land, a vast wilderness. It isn't hard to imagine, despite their early contacts with the indigenous people on the coast, why Cook and other explorers thought the land was, relatively speaking, uninhabited. Even now, there is nothing indicating human intrusion. No roads, tracks, railway lines or telegraph poles. Nothing.

The first sign of habitation is Papunya, a scattering of homes and buildings literally in the middle of nowhere. We fly low over the airstrip to give them warning of our arrival, and then land. As we taxi to a halt, a policewoman, the principal of the school and a road maintenance worker, separately drive up to the aircraft to collect the mail and supplies. Each of us passengers has been given a map of our Outback mail flight on the back of which is a written message advising us how to approach the local residents:

Two aspects about the culture of our clients that we feel we need to mention:

- The taking of photographs of the scenery is encouraged, however, if you wish to take photographs of people during our time on the ground, please respect the individual's right to privacy by using discretion.
- Central Australian Aboriginal people are comparatively reserved by nature.
- Please avoid asking direct questions as English is not their first language. If unsure, then please ask the pilot for guidance.

The only Aboriginal person on hand to meet us is a young boy holding onto the skirt of the school principal. We say goodbye to the pipe-smoking town advisor and have barely five minutes on the ground to unload mail and supplies from the bulbous baggage compartment under the fuselage before we are off again.

We fly along Haast's Bluff, past Mount Liebig at 1,274 metres, over a ridge and land at another airstrip tucked behind the mountain. As we taxi in to a halt, to let in air Gil opens my door as soon as the props have stopped turning. I don't know which is worse: the air inside the aircraft heated like a solar oven through the cockpit windows, or the stifling sun-baked heat from outside. The local 'advisor' or town clerk is there to greet us. Eager to socialise and with little prompting from Gil, the town clerk fills the silence with non-stop commentary as I flick flies away from my face.

The two Aboriginal women walk away without saying goodbye.

'Footy is bloody religion to the mob out here,' the town clerk tells me as I stretch. 'We had a footy game the other day; thought it was going to be a blood bath. It gives the Aborigines a way to settle a few tribal scores. Ended up OK, no serious injuries.' He relishes telling these details of life at an outstation. I don't have to ask any questions before he continues. 'Someone came into the clinic the other morning with a spear clear through his leg.' He shows us on his own thigh where the spear had gone. 'Stupid bugger had been caught in the swag with another man's wife.' The curious Perth couple open their eyes wide at the stories. 'His punishment was to take a spear in the leg from the aggrieved man's family. He did a runner instead of taking the spear. That was three years ago.' He waxes lyrical, realising he has a captive audience as Gil busily sorts out the supplies to be dropped off here. 'The elders put a curse on him, in the form of a guy with a red headband. For three years he kept seeing some guy with a red headband following him.'

'There's plenty of guys with red headbands wandering around,' I comment.

'Exactly. Eventually he got so paranoid he came back and took his punishment; hobbled to the clinic with an eight-foot spear through his thigh. If he had been a good footy player though, the tribe wouldn't have required him to take the spear; would have found some other punishment. If they take traditional punishment nowadays, they don't have to take white man's punishment for the same crime otherwise that would be like punishing them twice.'

The mail is taken off the aircraft and Gil hands out lunch boxes containing sandwiches, fruit and other goodies to the Perth couple and myself. He shares his own sandwiches with the Aboriginal cowboy. I feel badly that each of us white passengers has been given a boxed lunch, but not the Aboriginal passenger. I don't ask, but rationalise that it must be because we have paid more than he has.

Gil ushers us back into the Cessna and the advisor keeps talking as we climb on board. Gil shuts the doors and soon the spinning props blow a sandstorm of dust, which lingers long after we have left the airstrip behind us.

Nyirrpi is remarkable for the numerous wrecked cars littering its outskirts. In all of these tiny communities, even if there are only a couple of dozen houses, there is always a circular, Aussie Rules football field. Must be the first bit of infrastructure they put in when they settle a place. As we begin our descent to the dirt strip, I tell Gil, 'The scenery reminds me of East Africa.'

'You've been there?' he asks.

'Including when I was a kid, ten years.'

'Can you speak the language?' he queries.

'One of them.'

'You'll have to meet the maintenance supervisor here. Surprise him, speak to him in the East African language.'

Peter McDermott is already sitting on the bonnet of the Landcruiser by the time we have taxied to a halt. I descend the stairs that pop out of the fuselage and speak to him in Kiswahili. He replies fluently in the same language. We converse some minutes before breaking off into English for everyone else's benefit. Born in Tanzania, he served in the British army before coming out to Australia to work in this isolated outpost as the maintenance supervisor. It isn't difficult to imagine him as a British soldier serving in a similar colonial outpost. I can imagine him in uniform sitting on the porch of the local club drinking Pimms. But it would be difficult, even impossible, to find a place more isolated than this, even in Africa. He tells me, 'I loved East Africa and the damn thing is, this place reminds me of East Africa so much, every day of my life. But it isn't Africa and sometimes I hate it.'

Like the advisor at the previous community, Peter doesn't stop talking and it takes several minutes before we manage to disengage ourselves. Even after we have taken off and are circling overhead to continue flying south, he sits there on the fender of his Landcruiser, waving up at us as long as possible, maintaining that tenuous thread of contact, as if reluctant to face his lonely existence once again.

'You made his day talking to him like that,' Gil comments.

I stare out the window as we circle above the collection of houses. 'These communities or outstations are entirely run and managed by whites. The advisor or the town clerk at the top of the pile, with a retinue of maintenance staff, school-teachers, nurses under him.'

Gil deflects my apparent criticism. 'Don't forget, for the people living out here, it has only been in the last fifty years or so that any real contact has been made with whites. They've been living their nomadic lifestyles uninterrupted for tens of thousands of years and they can't just change that overnight. Many of them don't want to. But for those settling in houses, in permanent communities, they need the whites to do the maintenance of the infrastructure, to work as teachers, administrators, accountants.'

We are almost on the Western Australian border and a half-an-hour flight from the northern edge of the South Australia State border as we descend to Docker River.

'How did these settlements get established?' I ask, amazed that a community could function in such total isolation.

'Docker River was one of the settlements established in remote areas during the Government's policy of assimilation when Aboriginals were expected to live like white Australians. Wandering "bush" groups were removed to settlements like Docker River. It didn't work because the policy was based on the assumption that they would willingly adopt the economic and cultural values of whites. They didn't. This was in the 1950s. In the 1970s the policies changed to self-determination. Some inhabitants at these larger settlements then set up smaller outstation communities in the bush where they could restore their traditional links with the land and culture. It's a bit of a contradiction because they'll often have guns and vehicles, satellite television, videos, fridges and telephones.'

On the ground to meet us is a white woman working as a community schoolteacher. Unlike the other whites we have met during our quick stopovers, she seems happy, or at least she smiles a lot. The mother of one of two excited pre-teenage girls running around the stationary aircraft helping Gil unlock the baggage compartment under the fuselage, she explains, 'My twelve-year-old daughter "met" her friend on the School of the Air when they were eight and they visit each other every school holiday. My daughter's friend lives on a farm to the east of Alice Springs. They are both isolated from other white children their own age so they keep in daily touch with each other on the radio after the official School of the Air is finished, when there isn't much radio traffic.' The two girls giggle and laugh, happy to have each other's company and not just talk on the radio with a discombobulated virtual-reality friend.

'What's it like to go to school over the radio while sitting at home?'

'Not as strange as you might think. They get to know the teacher, they're all on a first name basis, the teacher even recognises their voices. Homework is sent by mail and returned by mail. It takes some discipline, but it works well.' She looks proudly at the two girls. 'But it makes a big difference when they can actually meet like this. Then they keep the friendship going over the radio until they meet up again.'

It's tantalising to get a whiff of what life must be like out in the Outback, and it's frustrating only having a few minutes at the airstrip to talk to these people and get an insight into their very different lives. It's better than nothing, but the experience makes me determined to get onto one of these Aboriginal communities before I leave Australia.

From Docker River we fly north-west, crossing the invisible Western Australia State border, to Kiwirrkurra outpost, where an ostentatiously hand-painted signpost informs us as we taxi to a halt that this is 'The Jewel of the West'. There isn't much to indicate how it became 'Jewel of the West'. Apart from the few houses, which are out of sight, there is just a toilet, strangely enough with a mattress scrunched inside, which makes it a bit of a jewel of a toilet. The only other luxury item qualifying this airstrip as a jewel is the corrugated tin roof supported by four poles providing shade over a bench and table. Four vehicles pull up in clouds of dust, each vehicle driven by a white. They studiously avoid eye contact with each other. There is no communication amongst them, despite the fact, or perhaps because, they live together in this isolated place. With the vigilant eye of hungry vultures, they wait in turn to pick through their mail and supplies, without acknowledging each other's presence. Even to a bystander like myself, the animosity among them is apparent. Their solitary lives, filled with rancour, must be absolute hell in a tiny place like this.

A bunch of children arrive, each stark naked. One rides a tiny motorbike, although he cannot be more than ten years old at the most. Three Aboriginals board the aircraft and the Perth woman pulls out her air freshener again and sprays the interior.

Some hours later, driving through the centre of Alice where we are dropped off by the airport transfer bus, I see the same inner-city graffiti I had seen in downtown Sydney, spray-painted on the side of a building: 'You are on Aboriginal land!'

For the second day in a row I stand outside the backpacker's lodge in pitch darkness waiting for a bus to pick me up. It is surprisingly cold, almost freezing. The first passenger, I lay claim to seat 1A where I can easily talk to the Coach Captain. My Greyhound bus pass around Australia includes a tour to Ayers Rock, known more recently by its Aboriginal name, Uluru. Included with the three-day Uluru tour is a diversion to the Olgas and Kings Canyon. I wrap my sleeping bag around me as we drive into the concrete culvert crossing the Todd River, the headlights illuminating a sign warning of camels crossing. Dishevelled men stumble like ghosts at the edges of the bright beams of light. The driver glances at me. 'One and a half million dollars was spent on alcohol by Aborigines in Alice Springs between Wednesday and Friday. Frightening statistics. And if they're not drinking alcohol, they're sniffing petrol, destroying what's left of their brains.'

He tells me as we drive around Alice picking up the remaining tourists booked for the tour, 'The average thirty-year-old Aborigine getting on the Greyhound can't even read his boarding pass to see what seat number he has. They didn't even have a wheel fifty years ago and now they are travelling on coaches that could carry their whole clan. It's been too much, too soon. All they are interested in is booze, cigarettes, and if they have enough money, a vehicle. It's tragic.' We pick up a full coach load of passengers before heading on the straight highway leading south out of Alice Springs.

The Coach Captain continues on what is apparently a favourite topic, 'People think the Aborigines are not as intelligent as white folk are. I used to think that too when I first started teaching Aborigines brick-laying at a vocational school here. Sometimes I would give a class, and then ask them the next morning what we had learned the previous day. It was as if none of them had been there. One day we were outside doing practical work and because I didn't have my notebooks, I drew what I was trying to show them in the sand with a stick. The next day, I wanted them to repeat what I had taught the day before. One of the students drew everything I had drawn in the sand, exactly the same way. I experimented. I drew complicated patterns in the sand. The next day every single student could duplicate those drawings without any problem. Aborigines are as smart as we are all right; they are intelligent in different ways from us. They are intuitive, visual, they hear and smell things we can't, they have a sixth sense, and they understand animals better than us. These are all the things we have lost over the centuries being 'civilised'. It's just too bad that their capabilities have little use in our modern world.'

I still feel like a kid living a dream as I stare out the window at the passing scenery, half-listening to the driver.

'Straddling this stretch of road between Alice and Ayers Rock, there are eight properties, each between 1 and 10,000 square kilometres in size,' the Coach Captain tells me; the boredom of driving this stretch of track is too much for him to sit there silently. He needs someone to talk to just to keep awake. 'One of the farms was bought for the Aborigines as a pastoral-station, but it's gone to seed already, which is too bad because they are good stockmen and as I said, have a natural ability with animals.'

Maybe letting it 'go to seed', meaning back to its original state, isn't such a bad thing. It's the overstocking of cattle and sheep beyond the carrying capacity of the land that has stuffed up so much of the Australian Outback. It would be interesting to see what this desert landscape would look like now if there had been no cattle farms here, no exotic animals with cloven hooves to chop up the land into dust balls.

At the Erldunda Roadhouse, we turn west off the Stuart Highway towards Uluru and continue in a straight line until we drive into Ayers Rock Resort, a huge compound within sight of, but still some distance away from Uluru, the Rock itself. The Resort consists of several hotels, a backpacker's, and a campground for the adventure tour operators. It has a tour/information centre, shops, hairdressing salon, a bank, tourist souvenir shops, supermarket, cinema and outdoor theatre. This pre-planned instant village, with a ring road accessing the infrastructure, looks suspiciously homogenous and prefabricated. Even the backpacker's lodge doesn't look seedy, or for that matter much different from the fancy hotels. The way we are isolated in this compound with all the amenities, it is as if we were on a cruise liner in the middle of the ocean. One management company operates the whole affair, with a staff of 1,500. The entire staff is white, there is not a single Aboriginal to be seen on the compound.

The Resort is the antithesis of what I had expected Uluru, to be. There is no historical, cultural or spiritual merit to this planned tourist resort. On any given night, 7,000 tourists can be accommodated in a community artificially created so tourists can gain easy access to the Rock.

Once checked in to our accommodation, we continue for an evening scenic drive to Uluru, or Ayers Rock as the Coach Captain insists on calling it. As we approach the recognisable granite dome he tells us, 'This monolith, formed some 400 million years ago, is 8 kilometres in circumference and its summit is 347 metres above the surrounding plains.'

We enter a gate and a sign greeting 'Welcome to Aboriginal Land'. It's like entering a theme park or one of the artificial South African banthustan homelands that catered to wealthy South African gamblers during the days of apartheid. We all exit the bus and line up to pay the entrance fee. 'Twenty per cent of what you just paid goes to the Aborigines who call this place home,' our Coach Captain informs us as he puts the bus into gear and we continue towards Uluru. 'That's over ten million dollars a year for a clan of Aborigines that can't number more than some hundreds of individuals; less than half the Aborigines of this tribe live here now.' He only goes so far with many of his critical comments. It's as if he wants to say more, but doesn't dare in case it should offend the sensibilities of his passengers. 'This rock is supposed to be the modern symbol of Australia's indigenous people, despite the fact that there are 300 different tribes and cultures of Aborigine clans.'

The Rock looks as if it could swallow us. The closer we get, the more impressive it becomes as we drive on a two-lane sealed road circumnavigating the perimeter. Despite the profusion of four-wheel drive vehicles, there is no need for four-wheel drive. The tarmac road is smooth enough to roller-blade on. As if to prove the point, half-a-dozen Harley Davidson motorbikes on an organised Ayers Rock tourist tour from Alice overtake us with a thunderous roar. They are perhaps the ultimate symbol in the commercialisation of this once sacred site.

Along a side road, through the bush, we see several buildings with a sign at the entrance:

Warning, do not enter.
$1,000 fine. Aboriginal Freehold Land.

'This is where the original four motels and campground used to be located. It was closed off and the facilities given to the local clan. Now all the tourism to Ayers Rock is centred at the Ayers Rock Resort.' Being located further away, I suppose that is an improvement from an Aboriginal point of view. Numerous signs request us not to take photographs of sacred sites covered in rock paintings, which provokes anyone with a camera to take a quick prohibited snap.

We stop at the bottom of a chain scarring the rock face. Hundreds of climbers, like a line of ants, use the chain to grab onto as they ascend and descend despite a notice clearly informing tourists that the local clan would rather no one climbed up Uluru.

'This is just a preview,' our Coach Captain encourages. 'Tomorrow we will climb the rock and those who are faint-hearted and don't want to climb can visit the cultural centre.' We drive away. 'The bloke who has the record time for climbing Ayers Rock,' he tells us, 'is from New Zealand. He ran all the way, up and down. Can't remember how long it took him, but it wasn't long.' There is silence from the bus, no oohs and aahs. 'How many are going to climb it tomorrow?' he asks looking into the rear view mirror as we depart for the Resort.

Only three passengers put up their hands: two Frenchmen and a Japanese boy. I presume the rest of us are not climbing in deference to the Aboriginals' wishes and not because the climb is too daunting.

We pull in to the 'sunset viewing area', a vast stretch of tarmac where hundreds of cars, as if parked at a drive-in, are lined up facing Uluru. In a separate area sectioned off for buses, I count over fifty full-sized coaches. There must be at least 2,000 tourists on the buses alone. We disembark in the parking lot and walk towards a fenced-off area. Several tour groups stand around tables decked in white linen, topped with champagne on ice and plates of hors-d'úuvres. The clients watch the sun set on Uluru, occasionally lifting fly nets hanging from their hats to cover their faces, so they can sip champagne from crystal glasses or eat smoked salmon and oysters. They chat as if this were an outdoor cocktail party, which I suppose it is. Their guides dressed in immaculate khaki try to disguise looks of utter boredom. You can only take so many sunsets on Uluru before becoming jaded and blasé about the experience.

I walk for ten minutes on a slightly raised sand dune to obtain an unobstructed view of Uluru. Two helicopters buzz around ferrying sightseeing passengers for the sunset flight over the Rock. Traffic cruises up and down the road in front of us. The rock changes hue from bright yellow to orange, red, mauve and then purple. Finally, when the sun has dropped below the horizon, Uluru turns an undistinguished brown. Before the sun has set, there is a mad rush of cars and buses as everyone tries to beat the rush hour traffic back to the resort, to hotel rooms and dinner in a restaurant.

By the time of the Second World War, only a handful of whites had climbed or even seen Uluru. Now almost 500,000 tourists visit the rock monolith annually. What would it have been like a century ago to wander in here with a local clan, to have camped out here with them, and watched the sunrise and sunset? My romanticised notion of a walk in the desert with the 'noble savage', surviving off the land, is in stark contrast to the reality.

I remain on the sand dune staring at Uluru as long as I dare without getting left behind. I find myself alone. A three-quarters moon hangs suspended above. The sun's last rays hit skeins of clouds patterned around Uluru like supernatural, flickering red flames from a campfire. It's as if Uluru itself were the source of the conflagration. Apart from me, no one else seems to be watching this magical show.

In the early morning light, the Rock is magical. It rises massively out of the ground over the surrounding flat plains. It has a monstrous presence about it, like a slumbering prehistoric giant. There is a powerful, supernatural force about the place.

Our bus drops most of us off at the Cultural Centre while the three climbers continue on to Uluru to ascend the rock.

Inside the Cultural Centre an unambiguous sign reads:

Now a lot of visitors are only looking at the sunset and climbing Uluru. That rock is really an important sacred thing. You shouldn't climb it! Climbing is not a proper part of this place. There is a true story to be properly understood.

There is an emotional and sometimes funny video depicting the recent history of Uluru. While us foreigners sit avidly watching the video, an Australian wearing an Aussie bush hat can't stomach what he sees. He gives a derisive snort when the video relates how some time ago brutal white policemen chased Aboriginals to the Rock and shot them there. He gets up and walks away in a huff, his wife and two young children in tow.

Included in the video is a black-and-white news clip from the 1950s showing a Boy Scout group climbing Ayers Rock. The commentator refers to 'these indigenous primitive people' as if the expedition was an incursion into deepest, darkest Africa at the time of Stanley and Dr Livingstone.

The video film also shows Aboriginals working in the original motels around Ayers Rock, doing menial labour, making beds, sweeping. Now there are none working at the Resort; at least none that I could see. Last night when I asked the manager of one of the hotels why this was, he replied, 'It's all going to take time, mate.' But if they were working at the motels forty years ago, why aren't they working at the Resort now? Surely over forty years some could be in managerial positions? Maybe it's simply because they don't want to. Maybe they have enough money and employment is meaningless.

Although the video is tragic in its depiction of how Australia's indigenous people have been dispossessed, the film, true to their sense of humour, is also very funny in parts. Fast motion sequences show coaches driving frantically around Uluru, parking in the sunset viewing area, passengers climbing out like so many scurrying ants. Then the film slows down to normal speed to interview an American in his fifties. He says in a broad American drawl, 'Well, I wanted to climb that rock for some time and I've trained for it and worked hard and now

I've climbed it and I'm proud of myself.' Words to that effect. Then fast forward again as everyone climbs back on the coaches, the coaches take off, leaving the parking lot empty.

At the centre's café I talk to a driver, Coach Captain, from one of the luxury buses. He wears an authentic bush hat with crocodile skin trim. He tells me, 'I've been coming to Uluru for years. Every time I return, I get a headache. There's bad karma here. What is going on with tourism here is wrong. They should leave Uluru alone.' He stirs his coffee, ruminating. 'People climb that rock. They don't care what Aboriginal people think; otherwise they wouldn't climb it. To the local people it is *tjukurpa* and it establishes rules for behaviour and gives meaning to the Dreamtime stories.' He sips his coffee before telling me, 'When we look at Uluru, we just see a monolith. When the people from this area look at it they see a storybook, like our Bible, telling the story of creation. The paintings on the rock teach the *tjukurpa,* the relationship between people, plants, animals and the physical features of the land. Locals see meaning and significance in every crack, scar and waterhole of that rock. Uluru is sacred, because of its spiritual significance, and yet look how those tourists treat it.' His own busload of passengers is climbing the rock.

He finishes the cup of coffee. 'They've got boxes full of rocks in the administration building. Know where they come from?' I shake my head. 'Tourists who removed them from Uluru. When they got back to their homes, they airmailed them, sent them back by courier, whatever it took, to get rid of those rock pieces. Why did they return them? Because the stolen bits of granite brought them bad luck. OK, one or two instances and you would think it a coincidence. But this is not just a few. There's boxes back there, full of stones, rocks, bits and pieces that were taken from Uluru.' He raises his eyebrows at me. 'That's no coincidence. If taking those stones brought them bad luck, I reckon climbing up Uluru qualifies for even worse luck.' He contemplatively touches his fine moustache.

'Then why don't the Aboriginals stop people climbing if they don't want them to?' I ask. It's an obvious question.

'Ah, look,' he says, 'The Japanese will even ask for their money back if they can't climb up because there's too much wind or too high temperatures. If they weren't allowed to climb Uluru at all, many of them wouldn't bother coming to Australia. They fly to Cairns, do a Great Barrier Reef cruise and snorkel around the boat, then fly to Uluru so they can climb the Rock. Most of them don't even bother to go into Alice Springs. Then they fly out of Sydney. If they couldn't climb Uluru, we'd lose half of our Asian visitors to Australia.'

'The Aboriginals want the money, so that's why they let the tourists climb the rock?' I imply.

He shakes his head. 'It's the government, big business. The Aboriginal people here would just as soon close it down. Stuff the tourists, they'd say.' He studies the massive monolith. 'Can't say I blame them.' He looks back at me. 'The Aboriginals don't care about the money side of it. They've got enough anyway.'

'How do you know?' I ask.

'I talk to them.' He becomes agitated. 'There is a total contradiction between what this is now, and what it should be. It's an important spiritual place for the Aboriginal people. Tourists treat it as a climbing rock, trampling all over it. How would we like it if visitors and Japanese tourists started climbing all over our churches?' He pauses, upset at the whole topic of conversation. 'The Japs are crazy about climbing this,' he flicks his eyes at the rock outcrop, 'even if it kills them, and it does. Those that die, die from heat exhaustion, sometimes from heart attack, and some fall, especially during high winds.' He turns to look at me. 'It's really bad news for local people when someone gets killed on Uluru. Traditionally, if they permitted a stranger on their land, they were responsible for that person's safety. If anything happened to him, it was their fault and their lives were forfeit.'

'So, surely the Aboriginal people could close it down?'

He shakes his head. 'The Government handed over this land to the local clan in 1985, but on the same day the Government handed it over, they signed a ninety-nine year lease with them for the National Parks Service to run Uluru as a National Park. So the Government gave with one hand and then took away with the other.'

Our Coach Captain told us to be ready to be picked up at precisely a certain hour or be left behind. I see the blue Greyhound logo on the side of a bus as it approaches and have to run fast to catch it otherwise I'm sure he'd live up to his threat. The others are already on the bus as I reach the door. Panting with the effort, I swing into my 1A seat and sit back, the air-conditioning cold on my sweaty brow. The driver reprimands me for my tardiness and grinds the old bus through a succession of gears as the road crests a small hill affording a view over this vast expanse of dry red nothingness. It has an inherent appeal, these vast open spaces devoid of any sign of civilisation. As I catch my breath I try to figure out what it is about this landscape that fascinates so much. Maybe it's just the unabashed nothingness of the place.

We are given an hour's break to walk up the gorge at the Olgas, several Uluru-shaped rocks. It isn't long enough. In a way, the Olgas are more spectacular than Uluru, and this impression is probably enhanced by the fact that there aren't so many tourists competing for room on the path. In an hour we have time to quickly walk up the gully between the rocks and then return to the bus to tick the Olgas off the list of requisite Australian icons visited. We continue to the King Canyon Resort, an enclave of tourist facilities removed a respectable distance from the sacred Olgas. While Ayers Rock Resort could take 7,000 guests, Kings Canyon Resort can only take 700. There's less of a vacation spot feel to the place. I walk around the enclave and read off a brass plaque bolted to a boulder:

Kings Canyon Frontier Lodge—October 1991
A co-operative development by Aboriginals and Torres Strait
Islanders Commercial Development Co-operative, Centrecorp
Aboriginal Development Corporation Pty. Ltd., Australian
Frontier Holidays Ltd, Northern Territories of Australia.

Wanting to savour what it must be like to be alone in this
enormous sandy red desert, I change into running shoes and
shorts and jog down the highway away from everyone
and everything. In front of me are the red cliffs of Kings
Canyon. Parrots, pink galahs, black cockatoos and other
colourful birds return boisterously to their roosts in the
tangled branches of dead trees silhouetted against the sky.
Insects commence their noisy racket. I jog for half-an-hour
before I stop running and stand still to absorb fully the
experience. The intense colours flare brightly for several
moments and then fade in gradual sequence across the sky
until it is completely dark.

There is something deeply primeval about the Australian
Outback that touches me profoundly and I am still grappling
to explain the affinity I feel for this place. I could become
addicted to the sense of solitude.

We are up before dawn to continue to Kings Canyon.
Although we arrive early, already several 4WD Landcruisers
and a beat-up old Holden station wagon are in the parking
lot. Desperate to regain the sense of solitude I experienced
yesterday, I deliberately drift away from the others to walk
the trail alone. Pools of water in the crevices of the vertical
barren red rock are surrounded by lush vegetation. With the
surrounding dry desert these oases are like Gardens of Eden.
Appropriately enough, I bump into two temptingly nubile
Australians in jean shorts and T-shirts. They lounge beside
one of the idyllic natural pools high on the rock. Despite their
fair complexion they are as brown as berries.

They tell me their names, Penny and Cathy. 'We're been travelling around for three months in our car. You probably saw our old Holden wagon in the parking lot.' Despite the fact that they've been travelling in close proximity to each other for three months, I feel like I've interrupted their conversation. The one looks at the other and as if continuing their line of thought says, 'On the East Coast we met heaps of foreigners but they're so young and . . .'

'Inexperienced,' the other adds ruefully.

'Where do you come from?'

'Adelaide.'

'What do you do back home?' I ask, slightly smitten and almost tongue-tied.

'Well, we've taken three months off to travel around our country, but normally we work at the hospital in Adelaide.'

'Nurses?'

'Doctors.'

Hate it when I do that. There are probably more female doctors around now than there are male doctors and I still assume a woman working in a hospital is a nurse.

The two doctors are in their early thirties; by contrast to the inexperienced foreigners they met on the East Coast. They are also well travelled, worldly, intelligent and best of all they seem interested in talking to me. They have both travelled through Africa on one of the overland trucks. We compare notes on different corners of that continent.

'How do you like Australia?' Penny asks.

'I like it. Reminds me of Africa, especially this.'

'This . . . ?'

'This . . . emptiness. The colours of the earth and the sky and the sharp clear light. I love the fact that the sky is so big the clouds can never cover it. There's always a patch of blue somewhere. I love the smell, I love how empty it is . . .' Tongue-tied by their presence, I begin to repeat myself. Sometimes I can be quite articulate and then other times, typically in a situation like this, I find it hard to string three intelligible words together. Pitiful. 'Uh, it's hard to put a finger on it exactly, but . . . uh . . . oh, I don't know . . . I just like it . . . especially the Outback.'

'What about the people?'

'How do I like you Aussies?' I repeat the question, giving myself time to think of an appropriate answer.

'Yeah.'

'So far so good,' I reply eloquently.

'Have you met many Aboriginals?' Cathy asks.

There's a loaded question. 'In bars. It's hard to get on their communities. You have to ask permission from the Land Council or whatever and it takes a minimum of six weeks for that approval to come through. But what little I've seen of them, I've liked. Wish I'd met more.' Hope that was the right answer.

'It's surprising there's any left,' Cathy comments.

'What do you mean?'

'Oh, the whole confrontation business between the Aboriginals and the early settlers,' she says it casually, but the comment isn't casual at all.

Penny indicates the idyllic Garden of Eden waterhole beside us. 'We were just sitting here talking about how a waterhole like this was essential to their survival and how it's all been taken away from them.'

Cathy studies the pool of water. 'Aboriginals hunting around waterholes just like this would come head-to-head in conflict with our squatter-settler forefathers. Apart from polluting water holes and digging up the ground with their hooves, the settlers' domestic stock frightened the wildlife away. But if any starving Aboriginals speared any cattle or sheep, a posse of settlers would use that as an excuse to kill every man, woman or child they came across.' Her voice trembles, as if she had been an eyewitness to the event. 'They were shot, clubbed, decapitated, burnt and their bodies left hanging in trees as a warning to deliberately exterminate Aboriginals from areas they wanted.'

'I've just been reading about some of this history,' I reply, eager to ingratiate myself.

'You've read about Myall Creek?' Cathy asks.

'No.' I sit down on a boulder.

'The Myall Creek murders were a watershed in Australia's pioneer history because it was the first time white men were tried for murdering Aboriginals. After that, white massacres were more obscure. Rather than slaughtering them with guns, the settlers generously distributed bread laced with strychnine and blankets that had been contaminated with smallpox and other infectious diseases, or simply poisoned Aboriginal waterholes.' Cathy is so emotional about the issue she begins to cry.

Penny puts her hand on Cathy's shoulder. 'We've been talking a lot about this since travelling around Australia. It's sad to see what our ancestors did . . .'

She's right. The early settlers did a thorough job of ridding their new colony of its original inhabitants. Of an estimated one million people living in Australia in 1788 when the First Fleet of eleven ships of British convicts arrived with their wardens, by the time of the first Commonwealth census in 1911 the Aboriginal population had been decimated to 20,000. British settlers did an effective job in wiping out resistance by the Natives in North America, and the Maori in New Zealand, but the elimination of Australia's native people bordered on genocide.

I don't know what to say. In the short time I've been here, I've met other Australians who are as outspoken and emotional about this issue as Cathy is. In a bookstore in Sydney I had spoken to the manager to ask her for her advice on what to read about the Aboriginals. As she pulled out more and more books and told me about their history, she started to cry, right there in her bookshop. Conversely, I've been surprised by other attitudes, like the female bartender proudly telling me she is a racist.

Cathy recovers. 'I'm sorry.'

'No, no, that's OK.' I look at my watch. 'Damn! I'm going to miss my bus. I almost missed it yesterday and that Coach Captain definitely won't wait a second time.'

'Where are you going from here?' Penny asks quickly. 'It'd be nice to meet up again.'

My pulse accelerates instantly, ba-doom, ba-doom, as if I'd just received a shot of adrenaline. 'Coober Pedy,' I reply in time to my heartbeat. What a difference that would make; travelling around Australia in a station wagon and camping along the way with these two interesting women.

'Coober Pedy?' Penny asks. 'So are we. When are you arriving there?' There's a faint trace of a smile. I reckon she knows what's going on in my head.

'To-,' ba-doom, 'night,' ba-doom. Can't help it. My heartbeat is way out of control. Even if I'm not a pimply teenager, I'm definitely acting like one. I should buy a comic book to hide my blushing face.

'We're driving down in our car, but we won't get there until tomorrow afternoon. Let's meet.'

BA-DOOM, BA-DOOM, 'Sure,' ba-doom, ba-doom, I reply like a half-wit, stunned that they would be even remotely interested in my itinerary. I check my watch again and realise I only have minutes to get to the bus before it leaves. 'Look,' ba-doom, ba-doom, 'I gotta go,' ba-doom, ba-doom. 'I'll see you there.' Ba-doom, ba-doom, ba-doom, ba-doom. I turn around to run off down the rocky path.

'What's your name?' Penny asks as I scurry away.

I forgot to introduce myself when they told me their names. I turn to yodel back, cupping my mouth so they should get this crucial bit of information, but in my eagerness, trip and fall flat on my face. I pick myself up and scrape off the dirt. Blood oozes from both knees, which have taken on the appearance of miniature tomato and cheese pizzas. I've scraped the end of my nose too. Should get a helmet before I do some real damage. 'Andrew,' I yell back before giving the two women one last furtive wave and then hurtling down the path with more success.

Our Greyhound coach is returning to Alice Springs. Those of us continuing south are dropped off at the Erldunda crossroads roadhouse, where we wait for our scheduled late afternoon southbound coach departing out of Darwin. I take advantage of the washroom to tend to my knees. I wonder if the two Aussie women saw my pratfall. Just when you want to create a good impression, something like that happens. It seems to happen to me a lot.

Boarding the connecting coach, our new Coach Captain tells us, 'Those of you who climbed Kings Canyon and Ayers Rock, please keep your boots on you feet; we'd like to breathe something resembling fresh air.' He proceeds through his own version of the standard rules of engagement on board his coach: no smoking, no drinking, no recreational drugs. 'The toilet at the rear of the bus is for emergency purposes only,' he reminds us. We need a note from a doctor to avail ourselves of the toilet facilities. 'Please save your heavy artillery for our break stops. If you have to use the emergency toilet, make sure anything you put down the toilet you have eaten first.'

We barrel south, crossing the empty continent along an endless straight road, lulled into semi-consciousness by the constant hum of the engine and the thrum of the tyres. Occasionally we labour past a rumbling road train. Although I am doing nothing more than sitting semi-reclined in a comfortable chair, I am going somewhere, slowly making my way around Australia.

As the sun sets I am reminded once again of the savannah plains of the Serengeti in East Africa. It has the same flatness, the same type of flora, but the few wild animals visible here are kangaroos and imported camels from Afghanistan. And unlike Africa, there are no villages. The only evidence of human habitation is the occasional roadhouse, spread some hundreds of kilometres apart along this desolate stretch of road. Night falls and there is nothing but an expanse of black. We could be at the bottom of the ocean.

Our high beams illuminate a sign:

Welcome to Marla.
To help keep the cattle out of town, PLEASE ensure the town boundary fence gates are kept shut.

The bus rattles over a cattle grid. This place on the map doesn't seem to be a town so much as a roadhouse. The bar is lined with a dozen leathery Australians wearing bush hats sussing out the female talent brought in with the coach. The arrival of the bus is the highlight of their evening.

Back on board, the Coach Captain does a head count to make sure no females have been abducted, and then the comforting rumble of the engine and the rolling tyres lull me as I stare out the window and fantasise about the two Australian doctors. Penny was quieter and more athletic. Cathy was more vocal and outspoken, although her emotional outburst indicated a softer side to her.

A chance meeting like this changes my entire disposition. Not that I was disconsolate before, but now there's an atmosphere of anticipation—it sort of feels a bit like Christmas Eve.

The coach arrives at Coober Pedy just before midnight. My pack is thrown into the back of an awaiting utility vehicle and I am driven to the backpacker's, a converted old opal mine. At the top of stairs leading into this underground backpacker's is a posted warning: 'You are entering sleeping dungeons— please be quiet.' You wouldn't want to have claustrophobia in a place like this. A no-nonsense Australian leads me down stairs into a catacomb where dimmed lights provide barely enough illumination to see into open tomb-like rooms carved into the pink and red rock face. Each tomb has bunks lining the cavities with a sleeping body on each bed. At least, I assume it is a sleeping body. It *is* deathly quiet.

I climb out of the silent catacomb before anyone else is awake to wander around in the bright morning light of this strange underground mining town. At an above-ground delicatessen, the only place that seems open so early, I ask for a coffee and freshly made bread.

'We're not open, but is OK.'

'Polish?' I ask the man serving me.

'How do you know?' I tell him his accent is unmistakable, although in fact it was a wild lucky guess. He doesn't seem to mind my observation. 'I been fifteen years in Australia, and eight years in Coober Pedy. I like it here. I am geologist by training. In Poland, Australian embassy told I have no problem to get job here. When I get here, is different. Is difficult to get job if you cannot speak English. But here is good. Here is Greeks, Serbians, Croatians, Italians; every nationality working together, sometimes as partners. In Coober Pedy is no racism.'

'You're a geologist, but you're a baker?'

He laughs. 'Easier to make money.' He shrugs at the irony of it.

An Aboriginal walks by the delicatessen. I had seen several others already this morning, barefoot, dressed in tattered rags, wandering around the dusty streets. We have this notion that if people are barefoot they must be so destitute they can't afford shoes. But a lot of people, especially rural Australians, seem to have a preference for walking barefoot and it has nothing to do with poverty. Perhaps I shouldn't prejudge the Aboriginals with bare feet either.

The Pole sees me studying the man outside; he sighs and gives vent to his opinions. 'You see them walk by, so poor. You feel sorry for them, huh? They ask me for credit, but they never work. Do not lift one finger even this much.' He holds his fist up with an erect finger. 'They come to Coober Pedy, live off dole. I am not racist—or maybe I am—but I am just telling you how they live. They dirty, lazy, drink. They want land back, but for what? They don't want to live on land.

Look!' He points out the plate-glass window. They live outside 'church', is social welfare office, pick up cheque, go to discount liquor store.' He points his finger at me. 'You know, you people in Western Europe tell Polish people,' he hooks his thumb back at himself, 'we must forget past. We must make peace with enemies. We must forget old boundaries. We must forget what Germans and Russians did to Poles. We must think about future. Is strange, huh? In Europe we must forget past, but here they talk about past always.' He shakes his head. 'Aborigines want to take back Coober Pedy, but they cannot. They cannot show they lived here. Is no water before miners come; water is from borehole sixty kilometres away.'

He gets on with opening his shop, and I buy a loaf of bread and take my leave.

On the street a woman walks in front of me. Two other Aboriginal women sit in the dust on the other side of the road. One calls out to attract the others' attention and I watch as they communicate, non-verbally, in a series of hand and head actions, as if they were indeed telepathic.

Curious about what the Polish immigrant has told me, I walk into a Family and Community Services office and chat to the receptionist. She is so pale it doesn't seem possible she could live in a place where the sun is so evident; must keep totally protected from the sun in an underground dugout. I greet her good morning and try to make conversation with her. It is hard to draw her out initially, but soon she is cautiously spilling forth opinions about her clients. She takes her hands off the keyboard she has been working on and reaches around for a coffee sitting on the table beside her, making sure no one else is in the reception room with us.

'Ah look,' she says, preparing for the soliloquy she is about to deliver, 'I was brought up on Kangaroo Island, a fourth-generation Australian of Scottish, English, Irish, Italian stock. It's hard to take when Aborigines keep telling me I don't belong here, that this is their land. Where else do I belong, some European country?' she asks rhetorically.

I shrug.

'I've never been out of Australia. Neither have my parents or grandparents. Where can we go? Canada, America, New Zealand? Why? All the non-indigenous people should be thrown out of those countries too, for the same reasons. Aborigines tell me they were here before me, that it's their land. OK, so if someone is younger than me, I'm going to tell him I was here before him, and that it's my land?'

I shrug again.

'That's just as ridiculous as Aborigines telling me this was their land and that I don't belong here.' She looks down and shakes her head. 'I try to be empathetic with them, but it's difficult. I'm tired of being told that their way of life is better than ours is and that their culture is 50,00 years old.' She looks at me again. 'If their culture is so bloody great, why do they abandon their culture and accept ours so readily?'

A dishevelled Aboriginal walks in and the receptionist is conspicuously silent. When he remains sitting in the reception area she continues on a different bent, 'You'd have to spend at least a year with the Aborigines to get a glimpse into their lives, to even begin to understand where they are coming from. You have no idea of the issues and the problems at hand,' she says, effectively dismissing me and getting back to her computer.

On the way to the backpacker's crypt, I stop at an opal shop. Behind the counter a bearded man sells opals to two American tourists. He gives the classic line in a heavily, Greek-accented voice, 'I give it to you for same price I buy it.'

Anxious about my date tonight with the two Australian doctors, I diligently buy stain remover and do my laundry, dumping extra dosages of washing powder into the machine to see if I can remove a month's worth of grease that didn't quite make it into my mouth. I pour the stain remover directly on the dark spots. I want to look presentable, with a clean set of togs. I shampoo and then cut my hair with scissors where I can see it is too long, and trim my scraggly beard. By the time I have finished making myself reasonably presentable, dried and ironed my shorts, it is time for a tour of Coober Pedy. Satisfied that the fish and chip fat stains are mostly gone from my shorts and T-shirt, I join a bunch of other backpackers.

'Coober Pedy with a population of only 4,000 has 48 different nationalities speaking 50-odd languages or dialects; 70 per cent of the inhabitants live in dugouts, homes dug into the earth, preferably out of a hill with sloping ground. In an old mine area called potch, or Posh Gully, are some of Coober Pedy's finest homes.'

Driving through Posh Gully one could be forgiven for thinking this was nothing more than a rock quarry. The only indications that it isn't a quarry are TV antennas and ventilation pipes sticking out of the earth.

Our guide tells us as he drives through the rock quarry, 'Believe it or not, this is prime real estate. It's good tunnelling and good rock. You just need to get a tunnel machine to hollow out your home. Go in, turn left, turn right, and a three bedroom home can cost as little as 35,000 dollars. Some of the new owners in this neighbourhood found hundreds of thousands of dollars worth of opals when they were digging out their homes. One of these houses has fifteen bedrooms, not because the owner has fifteen kids, but because he kept finding more and more opal. One house has a thirty-metre lounge. The problem is, the area is zoned as residential, so mining for opals is no longer allowed. If the owners found opals here, they had to ask for an extension of the house because they weren't allowed to 'mine' it. That's one of the reasons it's one of Coober Pedy's best areas. Buying a plot of land and excavating a house could pay for itself, just in the opals taken out.'

The Flintstones might aspire to live in a mother lode of opal but not me, even if I could get rich burrowing out my own home.

'At night, in the winter, it can get to below zero degrees Centigrade. In the summer it can get to be over 50°C. But in these dugout homes, the temperature will remain constant at about 18–20°C. If you need more space, you simply drill out a new room with your jackhammer, and the new addition to the family has a bedroom to call his own. And it's very quiet in a dugout. You don't hear your neighbours partying. The front room is always the kitchen because that's where you need the most light. The bedroom is at the other end of the house. Midsummer it's so hot you can only work in the mines from four until eleven in the mornings. Then you go back to your dugout and dive into a nice cool and dark bedroom, even in the middle of the day. There's no lawn to mow and you'll notice there are no streetlights and no signs. That's for a good reason. No one can find these houses unless they've been given instructions. Helps keep the taxmen away and no one knows for sure how wealthy those homeowners are. Legally, you can work a twenty-hour week and still collect the dole; you just have to tell the unemployment office how much you earned from mining during the hours you worked.' He grins and nods, 'Miners may not be the brightest people in the world, but we're not that stupid.'

We drive by the local school. 'This is the only patch of greenery in Coober Pedy. It was put in when the kids were away on holiday. Underground pipes drip irrigated water into the lawn. The first day at school some kids cried when they were told to go out and play. They had never seen a green grass lawn like this before.' We continue on past the new police station. Confirming the Wild West atmosphere about the place, our driver/guide tells us, 'There's a lot of blokes who know how to use dynamite and some of it seems to find itself regularly blowing up under the police station.'

'Outside of town one-and-a-half million twenty-metre deep, one-metre diameter shafts lie in wait for unsuspecting tourists.' No wonder the Aboriginals called the place 'white man's burrow', or Coober Pedy. 'Three tourists have died in those unprotected mine shafts by stepping backwards to take a photo. So why don't the authorities fill in the shafts with the overburden to make it safe for absent-minded tourists?' He answers the question himself. 'Because a miner may be excavating horizontally in the adjacent claim and if he dug into a refilled shaft, the replaced rubble might avalanche into his, burying him alive and the elected authorities are more worried about local resident miners than passing foreign tourists.'

I try to sit so that my freshly-ironed shorts and shirt keep their creases. Difficult to do when it's so hot that I'm dripping sweat by the bucketful.

Boot Hill, the local graveyard, has a disproportionately large number of young buried there. 'Alcohol abuse,' our guide explains when I make this observation as we walk around. 'People out here have a tendency to drink themselves to death.' One grave has a metal beer-barrel for a headstone with 'RIP and take it easy' as an epitaph. 'In the seventies the ratio of men to women here was 400:1.'

Our guide points out a dozen satellite dishes outside a dilapidated mobile home. 'Belongs to a miner who found an opal worth 100,000 dollars. Bought a few satellite dishes and no one has seen him since.'

Coober Pedy's most famous inhabitant claims to be the original Crocodile Dundee, except his name wasn't Crocodile Dundee, it was Crocodile Harry. The guide doesn't explain how a Crocodile Anyone lives in an environment as unsuitable for crocodiles as Coober Pedy is. Nor does he explain how the 'real' Crocodile Dundee was shot dead by police in Darwin recently. 'Crocodile Harry isn't here today, otherwise he'd have you girls on his knees in no time,' our driver tells us. 'His home is a converted disused opal mine with car windscreens for windows cemented into the holes in the rock face.' In Harry's bedroom thousands of girl's names are inscribed on the walls. Bras and underwear supposedly left by female visitors add to the debauched atmosphere. There's a few photos of a younger Crocodile Harry wrestling with crocs but there's a lot more photos of an older Harry wrestling with dames of all shapes and sizes, some semi-clad. How he manages this is a bit of a mystery too; he must be in his seventies. 'Crocodile Harry's ex-wife, who came here from Germany after reading about him, lives in a mine across the road. She's been living there for twenty-two years after only two weeks of marriage.'

They are the only neighbours for kilometres around.

We get back into the bus. It's so hot I'm falling into a heat-induced somnolent stupor.

It takes considerable time to drive past a tiny portion of a farm that is larger than the size of England and the largest in the world. The earth is so dry the farm can only carry a single head of cattle per square kilometre without overgrazing the land. We are shown where *Mad Max* was filmed, and the Dingo Fence, a wire fence that stretches 9,600 kilometres north/south, to keep the dingoes out. But none of this stuff really impresses me. All I can think about are the two Aussie doctors who promised to show up tonight. The sun sets spectacularly and darkness sets in and I watch a full moon rising. Couldn't be more romantic.

I check my shorts. The carefully ironed creases have disappeared in the sweltering heat but the grease blemishes thankfully are barely discernible dark smudges since I washed them in stain remover.

The two doctors are waiting for me when the bus pulls in. 'We went to the other backpacker's place but you weren't registered there so we came here. We've been waiting for you all afternoon. We even drove around trying to find the tour you were on.'

I shuffle my feet around bashfully hoping they don't mind my haircut, which looks as if I took a chainsaw to it. I do hope they notice the fish and chip grease stains have largely gone, even if there is not much of the crease left on my shorts after sweltering in the bus all afternoon.

'So, what are you doing this evening?' one of them asks, studying the iodine-stained scabs on my knees.

'Scheduled to take the midnight bus to Port Augusta and then Perth. I've booked a bus up the West Coast from Perth.'

'We were hoping you would be around for a couple of days.'

I kick the toes of one sandal with the heels of the other and try not to look as embarrassed as I am. I need to get my head examined. They had said they would meet me here. Self-consciously I rub the scab on the end of my nose. Why haven't I thought this far ahead? I could have phoned and delayed the bus trip up the West Coast. For someone who for the first time in a long while is totally unattached, with no girlfriend and no commitments, I am remarkably obtuse.

'Anyway, we can go out to a restaurant. We heard there is a miner's club where they serve good dinners. Would you like to do that?'

'Sure.' My toenails need clipping.

We walk through this strange mining community until we find the miner's club. I'm glad I took the time to spruce up. We abandon pretensions to the material world, but when it comes right down to it, we are still hung up about how we look and what we wear. We sit down at a table. The miners stare at us. Or at least they stare at my two female companions. I stare smugly back at the miners. Eat your hearts out guys. An average of 400 men to 1 woman and I've got two of them sitting next to me. Penny presses her knee against my bad knee. I don't have that much sensation in it after multiple surgery cut most of the nerves and it's about as sensitive to the touch now as a rubber tyre. Maybe she's just resting her leg against mine quite innocently. On the other hand . . . it's hard to tell for sure.

We order another round of beers. The conversation becomes personal as we talk about how difficult it is travelling alone when friends or relatives have been left behind and tactile relationships are reduced to a minimum. As if commiserating with my predicament, Penny's leg presses against me. My heart starts thumping again, wildly out of control.

'Do you think we are lesbians?' Cathy asks.

'Of course not. Wouldn't even enter my head.' Gosh, that would change the picture.

They look at each other. 'Well, we're not, but it's strange how Australian men automatically assume we are, travelling around together like this.'

'Especially when we aren't interested in them,' Penny adds, with a not-so-subtle increase of knee pressure.

'It's just sour grapes,' I reply, currying favour.

Totally involved with my two companions and starting to feel very comfortable with a couple of beers on board, we order another schooner of beer and dinner: three orders of fish and chips. It doesn't occur to me that ordering fish in Coober Pedy is ludicrous.

We talk about Australia, where we've travelled, what we've seen. Penny grew up on a farm in New South Wales, not far from Bourke. 'What was that like?'

'It was OK. I mean, how would you answer the same question, what was it like growing up all over the world?' she asks.

'It was OK,' I repeat. 'I didn't know anything else, so how can I comment?'

'Exactly. It's the same for me growing up on a farm in the Outback. It was all I knew and it was OK.'

'This whole land issue thing, can you explain it to me?' I ask earnestly. They probably would both like to talk about sex more than anything else, and here I am nerdishly trying to engage them on a topic of conversation that would kill the passion of the most ardent of suitors.

Penny looks at Cathy. 'She's the expert. She grew up on an Aboriginal community. Her dad was a doctor in the Outback.'

Cathy takes a breath as if about to embark on something she'd rather not. 'You've heard of the Eddie Mabo case?' she asks me.

'Only vaguely.'

She takes a big breath. 'Are you sure you're interested?'

'Yeah, I'm interested.'

'OK. In the 1970s Eddie Mabo, a Torres Strait Islander, sued the Queensland government for dispossessing him of his land. The High Court of Australia decided, finally, in 1990, in Mabo's favour.' She takes a long swig of her beer. 'That ruling was crucial because it admitted that the indigenous population had existing developed social organisations and systems of law before the British arrived. In other words, it wasn't empty land.'

'*Terra nullius*,' I tell her, remembering the conversation with Trevor.

'Exactly.' She takes another long pull of her beer. 'If it wasn't empty land, *terra nullius*, then ownership should never have been vested in the Crown in the first place. Mabo was just one particular case on a tiny island in the Torres Straits, but the fact that the High Court recognised native title in the common law of Australia turned the whole legal framework based on the doctrine of *terra nullius* upside-down.'

'That's pretty significant.'

'That's an understatement. There would have been chaos if all of Australia's land titles became invalid, so a process was established allowing—here's the catch-phrase—"extinguishment of native title" in cases where a valid freehold title to land existed.'

It's hard to be earnest and focus on this rather complex issue when I can feel the not-so-subtle pressure of Penny's knee. 'Extinguishment of native title?' I gasp, my right and left side of my brain diverging for completely separate planets.

'Extinguishment of native title means my dad's urban house in Adelaide is not up for grabs. He bought it and has the documentation to prove he has the freehold title. The big question now is whether existing pastoral leases made by the government of Australia to farmers are also extinguished by native title. Technically, the farmers leased the land, they didn't buy it.' That's what I was trying to tell the American-Iraqi cyclist. 'That means that Penny's dad's farm, which is leased, *is* potentially up for grabs. Of course, the farmers are up in arms. Something over ninety per cent of Western Australia is subject to claim, including mineral-rich land which the original inhabitants could deny exploration rights to. That is a whole can of worms still to be worked out.'

'And that's where it stands?' I ask, sipping my beer and trying to look both suitably enlightened and captivated.

'No, because then the Howard Government brought in the Wik legislation to politically minimise the damage of the High Court of Australia's decision in another case.' She's starting to lose me as the beers take effect on whatever grey matter is left after the two halves of my brain separated down different tracks. 'One of the Wik bills says the indigenous people must "prove continuing physical connection with the land",' she raises both hands and indicates quotation marks with her fingers. 'How're people forcibly removed from their land a century to a century-and-a-half ago going to prove "continuing physical connection with the land"? Wik legislation provided all kinds of loopholes for the pastoralists to retain their land rights,' she says scornfully. 'The debate's been reduced to a legal question of land management issues, with hardly any reference to the human rights of Aboriginal people.'

While happily engaged in conversation with the two doctors, the waitress ambushes me from behind.

Loaded with the tray full of fish and chips and a jug of beer, she trips on the carpet. I see a startled look on Cathy's face before the whole load drops over the back of my head.

I don't believe it.

I've spent a good portion of the day trying against all the odds to make myself look presentable, and this clumsy waitress has completely sabotaged my efforts. Why do waitresses and waiters have an international conspiracy to make my life miserable? I sit there without budging, my hair plastered into a slick helmet by a jug of beer. Chips slide down my face. I pick a chip off my shoulder and put it in my mouth.

Penny, Cathy and the waitress fuss over me, trying to limit the injury, but the harm has been done. With a stoic stare, I ignore the hilarity of the miners standing at the bar. I will never ever be the same again. I shall *always* have this deep-rooted fear every time a waitress approaches me from behind. Penny takes me by the hand to the women's washroom to tend to my wounded sense of being and to clean me up.

I normally don't drink a lot of beer at the best of times, but in quick order we finish off another round. I suspect the two Australian doctors could easily drink me under the table. We don't converse about anything much, but it seems incredibly interesting whatever it is. Penny sits next to me again and although my rubbery knee tends to get more rubbery as the night wears on, I can feel the not-so-subtle pressure of her knee resting against it.

'It's almost midnight!' I exclaim at a quarter to twelve.

'So?' Penny says.

'I've got to catch the bus, I'm supposed to be in Perth in a couple of days,' I repeat. 'I've booked the Greyhound up the West Coast; if I miss the bus I might not get another booking for a while.'

'Is the bus *so* necessary?' Penny asks.

'There're not many buses going up the West Coast and I've heard you've got to book well ahead otherwise you have to wait for days,' I reply. Hate to be sitting in a city when I could be Out There. On the other hand, hate to be alone when . . .

At my insistence we walk back to the backpacker's and they drive me to the bus station in their Holden station wagon. They pull up beside the bus and I grab my pack and hurry over to the Coach Captain. The two Aussie women lean against the old car, hands in jeans, jean jackets buttoned against the cold, their battered vehicle stuffed full of camping gear. They look so cool and neat they could be the heroines straight out of a film. I look like an extra that accidentally stumbled onto the set after falling into a vat of frying fat.

The Coach Captain throws my backpack into the baggage compartment. With a row of passengers staring at us through the bus windows I self-consciously hug both of them and then reluctantly take a seat on the coach. Exactly at midnight, I transmogrify from a potentially lucky prince into a solitary pumpkin. As Cathy and Penny wave goodbye, the Greyhound grinds its way into an empty expanse of desert clearly illuminated by a full moon.

One thing about the Greyhound that is very different from the Alternative Coach Network for Like Minded Independent Travellers: there is no mollycoddling. Passengers arrive and leave destinations at the oddest hours. We bail out of the bus in Port Augusta before dawn. It is not an auspicious looking town even if there is a Greyhound Terminal here. The bus schedule's short description of the stops down from Alice Springs to Port Augusta speak for themselves: Orange Creek, mail box; Stuarts Well, roadhouse; Erldunda, roadhouse; Kulgera, hotel; De Rose Hill, mailbox; Indulkana, turn-off; Chandler, roadhouse; Wintinna, mailbox; Cadney Park, roadhouse; Coober Pedy, Greyhound Pioneer Terminal; Bulgunnia, mailbox; Bon Bon, mailbox; Glendambo, mailbox; Coonhambo, mailbox; Wirraminna, mailbox; Woomera, Banool St. bus stop; Pimba, roadhouse; Port Augusta, Greyhound Pioneer Terminal. At most of those stops, a mailbox, a roadhouse or a turn-off is about all there is on the Stuart Highway, or The Track as it is more commonly referred to.

Although the coach has arrived on time, the bus terminal is locked and closed for another hour. Passengers spill out and sit unhappily outside in the chilly air.

I now have a couple of days ahead of me, cooped up in a bus, to thoroughly reflect over my premature departure last night from Coober Pedy. How's the saying go? *Carpe diem?* Seize the day. I'm tossing my days away like an inept one-armed juggler.

There isn't much to do in Port Augusta at six in the morning. I wander around sulkily waiting for the town to wake up. An elderly couple walks by, picking up empty soda bottles. 'Is this the main street?' I ask, catching up to them as they rummage around in a waste bin. I'm desperate to talk to someone.

'That's it.'

'You on rubbish patrol?' I ask insolently.

'We get five cents per empty bottle,' she says contentedly, holding up a bag that probably contains an Australian dollar's worth of soda bottles.

In Ozzie's Coffee Lounge I sit by the window, watching the town wake up and listening to depressing music wafting in from Ozzie's kitchen. Frank Sinatra croons 'Whatever will be will be, the future is not ours to see.'

I pick up the local newspaper. It's the twelfth of May, my birthday! Travelling alone to forgotten corners of an empty continent listening to Perry Como and Frank Sinatra crank out a few nostalgic love songs in a dive of a coffee shop while drinking yesterday's re-heated coffee and watching a provincial backwater town wake up on my *birthday?* Last year I spent Christmas Eve by myself on a deserted beach on the West Coast of New Zealand. This solitary business has *got* to stop. And I could have been celebrating my birthday in the company of two intelligent women who seemed as keen on me as I was on them. I feel like crying.

Instead, I ask for another coffee.

'Not a problem,' the owner tells me with a grating Australian twang that makes it seem as if it is a problem. It's a good thing I don't have a semi-automatic tucked under my belt. I'd be headline news. I slump my forehead in the palms of my hands.

Ozzie serves me coffee, spilling more liquid in the saucer than the cup. I hold the chipped crockery up against my mouth and feel the drops from the bottom of the cup staining my shorts.

Imitation tapestries of birds and posters of scenic Europe hang nostalgically from the walls; silk flowers in brass containers, smeared plastic table cloths and that irritating out-of-date music drive me out of the coffee shop before I really do get carried away with my fantasies about wasting Ozzie. Too bad life wasn't a video you could put on rewind whenever you wanted. I'd definitely do that right now and get that Greyhound bus to zip backwards to Coober Pedy. Then I'd change the rest of the script.

But life isn't a video, or a dress rehearsal; it's the real thing. Forget fantasising about a potential romance that you just nipped in the bud, Andrew. My reality is this: I am about to embark on the mother of all bus trips, across the Nullabor Plain bordered by the Great Australian Bight. The trip to Perth in Western Australia is almost 3,000 kilometres and a bus journey time of 33 1/2 hours. I'll be celebrating my birthday on a Greyhound bus travelling across the bleakest part of Australia. If I fudge things, and calculate the time difference between Australia and Europe or even Canada, I'll still be on this bus for my birthday no matter what time zone anywhere on earth I use as a reference point. The Nullabor Greyhound timetable, just like the Track, indicates stops at roadhouses, turnoffs, general stores or motels. There's nowhere to even begin to contemplate celebrating my anniversary. If you did want to forget your birthday, this would be about the most effective way to do it.

As the passengers show up for the midday departure, it is easy to recognise the Australians: they all board with blankets and pillows. As usual, the women wear baggy but comfortable sweatsuits. There are almost no backpackers or tourists on this long bus ride. This trip is for the hardcore spendthrift unwilling to part with the extra money for a more expensive, but less strenuous flight across the continent. My own excuse for inflicting this mind-numbing bus leg on myself is because I want to experience all of Australia on the ground, if only because this will truly impress me with the immensity of the country and its vast emptiness. Regretfully, I can be stubborn and bloody-minded about these things sometimes. On the other hand, I am reclined in a bus seat most of the time, not cycling and camping by the side of the road.

We are an even rougher looking crowd than those who had boarded in Townsville. Guys with shaved heads, big beards and bigger beer guts sit beside others with the ever-popular short hair on the top and sides, long and permed at the back. Accessories include tattoos, stubby shorts, wrap-around sunglasses, black jeans and cowboy hats. As for myself, I am coated with the stains of three portions of fish and chips and a jug of beer that have been dumped on top of me and a recent saucer-full of Ozzie's coffee.

An amiable Australian from Victoria makes conversation with me as we sit outside the terminal waiting for our departure. Although initially happy enough to be diverted from my current life situation, he drives me to distraction with the way he manages to say, 'Yeah.' He modulates and drags out the 'yeah' into a multiple-syllable whine. Starting the 'yeah' with a low voice he modulates it high then dips it down again before leaving it hanging with an inflection on the end. He makes his 'yeahs' sound like a whinging question when he is in fact only agreeing, or making a point, or just indicating that he is listening. He sounds like a kid contradicting an adult. He also tells me he had a brain operation and has been travelling around Australia on the Greyhound since then. This is his third time circumscribing the continent by bus. At least he has an excuse.

We leave Port Augusta with a tag team of two drivers who will be our Coach Captains all the way to Perth. With the omnipotence of God, our Coach Captain tells us lowly passengers the rules of life in his universe, the Coach Captains' Umpteen Commandments of what we are and are not allowed to do on His coach. The list of 'Do Nots' is long. What we *are* allowed to do is sit absolutely still in our seats, hands on our laps, and breath quietly. Seems the more isolated the place, the longer the Coach Captain's list of things you cannot do in the bus.

The scenery is different from anything else I have seen so far in Australia. Wide horizons of rolling plains of brown cultivated earth and dry harvested wheat fields about to be ploughed under. Trails of billowing backlit dust where enormous tractors carve up the earth on the horizon. Great green paddocks dotted white with sheep. It is bucolic, but more than that, it is the immense size of these holdings that is so impressive. I like the gargantuan scale of things. Europe is cute with its quaint little villages and winding roads, but this massive under-populated landscape has its attractions too. We pass tall grain elevators marked 'South Australia Co-operative Bulk Handling'. It is odd travelling once again in an area that is cultivated.

I have noticed something, which at first thought was coincidence, but now I realise it must be company policy. The Greyhound booking offices, and their drivers, when they allocate seats, make sure males sit separately from females, unless it is a couple. When I think about it, this gender segregation makes a lot of sense, especially on an overnight ride like this. Lowering two adjacent seats into the reclining position is about as intimate as sleeping in the same single bed. On a fifty-hour bus ride, that's like spending a whole weekend snuggled in bed with your lover.

Take the two passengers across the aisle from me. A tiny young Japanese woman in the aisle seat sits squashed next to an overweight, Australian woman. The Australian has bosoms so large one breast spills over into the seat next to her. The tiny Japanese woman falls asleep in her seat like a rag doll, her head collapsed forward, chin resting on her chest. As we progress into the afternoon the young Japanese woman starts listing to the side, towards the Australian. The big Australian woman tries to move her considerable mass away from the diminutive Japanese but there is little room for her to manoeuvre in these coach seats. Despite her acute awareness of the Asian girl's encroachment into her personal space, the Aussie woman is unsuccessful in her attempts to squeeze away.

Her predicament moves from the sublime to the ridiculous when the Japanese woman's head slowly descends onto the bosom of the Australian, perfectly pillowing the Japanese head. The Australian stares in front of her, stoically ignoring the fact that the Oriental passenger's face is now slowly sliding off her voluptuous breast and burrowing into her equally ample lap.

Two more videos and we arrive at Border Village on the state line between South Australia and Western Australia. Similar in name but not to be confused with Bordertown sitting astride the South Australian border with Victoria, in the other direction.

The crossing of the Nullabor Plain coincides with nightfall and once again the only variation while charging through a black expanse of nothingness is the whooshing of the occasional road train coming the other way, or the thud of a kangaroo as it hops into oblivion on the 'roo bar.

Exhausted from the previous night's bus journey, I pull my sleeping bag out and fall asleep as the clock winds through my birthday wherever you want to measure the hour.

Red-eyed and barely awake, I watch the passing scenery as the sun rises. It is misty and cool. Contrary to its Nullabor name, we drive through plains covered in small trees. I guess we have either driven through the treeless plains during the night, or the road passes too close to the Great Australian Bight with its onshore precipitation.

My two companions across the aisle are fast asleep. During the course of the night, the Japanese woman's head has nestled securely in the middle of the buxom Australian's spacious lap. But the Australian woman's double chin is now comfortably drooped over the Japanese girl's shoulder. They are a picture of peace and harmony, two pieces of an intricate jigsaw puzzle fitting perfectly together.

When we stop at Kalgoorlie, an Australian man occupies the seat next to me. He greets me, 'How'ya going mate,' pulls out a glossy 4WD magazine and studies the latest fashion in utility vehicles with a glossy centrefold of a Toyota ute and numerous photos of curvaceous corner lights and protruding mufflers taken from the oddest angles.

Kalgoorlie and Coolgardie have the atmosphere of Wild West gold towns, which is exactly what they are. The most impressive architecture is the imposing Mining Registrar building. Gold discovered in the area at the end of the nineteenth century brought in over 200,000 prospectors into this dry desert. The two mining towns are still thriving. But when we stop in Yellowdine, it is a different story. A genuine ghost town, there is nothing here but the roadhouse and some dilapidated buildings. A wooden pipeline passes alongside the road channelling water all the way from Perth to Kalgoorlie. When the water was 'switched' on in Perth, in 1903, nothing arrived in Kalgoorlie and the engineer responsible for its design committed suicide. But a day later the water gushed into town. I ask the Roadhouse Person behind the food counter how many people live in Yellowdine now.

'Eight.'

'Eight?' I ask.

'Used to be over 1,000.'

Eight pear-shaped survivors clinging to survival at a roadhouse.

Keeping a watchful eye on our Coach Captain, we scramble back into the coach when he steps out of the roadhouse. No one wants to take the slightest chance on being left behind.

Apart from turning right at Norseman, then left at Coolgardie, we've been driving on roads straight as a survey cut-line since we had dinner in Ceduna in South Australia last night. I initiate conversation with the tough-looking cowboy next to me. 'What do you do in Kalgoorlie?'

'I'm a welder,' he tells me, putting down his 4WD magazine and adjusting his Stetson and crossing one cowboy boot over the other. 'Work in the mines, except I got into a blue with my boss so I quit.'

'Blue?'

'Fight.'

'And what's there to do in Kalgoorlie?' I ask, 'Besides beating up your boss?'

'Go on the piss.' He reflects. 'See a strip show, go to a knock shop. Only place in Australia besides Victoria where the prostitutes are legal.'

'Lots of Aboriginals there?'

'Yeah, same as Alice Springs; most of them are drunks. Central and South Australian Aborigines are a hard mob. Drink too much, go walkabout. Can't hold down a job. Aborigines on the West Coast, from Broome to Darwin, are a better mob. Same with the mob North of Cans; they're switched on, too.'

'Have you worked with them?'

'Nah. Problem is, they can't get jobs. I went to school with them though, outside Perth. One of my best mates was an Aborigine. He was the boxing champion at school. He had a lot of respect because of that. I see him now and he hasn't held down a job, not because he doesn't want to. He just can't get a job because he's black.'

After the settlement of Southern Cross, the land becomes agricultural again with expanses of brown fields. Studying my map, from the single ribbon of red marking the only route from the east, we enter a network of roads again. The second Coach Captain, sensing we are soon to arrive in Perth, comes out of the sleeping compartment at the back of the bus. He stands in the stairwell beside the door and banters with the driver and two Australian women sitting in the front row of seats.

'Hit two Abos once,' the driver recounts. 'One went through the windscreen; the other got knocked into the bush to the side of the road. Police came and I asked them what they were going to do about it. They said, "Book one for break-in and entry, and the other for leaving the scene of the accident".'

They all laugh.

# 3   Western Australia

On the international scale of friendly, laid-back citizens, Australia must rank near the top. But here in Western Australia they take their friendliness and laid-back attitudes seriously. People take the time to smile, ask how I'm going. I jog along Perth's Swan River, which is more like a large lake, all the way to Kings Park, where I sit and survey the city below. It's another spectacularly pretty metropolis, not so overwhelmingly large as Sydney—yet. Like Sydney, though, it's not hard to imagine living here, even if it is one of the most isolated cities in the world.

That evening, after a one-and-a-half-hour swim workout in an outdoor swimming pool trying to shrug off some of the kinks and coils accumulating around my waist from the long bus rides, I stroll through Northbridge, a swinging district with cafés, pubs, restaurants and night clubs. I intend to have dinner here, but I stand out like a grease-stained sore thumb amongst these fashionably dressed Australians. Many spill onto the sidewalk, drunk. This is acceptable behaviour for white yuppies having fun. I stroll around the block a couple of times but don't get up the nerve to walk into one of these popular restaurant pubs; too shy, believe it or not. Crossing the bridge over the railway tracks into the centre of town, I see a group of Aboriginal people collected in the shadows: young, old, male and female. Many of the adults seem to be drunk and yet this drunken scene is unacceptable in a public place, although the debauched sight of Perth yuppies drunk on a sidewalk outside a fashionable club, which is a public place too, apparently doesn't generate the same stigma.

On one of Perth's main pedestrian malls I approach a man in a wheelchair belting out his rendition of the Beatles' song *All the Lonely People*. It is so awfully sung I presume the singer must be mentally deranged. I stop and listen. When he finishes, I lie, 'Not bad.'

'Not good either,' he acknowledges in a more normal voice.

'Better than I could do, anyway,' I admit truthfully.

His shoulders slope down, as if they had melted into his body. His wrists are enclosed in metal braces. His stomach is unnaturally distended. He thumps his stomach a couple of times, as if it were a drum, and sings *Stand By Me,* the words 'I don't want to live in a world without love' full of meaning if not tone. When he finishes he pulls a piece of string attached to a bucket on the sidewalk in front of him. There are a few coins in it. He puts them in his pocket.

'You packing up?' I ask.

'I can't sing any more.'

'Why not?'

'I feel your presence,' he replies.

'Do you want me to go away?'

'No, I didn't say that.'

'Do you come here often?' I ask.

He thumps his stomach hard again to catch his breath. It must do him harm to whack his body like that. 'Often enough,' he replies. 'Too much; it's bad for my health.'

'Then why do you do it?' I can be a persistent little bugger.

'Need the money,' he replies.

'Don't you get money from the Government?' What am I, a legal aid lawyer?

He looks at me and smiles. 'You tried living on the dole with a wife and two children?'

'You weren't always like this?' Sometimes I think I am weird. I'd rather talk to this mate than chat up some woman in a bar. Maybe that's not quite the picture. Maybe I'd rather be successfully conversing with him, than unsuccessfully chatting up some woman in a bar. Never got lucky in a bar anyway. Rarely get the courage to walk into one on my own.

'Drunk driving; had an accident.' There is no self-pity in this statement.

'People ever take your bucket or money?' I ask, ever inquisitive about other people's lives.

'Stole my bag once.' He shows it to me. 'Took everything out of it. I asked them to leave my personal papers but they took everything.'

'Who?'

'Three Aborigine women,' he says, continuing to pack up.

'So how do you feel about Aboriginal people?' I ask provocatively.

'I'm married to one.' He laughs. 'Doesn't mean I'm not a racist.'

'How can you be a racist against Aboriginals if you're married to one?'

'Easy.'

'You still married?' I ask.

'Twenty-three years.' He is packed up and ready to go.

'Can I buy you a drink?' I offer him.

'Learnt my lesson. Don't drink any more.'

'A coffee?' I continue.

'Had too many already. Thanks.'

'What's your name?' I ask.

'Charlie. What's yours?'

'Andrew.' I reach out a hand. He stretches one of his braced wrists towards me and I shake it carefully.

Two young white Australians, a boy and a girl in their late teens, approach us. She shivers. The boy says belligerently to Charlie, 'Haven't you learnt any new tunes yet? You said you were going to learn some new tunes.'

The girl ignores her boyfriend and looks at me with pleading eyes, 'Can you give us some money for the bus fare home mister? We've been robbed. Look, they slashed my shirt.'

The boy says, 'They grabbed my bag, tried to take it and ripped it.' He shows me a plastic shopping bag with a hole in the bottom.

'Who?' I ask.

'Bunch of Aborigines down there in the park. They asked us for some money and when I pulled my money out, they grabbed the wallet and her bag and ran.'

He wears a woollen hat pulled low down over his head. Although they are young, she has dark shadows under her eyes. She doesn't look as if she has slept in a week. Something about these two makes me disinclined to believe them, let alone stand there and remove my wallet from my pocket and give them money. Realising they are going to get nothing from me, they leave.

'Was that a scam?' I ask Charlie when they are out of earshot.

'Yeah, they're here most nights, on drugs or something. Same story every time. The wallet line they told you? That's what they do. Good thing you didn't pull it out. Would have grabbed it and run. The line about the Aborigines taking their money, though, is a good one. A lot of people want to believe that.'

I guess it wouldn't have done Charlie much good to warn me. Being a paraplegic, he wouldn't be able to defend himself, and they know him.

The Greyhound Coach Captain adds a couple of innovative rules as we drive out of Perth. 'OK, folks, when you put your seat back into the reclining position, think of the person behind you and don't jam their knees into their chest. Folks, if you can see up the nostrils of the person behind, that's a good indication you've set your seat too far back and it might be an idea to put it up a bit. It's not a bed. No hands, legs, bags or dags hanging out in the aisle. During the trip we may have to brake hard for cattle, animals or woman drivers on the road, so be prepared, otherwise you'll be doing the one-second dash down the aisle and I'm sick of pulling people out of the windscreen. And finally, folks, if you do have to make an emergency visitation to the back, please do it quietly so that the other driver can get some sleep. We'll be heading up to Broome together for some thirty hours, folks, and we'll need all the rest we can get.'

In Australia, bus drivers are Coach Captains and their bus passengers are Folks.

Being one of the Folks on these long distance coaches is like being a passenger boarding a transatlantic flight. There's that same collective feeling of hunkering down for the duration, of travelling somewhere far away, to another world.

I examine the timetable. The trip from here to Darwin is an epic 56 hours or two and a third days or approximately 4,425 kilometres. I add up the different sections on the Greyhound timetable: Sydney to Cairns, Cairns to Alice, Alice to Port Augusta, Port Augusta to Perth, Perth to Darwin, Darwin down to Adelaide, Adelaide to Sydney. The total distance is something like 18,220 kilometres. The time spent on the bus is 248 hours: more than 10 full days surviving off roadhouse food.

Passengers climb on board with their blankets and pillows. We have a high percentage of authentic working Australians with us, confirmation that the Western Coast of Australia is different from the tourist frenzy on the East Coast.

Out of Perth, we cruise through cattle country, rolling green fields with the occasional heavy oak-like tree in the middle to give animals shade. Like gigantic golf driving-ranges, green paddocks are full of golf-ball round sheep. But where are the farmhouses and where are the farmers? It's as if the cattle and sheep are farming themselves. Occasionally we slow down for wide farm machinery taking up the width of the road. Flat, rolling downs of wheat, barley, oat and hay turn to scrub as we progress up the West Coastal Highway, back on the ribbon of Highway 1 that almost circumnavigates the coastline of Australia. Through the front window I see wild emu trotting away like female brown ostrich in an African landscape.

Although we should be segregated, a woman sits next to me. The bus is full; perhaps it's like musical chairs and it wasn't possible to separate everyone by gender and she is the odd one out. Or perhaps it's me that's out of synch. She is returning to Cervantes from a shopping spree in Perth.

'So what do you do for excitement around there?' I ask.

'Women go to Perth to shop. Guys drink.'

'That's all there is to do for fun? Go shopping or get drunk?'

'That's about it, yeah. Used to work in a bar in Port Hedland. You're a hero there if you get really drunk. You brag about it the next day. And if you're so drunk you're sick, that's even better. The less you remember, the more you'll boast about it. If you can make a big fart and clear out the pub with the stink, they'll talk about that for months.' She shrugs and lifts her hands. 'A guy I knew, he came into the pub every day, even Christmas Eve and New Year's. The way he spoke about his wife was as if she was fat and ugly, but one day she came in and she wasn't bad at all. But he was always at the pub. One day she left him to go back home to her mother in Perth. He just couldn't understand why. He told me, "I come home and give her my pay packet, so what's she got to complain about?" He couldn't understand what he'd done wrong. He placed more importance on his mates than his wife.'

She disembarks at the Cervantes turnoff. A disreputable guy takes her place. His breath reeks of beer and cigarette smoke. The Coach Captain slides a video in the machine and asks everyone to close the curtains to shut out the glare of the sun. A darkened busload of Folks sitting in a bus hurtling through the Australian Outback with the curtains shut watching *Dumb and Dumber, Home Alone* or a generic vacuous Mel Gibson action film. Because I didn't book sufficiently ahead of time, I sit at the back of the bus with tunnel-like vision out the front windscreen. To look at the countryside I have to peep discretely through the curtains.

Watching the video isn't any better; like looking at a cinema screen through the wrong end of a pair of binoculars.

When the video is finished, the guy in 1A, normally my seat, has to take The Long Walk.

He alerts us all to his intention by clambering over 1B, who is asleep. 1A wobbles to the back of the bus, lurching for the seat backs as he progresses down the aisle. Without the video to distract us, fifty pairs of eyes watch him. Despite the nonchalant look on his face, we all know exactly where 1A is going, there's not a lot of choice, and we all give him warning stares not to resort to the forbidden heavy artillery. Even the Coach Captain studies him in his rear-view mirror. If he is in there for more than a couple of minutes, we'll know what he has done.

The rough-looking passenger sitting next to me tells me he works on the pearl fishing fleets. He uses the word 'mate' and 'bro' in just about every sentence. 'Had a good job offer in Queensland, mate, gave it up for a bloody sheila, but she's gone and thrown me out. Wasn't around much anyway, bro. Should'a went and took the job offer. Been taking it easy, mate. No point working too much, government takes it off you in taxes anyway. Want to retire when I'm forty, eh?' Every Australian guy wants to retire when he's forty. He has a scraggly beard, long oily hair and mirror sunglasses. 'Where you heading?' he asks, breathing stinking stale tobacco breath at me.

'Broome.'

He says conspiratorially, jabbing me in the ribs with his elbow, 'Party town. Plenty of sheilas there mate. You're going to be busier than a one-legged man at an ass-kicking competition.'

'Ah yeah.' I bait him with the Aboriginal word and off the subject of sheilas.

Doesn't seem to phase him. 'Lots of good blackfellas out there, mate.'

'You got any Aboriginal friends?'

He laughs. 'Sure, mate. Some of my best mates are bros. Just stay out of their way when they're drunk.'

We pull into Geraldton for our lunch break. Whenever we are about to stop at a roadhouse, the Coach Captains inform their Folks of our expected arrival time like a good airline pilot would. The ETA is followed by intricate instructions of where the toilets are, the telephones, the food counter, followed by instructions to put our seats upright and not to disembark with bare feet or no tops. Then, to make sure we understand, the instructions are repeated again. Because Greyhound bus Folk are not the sharpest of people, the Coach Captains insist on repeating these instructions a third time for good measure.

Making conversation while waiting for the next video to start after the break, my seatmate says, picking up on our previous discussion, 'Blood will be spilled if the Government keeps giving away land to the Abos.'

'I thought your best mates were bros.'

'Yeah, but it's not my fault what happened years ago and anyway, every Aborigine is getting a million dollars a year from the Government.'

'What?' I exclaim.

'True. I put up with them, they're cruisey people, but their own half-castes are ripping them off.' The video starts. 'You know what the definition of an Aborigine is?'

Oh boy, here we go, another racist joke.

'An Aborigine is anyone who identifies as an Aborigine and is accepted as an Aborigine by the community.' He's serious. He looks at me to emphasise the point. 'And I know, mate. I checked into it. Even if I haven't got any blackfella blood in me, if I reckon I'm a blackfella and my bro friends agree, I can be one. Then I get all the advantages they get, including a million bucks a year. If I was an Aborigine, know what I'd do?'

'Uh-uh,' I reply, not sure I want to know.

'Separate and become an independent state.' He raises his eyebrows at me as if to emphasise the point. 'True. That's what a lot of them want. Two Australias.' Another film flickers on the screen distracting my companion. 'Why not? Bloody Yanks own Australia anyway,' my mate tells me, listening to the Yankee Hollywood accents. 'Full on true, bro. Now they closed down Exmouth they've got their US base at Pine Gap outside Alice Springs. Keep aliens and UFOs and anti-gravity propulsion devices there. Got an antenna that goes 2,000 metres into the ground to keep track of submarines going around Australia. True, mate. Don't mess around trying to get information on Pine Gap otherwise you'll disappear, bro. That's what happened to one of our Prime Ministers. Went for a swim on the beach and the Yanks got him.'

Against a blood-red sky, the setting sun silhouettes lone Southern Cross windmills: the pervasive image of the Australian Outback. And then it gets dark and the surrounding blackness envelops our tiny capsule of humanity as we are propelled through the void.

We emerge from the emptiness of the desert to an oasis of lights. Although it is marked on the map as if it was somewhere, Overlander is a fluorescent-lit roadhouse, toilets and nothing else, in the middle of nowhere. If I walked a hundred metres in any direction and turned off the roadhouse lights, I'd be lost forever.

I queue in the food line and ponder. Could the same Pear-shaped Roadhouse People follow and leapfrog a Greyhound coach and its Folks all the way around the country? The food *is* identical and so are the Roadhouse People. I'll put a little mark on a hamburger or a chicken leg and see if I recognise it later. I take a close look at three puckered apples sitting in a basket. One of the apples has tell-tale crescent thumbnail marks in it.

Someone else had the same bright same idea.

As if to compensate for what it lacks, 'Overlander Roadhouse' is printed on absolutely every souvenir item conceivable, including linen tea towels, crockery, place mats and postcards. It's as if Overlander were a favourite tourist destination and not just a roadhouse stuck in the middle of the Western Australian Outback. Although it is May, Christmas decorations hang from the ceiling to distract us from the missing linoleum squares on the floor. Country and Western songs, where the woman gone left him and the dog up and died and the whiskey bottle is half empty, are played over and over.

One half of the roadhouse is assigned to the maintenance needs of the human travellers: hamburgers, fries, hot dogs and Cokes. The other half is devoted to the maintenance needs of the motor vehicles that bring us here. Engine oil, fan belts, batteries, tow ropes. I help myself to dried-out hamburgers, which could usefully serve as the brake pads of a road train. The chips are so soggy they drip onto my shorts before I can plop them into my mouth. Judging from the viscosity of the fat, they could recycle the cooking oil as engine oil. Maybe it is engine oil. As I pay the Pear-shaped Roadhouse Person behind the counter, I think I recognise her. I'm sure she's the same one who served me at Border Village. Or was it Border Town?

Killing time outside, sitting at a picnic table, waiting for the connecting bus to Monkey Mia, a young woman sits next to me eating what looks vaguely like a Chinese spring roll. Her baseball cap is turned backwards; she wears a T-shirt and jeans. Bit of a tomboy I reckon. She puts her hand on her head and swivels the baseball cap so that it is facing the front and asks me if I am heading up north.

'Yep,' I reply, wishing I had a baseball cap I could swivel around too. 'What's your name?' I ask a stranger for the thousandth time on this trip.

'Gemma with a 'G',' she says with a clear Irish lilt, reaching out a firm handshake. She removes her baseball cap, revealing short-cropped rusty-coloured hair. A couple of centimetres of black roots accurately delineate how long she has been on the road. She could be a boy of about sixteen. Bit of a lad too, judging by the mischievous twinkle in her eye emphasised by a wry smile and a dimpled cheek and a nose covered in freckles. 'And just in case you're wondering,' she says in the broadest of Irish accents, 'I'm all of twenty-six and five-foot two and work as a computer programmer for IBM when I'm at home in Ireland.'

She doesn't look older than eighteen to me. 'How'd you like Sydney?' I ask.

'Love it. Were you there?'

'Yeah.'

'What'd you think?'

'Must be the most beautiful large city in the world: perfect climate, great setting on the coast with an extensive harbour. Sydney has just about everything you could wish for, especially if you live along the waterfront or near the beaches.'

'Did you go to Bondi Beach?'

'Yeah. If you had to live in a large city, you couldn't find a nicer place with so much to offer. Did you go up the East Coast?' She might have been a Like Minded Independent Traveller sleeping and drinking her way up the East Coast on the Alternative Coach Network. On the other hand, maybe that's why she is so specific as to her qualifications: she's trying to differentiate herself from the others.

She confirms my suspicions. 'East Coast,' she says, 'is full of partygoers.' She holds her hand up. 'Don't get me wrong now,' she adds quickly, 'I don't mind a bit of partying myself but it was just bloody endless you know. I didn't come all this way just to funnel beer down my gullet and party and then sleep all the next day on the bus. I came out here to see Australia as well.'

Common ground. 'What's that like?' I ask. She stuffs the remains of the Chinese spring roll into her mouth. 'I see them in all the roadhouses.'

'A Chiko roll. It's about the only thing with vegetables. Must be cabbage or something.' She wipes her fingers, greasy from holding the roll, onto a paper napkin. 'At least, it doesn't appear to have any meat in it. It's not easy travelling around Australia if you're a vegetarian.'

There isn't much else to do, so while waiting for a smaller bus, which will take us west to Monkey Mia on Shark Bay, we talk, for a couple of hours. I like Gemma with a G. She's got a wicked sense of humour and she laughs easily, a good combination.

'Been working in Sydney. Dead easy finding jobs in Australia; couldn't believe how easy it was.' She sucks back on a bottle of beer. 'Em, only trouble is, I miss my boyfriend back in Ireland.'

When the connecting minibus arrives the backpackers are stuffed into it so tightly there is little room to manoeuvre for the couple of hours that it takes to get to our destination. By the time we reach Monkey Mia, a caravan park and not much else, it is midnight. Gemma and I share a derelict caravan with two Dutchmen. Like exhausted soldiers on manoeuvres, we flop onto bunk beds and fall asleep.

Another dawn, another brilliant blue, cloudless Western Australian sky. Already it is hot. I walk down to the beach through the maze of broken-down caravans converted to accommodation. Spectators stand at the water's edge watching wild dolphins begging for fish. The bay, the sea, the ocean, whatever it is, is as smooth as an oil slick. There isn't a ripple breaking the surface, not a hint of a breeze. I've never seen such an expanse of water so glass-still. A Conservation and Land Management officer stands in the water up to his knees supervising the spectacle as dolphins swim around him, rubbing their bodies against his legs.

Tame dolphins performing tricks don't impress me. But these are wild dolphins that have learned over the years that fishermen here throw their scraps into the water. CALM has taken over the process and regulates the feeding of these wild dolphins. With the park rangers superintending the scene, it does seem a bit contrived. But it must have been amazing for the fishermen when the first wild dolphins came in, the equivalent of aquatic naughty neighbourhood dogs begging for food.

The other side of Shark Bay is too far away to be visible. The coastline on this side, an endless empty beach bordered by red desert dunes, seems to front the open ocean. Despite its reputation and the intimidating but apparently well-deserved name of Shark Bay, I swim for an hour along the coast. Wearing swim goggles, I see a turtle, several flounder, lots of other fish, but thankfully no sharks. At the end of the two-hour swim, I climb out of the water onto the beach where three fishermen are busy filleting fish on a makeshift wooden table. Four begging Australian pelicans are so cheeky they practically have their beaks resting on the table. When one of the fishermen drops a fish head in the sand, a pelican picks it up delicately and waddles down to the sea and rinses it before swallowing.

'See any dolphins?' one of the fishermen asks without looking up.

'Nope. Saw them this morning though.'

'Been fishing here for thirty-three years and feeding the dolphins scraps for at least that long too. Now the rangers have that stupid video with the ninny saying she was the one who started it all. Aborigine down the coast claims *he* started feeding them. Doesn't matter, it was fishermen who got them to come in like this. Now the wardens tell us not to feed the dolphins; CALM bludgers sit there on their arses doing nothing, paid for by my tax dollars. That's why we feed the pelicans scraps, so they'll hang out at the Conservation and Land Management office afterwards and shit on their fancy brickwork.'

I watch them finish filleting a mound of fish. As they throw the scraps to the pelicans, one of them says to the other two, 'Those T-bones should be thawed by now.'

'You must be joking,' I tell them. 'With all that fresh filleted fish, you're going to eat frozen steaks?'

'It's more fun catching the fish than actually eating them. We'll take it all back in freezers and eat it sometime at home on the barbie.'

The horizon doesn't change. The sea remains glassy. The only variable is the sun moving slowly across the sky and the dolphins searching in vain for more handouts.

That evening in the caravan, the two Dutch caravan-mates tell me, 'We're going to Denham where at least there's a bar. There's nothing to do here.'

'Perfect isn't it?' I reply.

Gemma walks in just as the two disenchanted Dutchmen walk out. The freckles on her nose have increased with sun exposure. 'Scammed some fish off the three old fishermen out there.' She asks me, looking like the Artful Dodger with that irrepressible grin creasing her face, 'Want some? I'd never be able to eat it all myself.' She holds up the fillets.

'You've got a couple of kilos' worth of fish there,' I tell her. 'You got them off the same fishermen I was talking to and they didn't offer any fish to me. Next time travelling around Australia, I'm coming back as a woman.'

'Good isn't it? I can score a beer any time I want. Just walk into a bar and say to the nearest Australian, "Howzit goin' mate?" I've had the use of cars, apartments, been out on boats, just because I'm a female and they're desperate to root.' She swivels her baseball cap around so it faces the front and the smile disappears from her face. Her eyes narrow to mean slits. 'I'd break their bloody arm if they so much as touch me though. Really strong language helps too.' I can't imagine Gemma using really strong language, so that might be a bit of an exaggeration. 'If they don't give up cracking onto yer, yer just get up and leave.' I can imagine that.

We fry up the fish fillets in butter, seasoned with salt and pepper and lots of garlic and lemon. I contribute a bottle of wine to a dinner eaten on the edge of the beach, watching the sun set. Dolphin dorsal fins break the surface so gently they scarcely leave a ripple.

The sea is as still as it was yesterday, a huge expanse of placid water. The dolphins drift in silently, begging. The park rangers don't feed them at regular hours, and never past the morning, to encourage the dolphins to look for their own food. A baby dolphin swims on its back flapping its flippers in its innate desire to show off. Like a realistic garden ornament, a pelican stands motionless on the green lawn beside a sprinkler, its massive mouth open, lower jaw spread wide, catching the water.

This caravan resort, which for decades was a basic facility catering to die-hard Australian fisherman, has been put on the Australian tourist map because half-a-dozen wild dolphins come in to the beach to feed off handouts. With 500 beds crammed into dilapidated old retired caravans, the owners of the caravan park plan to expand to 800 beds. Millions of dollars are being invested, and reaped, from these few wild animals.

Heading back to the caravan I overhear *Stand By Me* playing on someone's radio and I am reminded of Charlie in his wheelchair, belting out the same song late at night in Perth. He seems so far removed from this scene. I wonder if he would like it here.

As I enter the caravan, I see Gemma is awake at last, standing in front of the mirror.

'You've got to help me!' she says.

'What's the matter?' I ask putting my book down and opening the fridge for a bottle of water. It's so easy to get dehydrated here and I have to force myself to drink.

'I can't sthpeak,' she replies with a frantic tone, 'My tongue feelsth like iths flopping around my mouth like a fish in a bucket.'

I suck on the bottle while looking at her sceptically out of the corner of an eye, and then put the bottle down, empty. 'What's the problem exactly?' I ask, somewhat alarmed at the sight of an eloquent Gemma reduced to an Irish woman with a peculiar speech impediment.

'My breath thstank of garlic from dinner last night stho I thought I'd usthe thisth mouth sthpray. Now my mouth feelsth like itsth numb. I can't feel my lipsth or my tongue or the back of my throat.'

'Mouth spray?' I ask, suspicious she might be pulling my leg. If she is, she's a bloody good actress.

She says, holding the diminutive can up for me to see, 'It'sth a mouth freshener I found here and I sthprayed my mouth with it.' She gives the can to me then stares at her tongue in the mirror. 'You've *got* to help me.' She's on the point of tears.

'Where'd you find it?' I ask.

'Maybe one of the Dutch guysth left it here. It wasth sthitting on the counter.' She shows me where she found it. 'Unlessth itsth yoursth.'

I study the container. '"Stud Delay". That doesn't sound like a mouth freshener.' I read the minute directions and look at her. 'You're supposed to spray it on your penis, Gemma.'

'I don't have a penisth,' she replies.

'I could have guessed that.'

I re-read the relevant section of the can. 'You're supposed to spray this on your penis to desensitise it so you can last longer during sexual intercourse.' I look at her suspiciously. 'You haven't been having sthexual intercoursthe have you?'

'It'sth not bloody funny, Andrew!' she says, stamping her feet. 'How long does it lastht?' she asks desperately. 'I might sthuffocate.'

'I don't know, I've never used it before.'

She studies her tongue in the mirror.

I peer at her reflection. 'You know, you can't actually see anything wrong with you, Gemma,' I say, commiserating. 'It's probably like having a dentist's injection. Your lips feel like they are made of rubber and swollen out of proportion to your face although there is in fact nothing swollen about them at all,' I try to reassure her.

'What sthhould I do?' she asks looking at me in the reflection of the mirror.

'Phone a hospital, I guess.'

'Pleasthe help me,' Gemma begs, stamping her feet again. She's getting desperate.

'OK.' I grab her hand and lead her out of the caravan to a row of pay telephones outside the showers. I make a couple of calls to emergency numbers before getting through to a nurse at the nearest clinic some hours drive away. I tell the nurse over the phone, 'My daughter,' Gemma rolls her eyes at this subterfuge, 'accidentally just sprayed her mouth with Stud Delay and her mouth is completely numb and she is very frightened. Do you know how long does it last for?'

There is a long silence at the other end of the phone before the nurse replies, '*You* should know, mate!'

I put the dead phone down and take an educated guess at how long a penis would usefully be numb and lie to Gemma, 'She said twenty minutes.'

We both reserve bus seats to Coral Bay. Peaceful as it is here, I'm running out of time. Australia is so different to New Zealand where the landscape changed dramatically within a couple of hours' travel. Here one could drive for days and still see the same scenery. Despite the distances and the sameness of much of the landscape along the way, I could happily stay longer.

I spend this second day reading about Australia's indigenous people, and then take another long two-hour swim along the coastline. The water is so salty and buoyant it makes swimming effortless. By the time I return, Gemma is up and sitting on the beach.

'Feeling better?' I ask as I get out of the water.

'Sorry I was rude to you yesterday,' Gemma says unnecessarily.

'You weren't particularly rude given the circumstances. Anyway, I should apologise for thinking it was funny, but I couldn't help it.' I look around. 'You didn't bring that handy spray out here with you?'

She looks at me reproachfully.

'I meant for the flies. I wonder if it would numb these bloody flies. Where'd you put it?'

'Well, I assumed *you* don't need it,' she replies, 'so I gave it to the old fishermen in return for the fish fillets.'

My mouth drops. I look at her. 'You're kidding, right?'

'Thought I'd return their generosity.'

'Did they say anything?' I ask incredulously.

'Their wives said their husbands needed Viagra more than they needed Stud Delay.'

'Liar.'

Late afternoon sets in. We wander over to the same old fishermen filleting another pile of cod. One fisherman slices up a cod so large it overlaps both ends of the wooden table put up for the purpose. The others tease him. A few metres away, dolphins swim in water thick and viscous like molten gold.

'Tell these two visitors what happened to you today, George,' one of the old-timers says to another who is conspicuously silent.

'Yeah, tell us what happened,' the third says.

George replies, 'There'sth nothing to sthay.' It is hard to understand him; it's as if his tongue is flopping around like a fish in a bucket.

Uh-oh.

'What happened?' I ask him, glancing quickly at Gemma. I can see it in her eyes: we are both wondering the same thing. Nah, it would be too much of a coincidence, he couldn't have done the same thing to himself as well. He's definitely got a problem, though, and it has all the symptoms of Gemma's peculiar affliction.

'He couldn't have . . . sprayed himself with Stud Delay?' The fisherman's hearing isn't too good and I can get away with whispering this into Gemma's ear.

She recoils and stares at me as if I was a lunatic.

'George was fishing, had his rod over the edge of the boat when he sneezed,' one of George's friends explains. There's a conspicuous silence.

'And?' Gemma encourages.

'And he lost his teeth.'

'Lost his teeth?' I repeat.

'Yeah. He lost his teeth. He sneezed and his teeth flew out of his mouth. So he drops his rod to grab his teeth, but loses both the rod *and* his teeth. We spent the next half-hour trolling with a line and a hook off a sinker, and one chance in a billion he manages to snag the hook of the lost fishing rod. Retrieved it out of fifteen metres of water! With that kind of luck we threw our ham sandwiches overboard to see if we couldn't get his dentures to snap at them, and salvage them too.' They laugh. Then he continues, 'That's nothing. Last year when we were heading back from a day's fishing he leant over the stern of the boat to put the empty fish bin over the side to clean it out and it filled with water and pulled him overboard. By the time we realised and turned around to pick him up, he was sitting in the bucket.'

'Sitting in the bucket?' I repeat. 'In the middle of Shark Bay?'

'Yeah, the bin was full of water, and he was inside it.'

'Didn't it sink?'

'Well, it wasn't exactly floating; he was crouching in the bin. You could just see his eyes.'

'But why was he in the bucket?' I ask.

'Protection againsth sharksth,' George replies, gumming the words in a fairly good imitation of someone who had just sprayed his mouth with Stud Delay.

I look accusingly at Gemma. She rolls her eyes in exasperation. 'And what are you going to do with that huge cod fillet now that you can't eat it?' I ask, as if he might volunteer to give it to Gemma and me.

'Yeah, George,' the others chime in.

'Give it to them, George.'

'Got some Weetabix in the caravan,' one suggests helpfully, 'You could soak it in milk overnight so you'd be able to eat it.'

'And I've got some custard, George,' another offers.

'Join us for a barbie tonight,' one of the wives suggests on a more serious note to Gemma and me, taking the pressure off George.

'Yeah, come fishing with us tomorrow too,' one of the fishermen invites. 'We'll have some extra space. George'll be too busy gagging down his breakfast.'

We decline and walk along the beach back to our caravan, the only sound the laughter from the fishermen still teasing the silent George. The sun sets. Out on the end of the jetty a solitary figure sits transfixed by the spectacular sky. The burnished bronze water mirrors the dark silhouettes of the fishing boats floating so calmly their mooring lines hang slack from their bows. Pelicans glide by, their wingtips engraving the water in wide sweeping arcs. Further out, two dorsal fins quietly cut through the viscosity of the gleaming ocean.

I turn the alarm off at two minutes to four in the morning. The sky is black and it's deathly silent. We scramble to dress, having given ourselves only minutes to board our minibus to retrace out route back to Overlander to catch the Greyhound. Packed in tightly, the others nod off sitting upright, propped up by someone else's body. The only one awake, besides the driver, I stare sleepily at the beam of illumination from the headlights; it's too magical riding through this empty desert landscape to sleep. Rabbits scatter in zigzag patterns in front of us before finally having the sense to pull off the road. The occasional kangaroo floats through the head beams, weird creatures bounding across our path. Ungainly cripples hobbling pathetically within dusty pens at roadhouses, they are so elegant when vaulting freely over the landscape.

It is almost dawn when we arrive back at Overlander. Like an exhausted army still on manoeuvres, we bail out of the minibus and wait for the full-sized Greyhound travelling north. Lining up for morning tea, I recognise the three wrinkled apples in a basket. One has the same thumbnail incision. I wonder if the chicken wings, hamburgers and chips are that old too. It wouldn't be so easy to recognise thumbnail marks on a puckered hamburger or the shrivelled skin of a chicken leg. A desiccated woman doesn't smile when she hands Gemma and I our orders: anaemic eggs and burnt rubbery bacon. I'm tempted to put a thumbnail mark on her furrowed forehead to see if she doesn't reappear later some hundreds of kilometres away in another roadhouse.

Giving up on finishing the meal congealing before our eyes, we sit outside where mobs of pink galahs flap away noisily whenever a road train thunders by. The sun rises, the day gets hotter and the flies get worse. We sit there waving distractedly at buzzing insects, the conversation becoming more desultory as the day heats up.

By the time the bus arrives, we are catatonic.

It is two hours late. A passenger with bags under his eyes the size of half-doughnuts explains to the waiting passengers, 'The engine died and the Coach Captain spent an hour trying to fix the engine before one of the passengers suggested he might have run out of petrol. That's exactly what the problem was. He had to phone a 24-hour emergency service to get enough petrol to go the five kilometres to the next petrol station where he filled up with 420 dollars' worth of fuel.' Good thing it wasn't a plane. The Coach Captain with aviator sunglasses is forgiven his miscalculation as he reads my name off a computerised list of passengers and I am automatically assigned my special seat, 1A. Someone in Greyhound's central booking office is on the ball. Once on board and after the door closed, I surreptitiously spend the first half-hour using the curtains to squash buzzing flies against the window before Gemma sneaks up front to sit in the empty seat beside me.

'They don't allow boys and girls to sit together on the bus,' I whisper, squeezing as far away from her as possible while still remaining in my seat.

'Come on, they do if you're together,' she replies.

'We're not together,' I argue.

'Well, we sort of are. I mean, like we're friends and all.' She looks guiltily at the Coach Captain. 'Anyway, Andrew,' she says in a stage whisper, 'He doesn't know if we're not really together.'

'I'll tell him.'

She groans. 'Wish I had kept the Stud Delay.'

The air-conditioner on the bus doesn't work and it becomes unbearably hot. From our seats at the front, we have a contest to see who can count the most animal carcasses. We spot dead eagles, emu, monitors, feral cats, cows, lots of squashed kangaroos and a snake, which must be five metres long. We give up counting dead and crushed animals before we've decided who the winner is and before our eyelids slide shut.

Diverting off the main highway, we pass through sandy scrub to Coral Bay, another end-of-the-road destination bordering the Indian Ocean where two caravan parks provide facilities for recreational fishermen and now the increasing trickle of backpackers discovering Western Australia.

'Want to share a room?' Gemma asks.

'Sure, as long as you don't use any mouthwash.'

'Very funny.'

'Donga' the woman behind the counter calls the rooms. The 'dongas' look like a commercial walk-in refrigeration unit, with heavy door and latches like a walk-in freezer, lined up side by side in a shipping container. Each donga is only a double, with ducted central air-conditioning. We act as if we are 'together' and sign up for a refrigeration unit, close the freezer door and lie down on the beds, revitalising ourselves in the cool air.

Gemma says to me in her strong Irish lilt, pulling her baseball cap over her face as if she was about to fall asleep, 'If me father could see me now, sharing a room with a strange man and it's Holy Sunday and all.'

'I'm not strange,' I reply, lying down on my bed.

'I don't mean strange like that. Anyway, my father shouldn't be worried about me,' she adds thoughtfully from under her baseball cap.

'Why's that?' I ask.

'I'm all talk and no action. It's my own form of contraception.'

Despite the decadent luxury of lying in a semi-private 'donga' with air-conditioning, even if it is the size of a commercial freezer, neither one of us wants to waste the day, so we rent snorkels, goggles and flippers and walk to the empty beach.

'You a good swimmer?' I ask as we sit on the beach at the edge of the water, pulling on our flippers.

'Used to swim on the university team,' she replies.

'That's good enough.'

With none of the fanfare of the East Coast's Great Barrier Reef, we wade into the waters of Ningaloo Marine Park. No admission tickets, no dive boats, no dive masters, no wise-cracking dive guides. It's just a simple stroll down from the caravan park onto the sand and into the water.

Unlike the Great Barrier Reef where the closest coral is some twenty-odd kilometres off the coast, the coral here starts metres from the beach. We swim for two hours to the outer reef, where ocean rollers appear like moving mountains and rumble like an endless succession of road trains. The water is warm and the coral is patterned as a Persian carpet. Colourful antler, table, brain, cauliflower, carnation and finger coral are bright fluorescent green, lime, purple, blue, red and lilac. The coral is so thick there are few patches of empty sand and the sea is teeming with fish and turtles. It makes the more commercialised Great Barrier Reef pale in comparison. We swim on the surface like gliders as we float across valleys and mountains of coral, sometimes swimming in water just deep enough to buoy our bodies above the coral; sometimes in pockets of water so deep we would have difficulty diving to the bottom. The sun casts shadows of the waves like shimmering sunlight filtering to the ground through swaying forest leaves.

Swimming closely beside me, Gemma keeps a lookout for sharks. A school of mixed fish darts by, fusilier and mackerel, hundreds of shiny specimens in metre-deep water. Another school of fish swims rapidly past us. I hear Gemma scream into her snorkel. 'What are they all running away from?' she asks, pulling the snorkel out of her mouth when I lift my head above water.

'They're trevellay, swimming, not running, in a school for protection.'

'Protection from what?' she asks, removing the mask, her face circumscribed by the pressure marks of the rubber seal. She treads water so energetically her shoulders rise out of the water.

'Predators,' I reply, treading water with less vigour.

'What *kind* of predators?' she asks, a twinge of exasperation in her voice, her body ascending a smidgen more. She'll be walking on water at this rate.

'You know, *predators*,' I answer. 'Bigger fish.'

'You mean sharks?' she says accusingly, her chest rising out of the water.

'For example.'

'And what if those fish're swimming away from a marauding shark?' she asks, her Irish lilt emphasised by fear.

'The sharks eat trevally, not humans.'

'That's not what *I* heard,' Gemma says, her reproachful tone taking on a definite edge.

'You've been watching too many Hollywood movies. There are no dangerous sharks within the reef here.' Says me, an expert, although if Gemma weren't with me *I'd* be scared. Safety in numbers; if one of us gets eaten, I have a fifty–fifty chance it won't be me. Besides, she is more bite-sized.

Despite paranoia about rampaging sharks, neither one of us wants to get out of the water so we replace our goggles and snorkels and continue swimming, totally absorbed by the underwater life so different from anything we experience in our daily lives. It's as if we had arrived on a different planet. Another hour and a half later, Gemma tugs at my flippers and points at the goosebumps on her arms. I nod and we swim back towards shore.

Another decided point in its favour, Coral Bay has two bars full of authentic Australian fishermen. That evening, while sitting with Gemma eating fish and chips, I watch a woman walk up to the bar with a skimpy jean mini-skirt on. She leans over the counter, revealing a naked bum. Gemma follows my open-eyed stare.

'Scumbag. If I had a few more beers in me, I'd go up to her and tell her she forgot to put her knickers on,' Gemma says belligerently.

'How do you know she's a scumbag? Maybe she's doing her laundry. Happens to me all the time when I want to clean all my underwear at once.'

'But you don't wear a tiny skirt when you haven't got your knickers on.'

'I don't have a skirt to wear if I haven't got knickers on.'

'Well that's a step in the right direction.'

Back in the comfort of our air-conditioned refrigerator, the two beds so close there is barely any space between, I ask Gemma sleepily, exhausted by our long snorkelling expeditions, 'What's the worst thing you've ever done in your life?'

She thinks for a long time before replying. 'Em, stole some sweets out of the local corner store when I was young.'

'That's the *worst* thing you've ever done in your *whole* life?' I query, disinclined to believe her. The lights are off and I can't see the expression on her face. She could be pulling my leg.

She thinks for so long before replying that I assume she has fallen to sleep. 'I think it is. Em, unless you count the fact that I told my mother and father I'm working on a farm picking grapes.'

I sit upright and stare at the black space where she must be. 'You mean your parents think you're working on a grape farm while you're actually having fun travelling around Australia spending days like this snorkelling?'

'They're so conscious of me spending money and all. They know I quit my IBM job in Sydney and that I've come out to Western Australia. I had to tell them I'm grape picking. It's just a white lie,' she murmurs.

'But it's still a lie,' I remind her like a niggling conscience. I lie down. 'What would your father say if he knew you were spending money having fun instead of earning an income picking grapes?'

'He trusts me,' Gemma replies guiltily.

'And what if I phoned him and told him what you were up to?' I intimate, in what I think is a good imitation of her Irish accent.

'And whose story do you think he'll believe? His own daughter or a strange man he doesn't even know?' She thinks. 'Besides,' Gemma adds, 'I go all red in the face if I lie and my father knows it.'

'So he'll know then if you lie,' I say reasonably.

'That was *before* I came to Australia. I don't have any redness left in me any more since I've been living here and he doesn't know that yet.'

Swimming early in the morning over the carpet and canyons of coral we encounter sleeping green turtles wedged under coral, lots of blue-spotted rays, schools of juvenile garfish, convict surgeon, golden-lined spinefoot and trevally. In the crevices of coral heads we find a variety of cod. We follow an ungainly starry puffer fish as it floats about using its tiny flippers like miniature fans for propulsion. Painted and many-lined sweetlips with their Mick Jagger mouths swim about self-consciously. There are numerous giant clams with colourful swollen flesh spilling out from their shells. We dive down and touch the slimy flesh, despite the nightmarish image of the clams clamping their massive shells shut on our fingers and holding us down there until we drown. There is a sense of intimacy diving without scuba tanks, a sense of being naked and vulnerable that heightens the intensity of the experience.

Absorbed in this underwater life, I absent-mindedly dive and suck on the snorkel mouthpiece and inhale water. Half drowned, I splutter for some minutes on the surface while a concerned Gemma makes sure I have emptied my lungs.

'What happened?' she asks.

'Forgot I was snorkelling and not scuba diving.' I cough up more water. 'Thought it was a regulator in my mouth and inhaled water,' I explain, treading water and hacking out more phlegm.

'You know, Andrew, sometimes you are really scary.'

'It's not funny,' I tell her, for a change.

'I'm not laughing.' She puts her goggles back on and adds, 'Try to focus on what you are doing. This is a snorkel, not a regulator.' With that she shoves her snorkel into her mouth and swims away leaving me to follow her fins.

In the middle of the day the coral is lit in spectacular ripples by overhead sunlight. Neon blue damselfish mix with blue-green chromis; as the school shifts direction, their shimmering colours change instantaneously, with the speed and synchronism of a flashing electronic billboard at

Piccadilly Circus. Late in the afternoon, the long slanting rays of the sun catch the floating particles of plankton and eggs in shafts of light. An assortment of multi-coloured parrot-fish swim around, their lateral fins replicating the moving wings of a parrot; they don't use their tail fins for propulsion at all. Hiding shyly in the coral is a dizzying array of butterfly-fish. It is easy to recognise the blue-spot, the tear-drop, the oval-spot, the threadfin and the chevroned. Longfin bannerfish and semi-circular angel-fish seem to be less shy, aggressively defending their territory despite our overwhelming size. Tiny little headband humbugs are particularly unafraid as they swim at us as if to attack, before quickly retreating.

At low tide there is barely enough space for us to snorkel over sections of coral and we have to plan our route carefully over the maze of channels, sometimes having to backtrack to find a way through. Near the roar of the rollers breaking on the outer reef, the water is deeper with stretches of sand where the accumulated rubble of broken coral has collected. Bottom-dwelling goatfish move about with long feelers flicking through the sand looking for food. Occasionally we see a ball of juvenile striped catfish like overgrown tadpoles bundled together. When we near the outer reef the currents become strong and the visibility less clear.

Just as we turn and head towards shallower water, a white-tipped shark cruises by. Gemma's eyes expand to the size of her goggles. I pursue the slow-moving shark, which is heading into shallower water anyway, and Gemma follows me. About my size, the shark moves its tail with a languid sideways motion as it swims through the water. It is easy to keep up with as we pursue the unconcerned predator. The shark heads into the thick of the reef and we trail it for some twenty minutes before giving up. It is thrilling. This is not the Discovery Channel. This is for real. This is us. We are wet, we are tired, and we are scared. We are following a white-tipped reef shark. A real one.

'What did you do that for?' Gemma asks when I surface to clean out my mask.

'What?'

'Follow the shark.' She removes her goggles too.

'Why not?'

'It's a shark!'

'What did you follow me for then?' I ask Gemma.

'It's OK for you; you're bigger than me. He'd have to think twice before biting you, but he could've had me for breakfast as easily as look at me,' Gemma states with apparent authority.

'But he didn't,' I reply, based on empirical evidence.

'That was beginner's luck more than anything else,' she says.

That evening, Gemma phones home to Ireland to tell her mother in graphic detail how hard work it is picking grapes on the West Coast. She doesn't bat an eye as she lies and she tells me everything she tells her mother.

Then she phones her boyfriend. She doesn't tell me what she tells him.


Our last morning at Coral Bay we snorkel in the clearest water we have experienced yet. There is no current; the sun shining on the rippled surface makes the coral dance and jump out at us. When the sun disappears behind a cloud, the water becomes a uniform blue. When the sun reappears, the world lights up, especially the chromis and neon damselfish flashing as brightly as Christmas tinsel.

We barely make it back in time to catch the Greyhound. Exhausted from three days of almost non-stop swimming, we sit back in our front row seats as we cruise through long stretches of dry red earth, low-lying shrub and red termite hills.

'This Western Coast of Australia is so undeveloped. It must be what the East Coast was like 100 years ago. I could come out here again. I could live in Western Australia.' Gemma tells me.

'Me too and I didn't even go south of Perth, and everyone who's been there tells me it's even better.'

'Why do you like it here so much?' Gemma asks.

'It's unspoiled, undeveloped. I dunno . . . it's sort of more like what I had expected Australia to be like, even if the expectations were unrealistic.'

'You mean compared to the East Coast?'

'I mean, look at that emptiness.' We both look out the window, front and sides. 'There's nothing but desert. The coastal settlements are few and far between and mostly set up for Australian tourists rather than foreigners. Take the snorkelling we did just now on the Ningaloo Reef. All we had to do was walk down to the beach and swim and it was packed full of coral and fish it was amazing, and yet there was no one, not a single other person out there. I like that.'

We pass a series of ochre mounds rising vertically from the desert floor. From 1B, Gemma asks the Coach Captain, 'Em, what are the brown lumps of earth?'

'Fossilised dinosaur poo,' he replies, clearly not taking her seriously like I do.

'Termite mounds,' I whisper into her ear. 'Should have asked me in the first place.'

At Exmouth I check into a backpacker's lodge and book a trip the following day on an excursion looking for whale sharks. Before we met, Gemma had already reserved a seat on the bus up to Broome, leaving Exmouth at ten thirty the same evening. 'Are you sure you won't stay here for a couple of days and come whale sharking with me?' I ask. I enjoy Gemma's company, she's easy to get along with and has a great sense of humour and although she has a boyfriend, there's an unspoken affinity between us. Besides, making it clear she has a boyfriend dissipates any sexual tension there might have been. We're friends for friendship's sake and we've dispensed with any sexual innuendo in developing that camaraderie.

'I've already paid for an adventure tour through the Kimberley, and have to get up to Broome where the trip starts. If I stayed here I'd only have a short overnight in Broome before the adventure tour and I'd like to see Broome, too.'

She showers in the evening, using my dorm as a temporary base, and then dresses for dinner, where we have booked at a proper restaurant where they serve wine. I keep my greasy shorts on which haven't been washed since the accident at Coober Pedy, but change my T-shirt for a regular shirt, which has been sitting rolled and rotting in a ball at the bottom of my backpack. It looks it.

'You've got earrings on, and lipstick and everything,' I comment half way through the meal, keeping an eye on the waitress' movements just in case she sneaks up behind me.

'I'm a girl, or haven't you noticed?' she replies.

'Are you sure you won't be staying here?' I ask, imitating her Irish lilt.

There is a long thoughtful pause, then she says finally with resolve, 'No. I am definitely taking the bus tonight.'

'Whale sharks grow up to ten metres long and move up and down the coast off the Ningaloo Reef on the other side of the Exmouth Gulf,' our diving guide tells us on the bus as we head down the coastline to our boat early the next morning. I sit alone. I miss Gemma; it was nice having a travelling companion.

'The whale shark is the world's largest cold-blooded animal but we don't know a lot about them. Some 240 were killed last year in the Philippines for food. They hang around here, just offshore, because there's a 2,500-metre trench with cold-water up welling, stimulating plankton growth. These tours are into its tenth year and we are increasingly successful at finding our whale sharks. We'll be out all day looking for them, with two spotter planes up above to help us out. When you get in the water, stay to the side of the shark, not in front or behind. If you are directly in front, it can't see you and if you are behind, you may find yourself caught up in its tail. Either end, you lose.'

I spend the day with a dozen other passengers and a crew of three, making friends while bouncing on the sparkling waves off the reef. From this ocean-side perspective, a long line of white spray demarcates where the wind catches the cresting waves breaking on the outer reef. Behind the surf and the protected coral reef, the coastline is a deserted empty range with Exmouth on the far side of the peninsula. Two tiny Cessna 150 spotter planes fly up and down the coast looking for the telltale shadow of the whale sharks feeding just below the surface. It is late afternoon and it's beginning to feel like we have just spent a wasted day on the water, when the radio cackles abruptly from one of the aircraft. 'There's a large manta ray not far from you.' The pilot gives us its relative position and we rush over, engines humming, waves splashing off the hull. We slow down and the skipper tells us, 'OK, you can go in. Don't chase after it, it'll probably do figures of eight around you as it feeds off the plankton.' I can see the dark shadow of its back. The animal is huge; it must be the width of the boat.

First overboard, within seconds of entering the water, I am confronted with a manta ray, its underside white, its top battleship grey, heading straight at me, face to face. Enormous flaps channel the plankton into a mouth so big it could swallow me whole. Does this creature have a blind spot straight in front of it too? It approaches me without any indication it has seen me. I dive, hoping to get underneath it. The manta turns onto its side, avoiding me. As it completes its banking turn, it flips onto its back as it swims by under-neath, the wings moving in graceful sweeps. Repeatedly the immense creature swims by, over, beside, right side up, upside-down, a gentle elegant giant gliding through the water. It's an experience not soon forgotten and by being so quick to enter the water it seems I had a front row seat. Although there were two other mantas, the one that executed figures of eight around me was by far the largest. When the mantas finally leave the area, we climb back on board the boat, all of us high on adrenaline.

Later in the day we head back to the mooring at full speed. It is a disappointment not seeing the whale shark but swimming with the manta rays is an unexpected plus. We moor off a buoy, take a small boat ashore and board the shuttle bus for Exmouth. Still high on the manta encounter, sitting on the bus on the drive along the coast watching the sun set, we cruise parallel to a herd of wild horses galloping alongside the road, the setting sun dramatically back-lighting their flowing manes and tails. It's the kind of image you remember years later, and it'll still bring a smile back to your face.

The dive companies guarantee that if you don't see the whale sharks on the first attempt, you are entitled to a second day out, dependant on availability of space. Taking advantage of the generous offer, I book to go out again. For the second day I bounce on the waves with the crew and fellow passengers for more than six hours before one of the spotter planes radios us late in the afternoon, 'We've got a ten-metre whale shark in sight.' We are directed to a long black shadow in the water.

With goggles, flippers and snorkel on, sitting right beside the captain at the wheel, I'm at the ready. The skipper cuts the engines and tells us to go in. Already perched on the gunwales, I roll in backwards as if I was entering the water with a scuba tank. I hit the water on my back with a loud splash, blow the water out of the snorkel and look around. The water is unbelievably clear but I cannot see the whale shark anywhere, which is strange, considering its size, and the fifty-metre visibility. There are lots of balloon-sized jellyfish though, which make me nervous, especially as I haven't bothered with a wet suit. Beginning to feel the cold temperature and to wonder why no one else is in the water, I notice a hammerhead shark deep below me.

I swim so fast I'm sure only the tips of my fingers and flippers actually touch the water. You couldn't get me out of that ocean fast enough.

'How come no one else was in the water with me?' I ask cockily as I climb onto the tray at the back of the boat. No one says anything. 'Is something wrong?' I ask, removing my flippers. Everyone in the boat averts his or her eyes. The mood has changed. There is a mutinous feel on board, except the distinct sense I get from the overt hostility is that I am the pariah, and not the captain. The engines start up; the dive master puts away her binoculars having given up on relocating the shark. Sensing a degree of animosity, nobody has said anything to me; I sidle up to the dive master with whom I have spent some hours talking during these past two days. I thought we had established a reasonable level of communication. 'What's wrong?' I question her.

She doesn't look at me. 'You hit the water with a splash when you rolled in like that. Scared the whale shark away,' she replies, occupying herself busily with putting equipment in its proper place.

I stand there nonplussed. 'I didn't know.' Don't feel so cocky.

'I guess you missed that part of the pep talk.' Not surprising. Never listen to what I'm told anyway. 'Got to slip into the water from the rear of the boat so you don't disturb the animal. Not all of them are that sensitive, but this one was. You whacked the water before anyone else had a chance to move and by the time the rest of the divers were ready to go in, the shark had gone.' She glances at the other passengers. 'If I were you, I'd keep a low profile for the rest of the trip. I think the others could easily put you through a meat grinder right now. Lucky for you, we don't have one on board.'

She is right. No one talks to me for the rest of the trip, a couple of long hours back to the mooring. Not a comfortable place to be, on a small boat when no one will acknowledge my presence never mind converse with me. Most of them quite clearly would happily dump me overboard with the boat's full load of lead weight belts wrapped tightly and securely around my neck. I find the least conspicuous spot on the vessel, and sit there very quietly, very still, as unobtrusive as a toad in a dark corner, just in case those lead weight belts prove to be too much of a temptation.

In the evening I avoid the backpacker's lodge where my irate fellow passengers have worked themselves up into a real tantrum by telling new arrivals how I, pointing at me with accusatory fingers, ruined their chances of seeing a whale shark. They sit drinking beers and every time I walk by them there is a sullen silence, so I know they are talking about me. Likely to get lynched if I hang around much longer, I disappear to a local bar where there are no backpackers and frustrated whale shark divers.

'How'ya going, mate?' the Ocker slouched at the bar asks.

'Prematurely and too noisily,' I reply sullenly.

That doesn't seem to put him off, which I take as a good sign. Scott reaches out a hand and makes me feel welcome into the human race again. 'It's a beautiful day but,' he says before asking, 'What'll you have, mate?' Anywhere else in the English-speaking world, a friendly stranger at a bar offering to buy me drinks would be an indication he was trying to pick me up. Taking a good look at him, I can't imagine anyone, of either sex, no matter how desperate, trying to pick up Scott, or for that matter, being remotely interested in being picked up by him.

He tells me he puts up fencing for a living, and spends most of his time sleeping out in the bush. He looks it too. Half the dirt in the Outback seems to have encrusted itself on him. He keeps winking at me conspiratorially and nudging me with his elbows. He has a nervous habit of readjusting his grimy Aussie hat over his long unkempt hair every couple of minutes. He is filthy, his T-shirt brown with earth, his fingernails black with grit. 'L-O-V-E' is inexpertly tattooed on the knuckles of a fist.

Everyone around this whale shark-oriented town knows I'm the guy who flopped out of the boat and scared the whale shark away. I need all the friends I can get. Putting up fences all day, I guess he hasn't heard about my blunder. He's my mate and most of the things he can think of talking about are all 'fucking A' and he emphasises the point by throwing both his arms in the air as if he were throwing salt and pepper over each shoulder. Running out of 'fucking A' things to say, and well lubricated with several beers, he tells me a series of jokes. The cleanest crack, the only one I could repeat, is about three bragging rats. 'Three rats at a bar. First rat says, "I'm so tough I can eat rat poison." The second rat says, "That's nothing. I'm so tough I can eat the cheese out of a mouse trap and eat the mouse trap too." The third rat says, "I'm off to fuck the cat".' Scott throws both arms in the air. 'Fucking A.'

'Ha ha ha ha,' I laugh enthusiastically. In the whole of Exmouth, Scott is the only guy in town who will befriend me and I don't want to offend this last ally by not laughing at his stupid jokes. 'Ha ha ha ha ha ha ha,' I laugh hysterically, realising how lucky I am to have a mate.

He looks about him to see if anyone else has witnessed how funny I think his wit is. Four women at the end of the bar giggle, although I doubt they are laughing so much with us as at us. They wear sexy black lace. Two of them get on the dance floor to dance together to music played by what I presume are a live band of Irish singers judging by the green Leprechaun outfits they wear, but based on the actual tunes, it's hard to know if they are Irish balladeers or Bulgarian gypsies. The two women give up jiggling to the Bulgarian or Irish folk music and return to suck on straws immersed in tins cans of Bundaberg rum concoctions. 'You're either a Bundaberg man or a Jim Bean man,' Scott tells me, appraising the women's tattoos and throwing his hands over his shoulders again. 'Know the difference between a slut and a bitch?'

'No,' I reply, getting ready to brace myself for another bout of hysterical laughter.

He simultaneously throws his arms in the air; salt over the left shoulder and pepper over the right. 'A slut will fuck everyone in town. A bitch will fuck everyone in town except me.'

'Ha ha ha ha ha,' I respond eagerly again.

He studies the women in lace with a jaundiced eye and adds, 'And those sluts are bitches.' For emphasis he adjusts the bush cap disguising his year-old bush head.

It is a Saturday, and this is a live band, although even this statement is debatable on a number of counts. The blokes in the bar are a rough crowd: Rastas talking to skinheads with shaved skulls talking to hippies with ponytails. The only unifying element seems to be black accessories. Black lace for the women, black jeans for the blokes, except Scott. He is just a uniform grubby brown. Cowboy and Aussie hats are mixed and matched with varying degrees of consistency to black tank tops and black leather vests; Blundstones vie with pointy cowboy boots. The guys are more mesmerised by the footy on the television than the women in lace at the other end of the bar. The only mixed group is a foursome playing pool. A black dog sits outside the open doors patiently waiting for something or someone.

'Want to come fishing with me Wednesday?' Scott asks, readjusting his Aussie hat and throwing both hands over his shoulders.

'Can't. Heading off to Broome tonight. Besides, I'm a jinx on a boat. But thanks for the offer anyway.'

Taking the ten-thirty minibus to the Giralia turnoff just as Gemma did the other night, I arrive at the T-junction turnoff at one in the morning. There is nothing but the strip of tarmac of Highway 1, and the side road 'shortcut' we have just come on from Exmouth. Not even a roadhouse to grace this intersection. This must be the only place in Outback Australia where two sealed roads meet and there isn't a roadhouse. Bet within a few years some Pear-shaped Roadhouse People immigrate here, build a roadhouse and fry up second-hand roadhouse grub to sell to innocent Coach Folk.

We bail out of the minibus and scatter on the side road. This definitely feels like the middle of nowhere. Adding to the sense of isolation, there is no moon and it is really dark and no traffic. Three Japanese sing songs quietly as one strums a guitar. Others sit grouped together talking quietly. The rest lie down on the side road in sleeping bags. The sound of muffled voices is amplified by the silence of the desert. I walk some distance down the side road until I am alone in this emptiness, lay my sleeping bag out and lie back. The Milky Way is a bright smudge of countless stars. The only disturbance to this peace is the occasional road train, its presence preceded by an eerie white glow on the horizon, almost like a moonrise except this moonlit glow becomes so intense it lights up the world in powerful multiple beams of light. There is a mighty roar of the engine and the whoosh of disturbed air as the truck pulling three long trailers tears by with the momentum of an express train. A blur of yellow running lights, the gleam of trailing red tail lights, and then silence as the road train is swallowed up in the considerable darkness of the desert.

It is almost four in the morning when the Greyhound appears, some hours late. But the bus's tardiness has given us an extension on one of the best experiences one can have in Australia: sleeping out in the middle of the Australian desert. I could do it indefinitely. I'd rate waiting for the connecting Greyhound bus while staring at the stars in the middle of the Australian Outback on a par with climbing high mountains, walking in the rainforest, swimming along a fish-infested coral reef.

It will be an eighteen-plus hour ride from the Giralia Turn-off to Broome. At first there are some ranges, but then it flattens out and becomes red dirt. Even the driver has difficulty staying awake. I watch him as he chews gum, stretches his arms, drinks copious amounts of Coke, wipes his hands over his face. It must be hypnotising driving down this straight road with the glare of the sun tiring the eyes. There is virtually no other traffic. Not even the road trains.

At Port Hedland we stop for a meal break. I pick up a local paper and sit outside on a bench to read. The headlines declare that it is Sorry Day. I read how white parents are taking their kids out of school because the parents object to Sorry Day. 'Why should Johnny say he's sorry for something that happened three generations ago?' is the caption under a photo of an angry, overweight woman holding the hand of her son. She looks as if she has had a lifetime of being angry. Wouldn't want to be the kid.

An Aboriginal woman sits next to me on the bench outside as we wait for the bus. She sees me reading the paper. I break the ice and say hello to her and ask her what Sorry Day is all about.

'I was one of those children,' she says, pointing at the headline with a bony finger.

'You were?'

'Yeah. When I was six when the station manager where I was born took me to another station and left me there. I cried and cried and cried. Imagine you are suddenly made an orphan like that. It was like an accident and everybody I knew was killed.' Recounting the event, she struggles to fight back the tears. 'I haven't been talking about this for years. Yeah,' she says, 'Now the government paid for me to go to Broome for Sorry Day. I don't know why.'

'How long did you stay on the station you were taken to?' I ask, filling the silence.

'Many years. They changed my name and I lived with a bunch of other girls camped out in the back of the house. We didn't get much education but when we were old enough we had to work cleaning. That was the only time we entered the house. We waited on the white folk hand and foot. The boys did stock work, repairing fences, things like that. The white kids went to school. We didn't see the vegetables we grew; they were for the white people. We ate the turnip tops and the outer cabbage leaves. If we didn't kill a bird during the day, we wouldn't have had any meat. I met my husband there. He has a Scottish father and an Aboriginal mother like me. When I fell in love with my husband, we had to ask the manager to write away for permission for us to marry. We worked there for twenty years. Then the station was sold and we had to leave overnight. Once I tried to go back to the station where I was born, where my people are, but I was turned away at the gate by the station manager.'

'When were you born?' I ask.

She laughs, but it is a bitter laugh. '1929. We were all born on the first of the first. Thousands of Aboriginal kids born on the first of the first. That's how much they cared for us.'

I offer her some of my chocolate bar. She declines. I say, 'Some people say it was a good thing you were taken away. That you were saved from alcoholic mothers, given an education, given a chance to work.'

She shakes her head sadly but doesn't take offence at my comment. 'I resent the fact that my Aboriginal life was taken from me. It wasn't much of an education we got, and at the stations we worked hard for almost nothing, for food, clothes and maybe some tobacco, just like slaves. It's still happening on the farm stations. All our lives my husband and I have struggled to survive. The only time we have been given something is when the Lands Trust gave us a bit of land to build a house. Even now we struggle to survive. We live as Christians, we are taught forgiveness, but it is hard to forgive what the white people did to us.'

There is an awkward silence between us. I don't know what to say.

'Sometimes I wonder what my life would have been like if I had stayed in the bush,' she says finally.

The bus leaves and soon we pass the edge of the Great Sandy Desert, a vast uninhabited region of red sand dunes running parallel to one another. Here the world's record for the longest heat wave was recorded: almost half a year of temperatures not dropping below 100°F or 37.8°C.

Witnessing this empty domain, the thought of flying through it in a small plane has a pioneering appeal that goes back to a vivid imagination stirred by readings of Antoine de Saint-Exupery's books *Night Flight* and *Mail Plane*. Seeing this vast expanse of desert, I regret not being more persistent with my original idea of flying across Australia. The terrain brings back memories of flying my Cessna 182 in the East African bush over a five-year period. Those are some of the happiest recollections I have.

That evening Gemma is waiting for me when I arrive in Broome. Everyone is barefoot. 'You can tell the surfies around here; they've got broad shoulders, big upper bodies and spindly little legs sticking out from baggy surfers' shorts,' Gemma informs me before adding, 'I missed your company.'

'Missed you too,' I reply, happy to see a familiar face and not have to explain myself again to a whole new set of strangers. Feel a bit of a loser arriving somewhere entirely on my own; it's like I don't have any friends at all. 'What've you done since you've been here?' I ask as she shows me around the town.

'Em, rode a camel at sunset on the long stretch of beach. Went to the cinema with its open roof under the stars; strange when the flights come in to land overhead. Sort of wished I had stayed in Exmouth though, to see the whale sharks.' She adds quickly, 'Did you see any?'

I tell Gemma how I blew a dozen backpackers' 300 bucks each invested in a whale shark trip by doing a back flip into the water and scaring the whale shark off.

'Somehow it doesn't surprise me, Andrew.'

'Why?' I ask, hurt.

'You're . . . well . . . special,' she replies evasively.

'What?'

'Well, em, you know . . . you're good at the big picture and all, but sometimes the details elude you,' she mumbles. 'You're not part of the programme and all.'

'I don't want to be part of the programme and all.'

'That's obvious,' she says almost inaudibly.

'And what's that supposed to mean?' I demand.

'Em, you need someone, you know, practical, around you; your head's up in the clouds half the time. And your feet aren't exactly touching the ground either.'

'You mean I really am a space cadet?' I ask rhetorically.

'Em, yes.' She shrugs helplessly.

I guess if you're a space cadet you're a space cadet, and there's not much anyone can do about it.

We head into the backpacker's. 'I've made you non-greasy pasta dinner,' she adds quickly to take my mind off being a space cadet. 'Em, and besides that, your T-shirt's inside out and backwards. Do you do that on purpose?'

If she starts a sentence with 'em' again, I'm going to call her Emma. 'Gemma, what time do you leave on your Kimberley adventure trip?' I ask idly when we sit down to eat, my T-shirt on the right way again.

'They're picking me up at five tomorrow morning.' She lets that information sink in. 'Do you want to come? There's a 24-hour booking service, if you're interested. It's an eight-day trip,' she reminds me.

'Haven't seen Broome yet,' I reply between mouthfuls of the first non-greasy food I've had in months.

'There's not a lot to see,' she says dismissing the town. 'Cable Beach, the camels, the open-air cinema. It's a nice place, but it's the party-town of the West Coast of Australia and touristy.' She knows how to push my buttons. 'I'm sure if you phoned their booking office they'd have an opening for you.' She gives me the colourful brochure that she handily has with her. 'There's the phone number, at the bottom of the page.'

'It's ten thirty at night and they're picking you up at five in the morning,' I protest.

'It's a 24-hour booking service,' she repeats. 'I checked.'

'The booking office is in Darwin and that's an hour-and-a-half time difference. It's midnight there already.'

# 4   The Kimberley

Sharing the dormitory with Gemma, our fitful snooze is disturbed at three in the morning by one of our five bunkmates who crashes drunkenly into the room and attempts, noisily, to play the *didgeridoo*. Gemma, in the bunk bed closer to the aspiring ethnic musician, orders him in no uncertain terms to stop. At four in the morning I am woken again by the shaking of my top bunk, as if there was an earthquake. I peer over the side to see the quivering buttocks of my bunkmate on the lower bunk intimately entwined by a pair of woman's legs. At five in the morning we get up. I go to the washroom. I can't open the door beyond a few centimetres. Someone has fallen asleep inside, curled up in a pool of vomit.

Half asleep, we sit outside the backpacker's under a light so that I can read and study the glossy brochure describing the 'adventure tour' while waiting to be picked up. According to the slick marketing, we are headed into one of the 'most desolate areas in the developed world'. Three times the size of England with a population of only 25,000, the Kimberley is one of the least densely populated places on earth.

Before dawn, the four-wheel drive vehicle lumbers in front of the backpacker's. Our guide introduces himself: 'Bruce,' he says and shakes our hands firmly. 'But you can call me Croc, as in Crocodile Dundee. Everyone else does.' He has sun-bleached rusty hair from what we can see under the Aussie hat, startling blue eyes and a chin so rectangular it looks like a caricature of a square jaw.

'Seems every Ocker in the Outback wants to model himself on Croc Dundee. Crock o' Shit is more like it,' Gemma whispers to me as he takes our packs and throws them onto the roof and ties them down under a tarpaulin.

The vehicle, an Australian-made Oka, is as square-jawed as Crock. Shaped like a shoebox with a 45° angle cut out of the top front where the windscreen is, the body is mounted on large wheels almost in the middle of the undercarriage. The roof rack is so loaded with supplies it looks as if we are heading out on a major transcontinental expedition. Getting up this early in the morning when it is still dark adds to the impression. Gemma opens the door to the separate rear passenger compartment and hydraulically powered stairs descend out of the chassis automatically. I climb into the forward cab. It's a cross between sitting high up in front of a forward-drive Land Rover and sitting in the comfortable laid-back position of a reclining seat in an airliner.

Crock jumps into the driver's seat. Outfitted in matching khaki with the company logo on each item, even the belt, he explains, 'It's for tax purposes, so I can deduct the cost of my clothes from my income.' He wears an Aussie hat, Blundstone boots with white ankle socks, and crippling tight stubby shorts. Anywhere else, dressed in short shorts, ankle-high boots and white socks, you'd be accused of being a bewildered cross-dresser with bad taste.

We drive to the Youth Hostel where we wait half-an-hour for a client who was asleep until Crock woke her. She wears platform shoes with soles the thickness of a London telephone book, tight-fitting-around-the-bum black bellbottom trousers, and mismatching brown leather jacket with oversized rounded lapels. Tilted at a 45° angle, she lugs a suitcase banging about her knees. She's obviously not a backpacker and equally obviously not in a good mood at being woken up. 'Spice Girl', Gemma christens her immediately, 'looks as if she hasn't had any sleep.' From her accent, we can surmise Spice Girl, despite her appearance, is Australian.

By contrast, we pick up an eagerly waiting, bright-eyed bespectacled Chinese-descent Canadian from the next hostel. He wears mandatory cool name-brand outdoor clothing and says 'Neat! Wow!' when he sees the hydraulically operated stairs flip out from the Oka body as he opens the door handle. He has a Leatherman multi-tool attached to his belt on one hip and a Swiss army knife and Maglite on the other. He says 'Neat! Wow!' so often we don't have to give him a *nom de voyage,* he effectively christens himself.

From another backpacker's lodge we pick up a young woman with a backpack covered in embroidered flags from countries she's visited between India and Australia. She's been travelling for six months and is apparently so exhausted she is still asleep. She says something to Crock but he doesn't hear her.

'Squeeze me?' he replies, admiring her good looks.

She repeats her question.

'Don't worry about me, I've had a vasectomy.' Crock opens the door to the passenger compartment of the 4WD and the stairs automatically lower. 'Jump abroad,' he says, extending a hand to her.

'What's a vasectomy?' she asks with a slight German accent as she climbs into the back of the Oka with Gemma. She looks like Marilyn Monroe with copper-tinged hair.

'Same thing as a lobotomy,' our hard-boiled Gemma whispers to her when the door closes, 'except the lobotomy didn't work on him so they gave him a vasectomy and that worked fine.'

The German girl promptly falls asleep in the reclining aircraft chair. 'Sleeping Beauty', Gemma dubs her, 'must have been partying all night.' Our final stop is at a swish hotel to pick up two middle-aged American women, both disguised in matching khaki outfits under khaki bush hats with anti-fly netting drooping from the rims. They could be the female counterparts to Laurel and Hardy, except one is tall and thin and the other is short and fat, rather than the other way around. With the anti-fly net veils and their khaki Desert Storm outfits, they could be widows on manoeuvres.

The shorter, fatter one has a loud voice, matching big face and a mouth that doesn't ever seem to shut. Besides having the shorter stature of a female Hardy, she reminds me of a smiling and vociferous bullfrog. Her tall, lean companion, a stretched-out Laurel, 'Dr Dizzy', I think she says when introducing herself, has a doctorate in oceanography and is the physical opposite of Big Face, right down to her prim and proper tiny mouth. Although it is hard to discern their features through the fly-nets, Dr Dizzy seems as dismayed as the rest of us every time her friend Big Face opens her voluminous chops. They have been travelling around Australia for two weeks and one can sense a palpable friction between them.

I am determined not to get into the thick of things with this group. I want to position myself on the sidelines as much as possible, as an observer. Never been a client on a group tour before, and I'm excited to witness the dynamics.

About 200 kilometres along the Great Northern Highway the Oka develops problems with the alternator; the battery doesn't seem to be charging. The Kimberley version of Crocodile Dundee parks at a Derby petrol station and wanders around the settlement trying to find someone who can fix the fault.

While waiting I buy two local papers. *The Kimberley District Times* has the headline: 'Sorry Day—"emotional nonsense".' Accompanying the article is a smiling white Federal Member for Kalgoorlie denouncing 'Sorry Day':

Yesterday's National Sorry Day was simply "white guilt-ridden emotional nonsense that did less than nothing for Aboriginal advancement" said Federal Member for Kalgoorlie Graeme Campbell.

As the Times went to press on Monday night indications were that many Kimberley parents intended keeping their children away from school yesterday, or at least not allowing them to participate in any National Sorry Day and Reconciliation Week celebrations at their schools.

The other paper, *The Kimberley Echo,* has a photograph of an Aboriginal Woman with a stocky white man who looks as if he could be the archetypal redneck farmer except for the fact that his hand is draped over her shoulder. Both were participants in a course for those interested in learning about the Aboriginal way of life. I sit outside on the curb in the sunlight and read the editorial on the following page:

It is ironic that Sorry Day has divided the community in its attempt to unite it.

Part of the division is rooted in language and two different understandings of the word 'sorry'. Where Aboriginal people use it to mean grief, white Australians take it to mean guilt.

National Sorry Day was not a day of white guilt but a symbolic occasion for all Australians to recognise the pain of past policies, the terrible suffering of children who were forcibly removed from their families over a period of 150 years (into the early 1970s) and to use that understanding as a basis for a strong and united future.

It is regrettable that some people felt threatened by this sharing of grief and refused to attend the event.

Crock walks by. I ask him, 'So, what was Sorry Day all about?'

'Sorry mate?' When it comes to guys, he doesn't say 'Squeeze me?'

'Sorry Day, what was that all about?' I ask again.

'Sorry Day?'

'Yeah,' I reply, holding the paper so he can see the front page.

'Don't know mate, never even heard of it. Was it advertised?' he asks before he disappears in search of a mechanic.

A Toyota Land Cruiser with 'Kimberley Land Council' printed on the doors pulls alongside. A man gets out to pump petrol. I greet him. He recognises the adventure tour vehicle and gauging that I am a sympathetic bleeding-hearted foreigner from my persistent questions, he bends my ear, 'You know, us Aboriginal people are treated in our own country as second-class citizens. To get our land back, we must show we come from here. Where do the whites think we come from? Outer space? We have to prove we come from this country to get our own land back, land we owned in the first place.'

'Nice fella, mate?' Crock asks me pointedly after overhearing the remark. Funny how the word 'mate' can sound so matey and sometimes it can sound like a verbal punch to the stomach.

There's no mechanic in town; regardless, we head down the Gibb River road, an unsealed but well-maintained track through the Kimberley. Increasingly, it feels as if we are off the beaten path. The earth is red-brown, the bush is green, the road straight as a jet contrail bisecting an empty sky. The strange boab trees are almost identical to the baobab trees of Africa. We bounce down the dirt road to Tunnel Creek, where we walk into a massive cave carved out of a limestone range by a river. We tread timorously, each armed with a flashlight. In addition to what Crock gave him, Neat!Wow! has his own halogen headlight, a Maglite, a miniature flashlight that comes with his Swiss army knife, and a luminescent compass on his wrist. Croc says he's surprised Neat!Wow! doesn't have a collapsible bayonet and an inflatable raft.

'The cave is almost a kilometre long, some twelve metres high and fifteen metres wide and was formed when water seepage gradually cut into fractures in the limestone,' Crock tells us. Stalactites drop from the roof and stalagmites protrude from the floor of the tunnel, their loud dripping and our echoing voices the only sound. 'We're going to have to wade through some pools of water,' Crock continues nonchalantly.

The air is noticeably cold. So is the water. In places we are knee-deep, wading through pools of cold freshwater. I look around at Gemma. The water is up to her thighs, same as Big Face.

'What's that?' Big Face hollers, her loud voice amplified by the sound chamber of the cave.

In the unsteady beam of her flashlight is a three-metre crocodile sitting to the side of the pool we are crossing.

'It's a croc!' someone says in a high-pitched voice.

'Dear Jesus, and what are we going to do now?' Gemma asks no one in particular.

We bring our light beams to bear on the crocodile. The croc's eyes are open but it doesn't budge. With our light beams focused on the crocodile, the rest of the world becomes spookily dark. There could be more out there, behind us, to the side, underwater.

'It's a freshwater croc,' Crock says coolly, taking his time in telling us this. 'Only place in the world where you find freshwater crocs, is Australia,' he adds.

'Ah look, I don't care what kind of crocodile it is,' Spice Girl snaps back with her Aussie accent, 'Or where you find them. It's still a fucking crocodile and it's looking right at me.'

Crock tells us, 'You could walk up to that croc and the water would only be up to your knees until you got to it. Then you'd be up to your hips. Keep walking and you'll be up to your neck.'

'What's he mean?' Sleeping Beauty, who looks wide-awake for the first time, asks.

'He means, if you walk any closer, the croc will bite you off at the knees, and if you get even closer, he bites you off at the neck,' Gemma replies. She doesn't have far to go before she is up to her neck in it anyway, croc or no croc.

Crock starts walking to the other side. The rest of us remain frozen, watching for the slightest reptilian movement. The crocodile looks as if it could be made of rubber, until it slithers into the water with surprising speed. 'That croc is underwater right now watching us,' Crock says. 'Now, if I were a *really* good guide,' Crock goads us, 'I'd probably wrestle it to the surface so you could get a flash photo. Unfortunately, there aren't too many *really* good guides left and I'm not about to become one of them.' He continues walking to the edge of the pool. 'These crocs are the fastest growing crocs in the world. By the time you get home, that two-metre croc you just saw will be three-metres and by the time you get to the local pub, it'll be four.'

'Why didn't you tell us there were crocodiles here?' Spice Girl exclaims angrily, safe on dry ground and not so dependent on Crock's goodwill should the crocodile attack. Spice Girl has done her big OE, spending most of her twenties in England and travelling around Europe, but this is her first trip in Australia outside of Melbourne and Sydney and she's as out of her element as we are.

'Wanted to surprise you.'

'And what other surprises might you have in store for us?' Gemma asks.

'Look up there.' Crock directs his beam of light upwards. Thousands of bats hang upside-down from the roof of the cave.

'Ah bloody Hell!' Spice Girl says. 'What are those?'

'Bats. There's five different species in here, probably millions of them,' Crock replies emphatically.

Half way through the tunnel, light filters in where the roof of the cavern has collapsed. The cavity is overhung with vegetation. Roots of trees, which have worked their way from the surface to the roof of the tunnel, hang eerily down to the pools below.

'How much further have we got?' Gemma asks nervously.

'We're about halfway. This is the cave where the famous Aboriginal called Pigeon, or Jandamarra, used as his hideout when he terrorised the whites in the area. They could never figure out how he disappeared into the range when they tried following him, until they found this cave. Finally they followed him through here and shot him at the far entrance.' Crock plays his beam of light on an erotic Aboriginal painting of a male with giant sexual organs, painted on the roof of the cave high above us.

'How'd they get up there to paint that?' Neat!Wow! asks, shivering uncontrollably despite several layers of high-tech mountain gear.

'Spirits did them,' Crock replies.

'Sure, like pigs can fly,' Gemma adds.

We return through the cave because we have to, there is no alternative, but this time when we reach the waist-deep pool there is no crocodile visible on the bank. We probe the dark edges and water with our torches but to no avail.

'Could it be underwater?' Gemma asks. 'If it is, I'd like someone to give me a piggyback. I'm a lot shorter than the rest of you and the water is up to my neck.'

'No it's not,' Spice Girl quibbles, pointing her light beam at the ground around her to make sure she is safe.

'Don't worry, freshies don't attack humans unless they are provoked,' Crock tells us as we stand at the edge of the pool, reluctant to enter.

'How do we know if we are provoking them?' Gemma asks reasonably.

'They attack you,' Crock replies.

'And how do we know if there are any salties in here?' Gemma pursues, sensibly.

'Same thing,' Crock replies.

'Someone should rewrite your script,' Gemma says as she wades into the cold water.

Surviving the return trip through the tunnel, we push-start the Oka and drive to the campsite at Windjana Gorge. Crock backs up onto a small incline so that we don't have to push-start the vehicle in the morning. He throws our swags off the roof onto the ground.

'How do these work?' Spice Girl asks, unravelling her swag, which looks vaguely like a sleeping bag. She still has her bell-bottoms, leather jacket and platform shoes on.

'You're an Aussie, you should know how a swag works,' Crock tells her.

'Ah look, don't give me that bullshit,' she replies angrily.

'She's a hard nut,' Gemma whispers a warning to me. 'Stay away from her.'

To silence Gemma's asides, Crock throws a swag at her. She ducks. Croc answers Spice Girl's question: 'You unroll the outer canvas bag and lay it out where you want to sleep. Inside is your sleeping bag. That's your swag, your bed, your room, your home for the night, unless of course you get lucky with me up here.'

'You wish,' Spice Girl says. She unrolls her bed, her room, her home for the night and takes a more conciliatory tone after moving in. She asks Crock, 'Is there any way you can inflate the swag? It's incredibly hard.'

'Em, are there any snakes here?' Gemma queries. She has a phobia about snakes and sharks and crocs.

'No,' Crock lies.

'Then why is it that you sleep on the roof of the vehicle and we sleep on the ground? Is it something you are frightened of?' Gemma asks.

You have to give Crock credit: he cooks amazing meat spaghetti in no time, single-handed. After dinner, while we clean up, Crock tells us, 'Two trips ago we broke the main axle and had to wait two days for another axle to arrive. Luckily we had plenty of booze on board so we just camped out by the Oka and got drunk until the replacement parts arrived.'

'This is my first night sleeping out, ever,' Spice Girl confesses meekly, interrupting Crock's description of how he got lucky with two Danish girls on the trip. 'I hope I can get to sleep.' She puts her plate aside and crawls into her swag, which is dangerously close to the campfire. She looks imploringly at Crock, 'I'd feel a lot happier sleeping on the roof of the Oka too, you know.' She doesn't play hard to get for too long.

'Not enough room, mate,' Crock replies.

The quiet Chinese-Canadian, a foreign exchange trader with one of the banks in Toronto, is pensive. He kneels beside his top-of-the-line backpack so spotless it looks as if he just pulled it off the shelf at Mountain Equipment Coop and fiddles with the locks on his pack before asking, 'Where can I change into my pyjamas?'

There's a stunned silence. Everyone stops doing what they were doing except Sleeping Beauty who is already in her swag fast asleep.

'What do you mean?' Crock asks.

'There's no changing rooms or anything,' Neat!Wow! replies straight-faced, looking around him.

'Use your towel, wrap it around your waist,' Gemma says, studying him hard in the firelight to discern whether he is joking or not.

'How?' Unbelievably, our currency trader is genuinely perplexed.

He doesn't have an old-fashioned towel; instead he has the latest in highly absorbent lightweight synthetic material the size of a handkerchief. Gemma lends him her full-sized low-tech towel and shows him how to wrap it around his waist.

Once you've done that, you can change underneath it. Look, like this. Have you never done this before?' she asks incredulously.

'No,' he replies.

'Are you sure? You're not pulling my leg and all?' Gemma questions.

'Yes. I mean no, I'm not pulling your leg.'

'How have you changed out of clothes in the past?' Gemma asks, still not believing him.

'I don't know. There's always been a changing room somewhere around.' Neat!Wow! has never camped out before, either.

Big Face and Dr Dizzy have camped out together all their lives it seems. In fact, Big Face talks non-stop about all the places they have camped in the Rockies as the two of them prepare to get into their swags. She doesn't stop talking until she falls asleep and then, in mid-sentence, she starts snoring loudly.

A laughing kookaburra wakes me before dawn. I collect firewood, light a fire, and begin boiling water. Crock descends from his penthouse perch on the roof of the Oka. 'That was a two-dog night, mate.'

'What's that mean?' Gemma asks from the warmth of her swag while staring bug-eyed at Crock's vacuum-packed buns negotiating the ladder on the back of the Oka.

'That's how the Aborigines measure how cold it is. You either slept out with nothing, one dog curled beside you, or, if it was really cold, with two dogs curled up on either side. It's either a one-dog night or a two-dog night.' Crock smiles at some secret joke as he makes billy tea from the hot water I have boiled. He pulls out what looks vaguely like a loaf of bread, what he calls damper. We stuff ourselves on the damper made of flour and water, and wash it down with billy tea. 'The damper fills ya up and the billy tea makes ya squit through the eye of a needle at 100 paces,' Crock tells us after it's too late to change our minds about the regularity and accuracy of our constitutionals.

As Crock bends over and ties everything securely to the roof of the Oka, Gemma whispers to me, gaping up at Crock's crotch, 'Do you see the tiny stubbies your man has poured himself into? They're so tight I can not only tell how many testicles he's got, which would be an educated guess anyway, but also which way he lies and I bet you I can correctly predict that he's circumcised.'

Following Crock's lead, Spice Girl sports tiny shorts like hot pants, which don't quite cover her dimpled buttocks sagging sadly beneath the flared lower edges of the hot pants. Her white socks are pulled above the knees.

'Ya look ridiculous,' an agitated Gemma pulls at her back-to-front baseball cap and remarks to Spice Girl, 'like you're advertising sexy lingerie or something. Have you not got something decent to put on? Why have you got your socks pulled up so high anyway?

'In case there're any snakes around,' Spice Girl replies a tad testily.

'Pulling socks up above your knees isn't going to protect you against snakes,' Gemma advises. 'They can spit their venom at your eyes and you'll die anyway. With a pair of white socks pulled up to your kneecaps and all, you'll look ridiculous when your parents collect you at the morgue. Will I lend you a pair of my jeans?'

'You're too short.'

'You'd look less ridiculous wearing my jeans than the outfit you've got on.'

The only mitigating factor compensating for the incredible heat is the dryness of the air. At Lennart's Gorge we bail out of the dusty hot vehicle and wait for Neat!Wow! to strap survival equipment on his body to cater to different potential emergency situations, then we head towards the gorge, clambering down the sides of the nearly vertical rock. Water tumbles in at one end of the natural pool and pours out the other end into another series of rock pools below. Crock stretches on the rocks and falls asleep. The rest of us jump into the numbingly cold but refreshing waters.

'Aaargh!' Spice Girl yells from the middle of the pool immediately after surfacing. 'There's a snake in here.' She's out of the pool so fast it's as if she'd dived in and bounced off a trampoline. The 'snake' climbs out on the other side and suns itself. It's a metre-long monitor lizard and there are four more monitors nearby, totally unconcerned by our presence.

Gemma starts giggling, lying on her back on the warm boulders.

'Why are you giggling?' I ask. It feels good to have the sun warming us up after the cold water.

'Because the water is dripping out of my ear and I love that feeling,' Gemma replies.

I like her giggles. She does it a lot. 'Tell me when it's empty and then I'll put more water in for you, just to keep you happy.'

'I am happy.' She giggles again. 'What do you think of Crock?'

I look around. He's out of earshot and anyway, I can tell by his rhythmic breathing that he is fast asleep. 'He's a good cook. What do you think?'

'He's OK, less hyperactive than the guides in Kakadu.'

'Hyperactive?'

'You know, he doesn't crack onto the women as much as the others do.' She turns her head to the other side to let the water drip out her left ear. Then she starts giggling again.

'That's not hyperactive,' I correct. 'Besides, he had his fill on the last trip with two Danish girls. He said the night before he started our trip that they each had a bar bill of 150 dollars. He's probably still recovering.'

Crock is unconscious. Or perhaps he isn't. He wakes up and looks at his watch. 'OK folks, time to go if we're going to make our next campsite before dark.'

The others climb up to the Oka. Wanting to have some time down here on my own, I wait, knowing I will catch them up. When I do head up after the others I see Spice Girl alone, bent over double in the path, her white socks still pulled above the knees in case of snakes. 'You OK?' I ask.

'I'm going to faint,' she replies, her voice barely audible, her face hidden beneath brown hair hanging limply from her upside-down head.

I get her to sit on a boulder and offer her my bottle of water. 'You're dehydrated.' She's as pale as a ghost despite her numerous freckles.

'I tried to tell Crock that. He just went on ahead, said he had to fix something on the Oka.' She mumbles something, then slumps over and I realise she has passed out. I lay her flat on the ground. Her hands and feet twitch.

'I'm giving you some water to drink,' I tell her. I hold it up to her mouth and gently pull her head back. 'Can you hear me?' She nods. 'OK, drink as much of this water as you can.'

Gemma yells from the cliff above. 'What are you two doing?'

What the hell does she think I am doing? Out on a hot date? 'Spice Girl's just fainted. Can you bring down some water,' I yell back.

Gemma comes skipping down with Neat!Wow!'s Camelback. 'Where's Crock?' I ask.

'He's under the Oka,' Gemma replies, studying Spice Girl.

'What's he doing there?' I ask.

'He said he was going to work on something, but if you ask me, I think he's asleep. He's borrowed Neat!Wow!'s inflatable pillow and he isn't moving much.' She adds, 'The walk back up here must have tired him out.'

I help Spice Girl up the steep path. It is the middle of the day and hot. It's even hotter in the vehicle. We remove the packs stuffed in the back seat of the Oka and get Spice Girl to lie prone. I soak Neat!Wow!'s highly absorbent synthetic cloth in water and place it over her forehead.

Crock emerges sleepily from under the Oka. 'What's going on?' Gemma was right; he was having a siesta.

'Spice Girl, I mean, Linda just passed out,' Gemma replies, checking guiltily to see if Spice Girl heard her. 'She's OK now.'

With Spice Girl prone in the back seat, Crock orchestrates us push starting the Oka and we proceed down a track so bumpy it feels as if we are being tumbled inside a mobile drying machine. Sometimes we lurch at such steep angles it seems the Oka must capsize. Back on the Gibb River Road, instead of camping at a campsite, Crock parks on the shoulder where the dirt road comes off the Napier Range, overlooking the valley fronting the King Leopold Range. From this vantage point is an expanse of . . . emptiness. The Kimberley's rugged terrain and oppressive summer heat have kept this corner of Australia virtually undeveloped.

We each do separate jobs in preparation for the evening. Gemma and I are responsible for the campfire. After dragging logs in from the surrounding bush, I show Gemma how to make a fire using kindling and twigs to create glowing embers before loading up with heavier sticks and logs. We have dinner around the fire but this time, when we lay out our swags, I wait until Big Face has chosen her spot for the night before I position my swag far away from her. Gemma follows me. 'If she's not talking, she's snoring,' she says unkindly but truthfully.

There's a slice of a silver moon bright in the sky. We climb into our swags and lying back, stare at the heavens. I ask Gemma, 'Do you know why the moon isn't full?'

'What do you mean?' she asks, turning her head to face me.

'I mean, why sometimes there's a full moon, a half moon, or a quarter moon, or like tonight, just the sliver.'

'Is it because the earth is creating a shadow on the moon,' she answers, her Irish lilt as pronounced as ever.

'That's an eclipse. I've been doing a survey on this for the past year and ninety-seven per cent of the people I ask give me that response, two per cent have a vaguely correct idea of why, and only one per cent really know. An eclipse of the moon occurs every few years, not every night.'

She is quiet, staring at the moon, the back of her head cradled in the palms of her hands. 'OK. So why is it only a quarter moon then?'

'Where did the sun set?' I ask.

'Over there,' Gemma replies pointing over our feet.

'And where is the moon?'

'Over there, sort of in the same direction,' she repeats, catching on, 'where the sun went down.'

'So how is the earth between the moon and the sun?'

'It isn't,' Gemma says.

'Exactly. So why . . . ?

'Is it because we are looking at the backside of the moon, mostly in its own shadow?'

'Yes. If it were a full moon, the moon would be on the opposite horizon, behind our heads, 180° in the opposite direction from the sun. When there is a full moon rising, the sun is setting at exactly the same time. If you look at that sliver of a quarter moon, like when it is as clear as tonight, we can vaguely see the whole circumference of the moon. Can you see it?'

'Would it be from the sunlight reflecting off the earth and although it's not as bright as the direct sunlight, it still lights up the back of the moon a bit?'

'Simple isn't it?'

'It is,' she replies.

'Tell everyone you know,' I preach.

'I'll be a moon evangelist.'

'Don't joke with me now, Gemma. This is serious. People should know this just as much as they should know not to spray their mouths with Stud Delay.'

I wake up to a limitless horizon over the King Leopold Ranges bloodied by a magnificent sunrise staining the ochre dust in the air a deeper red. The blue-black sky is drained of most of the stars and it is only the bright planets remaining. One of the planets has a tiny moon beside it. I shake Gemma. 'Look Gemma, there's a planet and you can see its moon with your naked eye. Only seen that once before without binoculars, in the Himalayas.'

'You've got moons on the brain,' Gemma says, rubbing the sleep out of her eyes.

'I'm serious. I bet that's Jupiter and one of its moons.'

An alarm clock sounds on the other side of the campfire and whoever it belongs to doesn't wake up. The alarm rings for several minutes.

When all the stars disappear and only the planets remain visible, Gemma believes me. 'Didn't know you could see a planet's moon.' We stare until even the planets have gone from the increasingly light blue sky.

Spice Girl remains buried in her swag until breakfast is ready to eat. When she emerges from the depths of her swag she gives vent to her anger. 'Ah look, whose bloody alarm clock was that this morning?' she demands to know, getting out of her swag already clad in her tight-fitting black bell-bottoms and brown leather jacket. 'I don't want to wake up in the morning to that shit,' she tells Crock when he admits it was his.

Spice Girl is definitely out of sorts this morning.

'What's wrong?' Crock asks.

'I can't have a you-know-what,' she admits.

'A Jimmy Riddle?'

'No, the other one.'

'A Johnny Jack. Why not?'

'I don't know. I just can't without a toilet.' She sits cross-legged on the swag. 'Haven't since this trip began,' she pouts.

'Why didn't you have one in the campgrounds when we were there?' Big Face asks.

'It's gotta be a flush toilet,' Spice Girl replies sulkily.

We push-start the Oka and democratically decide whoever rides shotgun up front with Crock gets to choose the music we play. Big Face is so short and fat we have to help her get into the forward cab. I kneel on all fours and she places a foot on my back and the others hoist her aboard. She has a few tapes of her own from the 1960s and she sings happily with Joni Mitchell, Willy Nelson and Cat Stevens.

For Spice Girl's sake, we stop at Mount Barnett Roadhouse where they have 'water-driven toilets'. It's another 400 kilometres to the next service station. I ask the sympathetic-looking white woman behind the counter of the general store, 'Who owns this place?'

'It's part of the cattle station, owned by the Aboriginal community here. They own the service station and this business as well.' She doesn't have that broad Australian accent others do around here. She sounds as if she could be from one of the big cities on the East Coast.

Dr Dizzy stands in line with me. It's one of the few times I've seen her without her fly net draped over her face. She asks, 'What do you mean exactly by the "Aboriginal community"?'

'Good question,' I comment. 'It slips off the tongue easily enough, but who is the 'Aboriginal community'?

'Travelling through here a century ago, you'd have encountered as many different languages and cultures as you would have in Europe a century ago.' She helps a small child count out the change for several chocolate bars before continuing. 'There wasn't an Aboriginal 'community' as such. The people who live on this station now weren't from clans that were necessarily even friendly with each other, although they had to get along in order to survive.'

'And they run the place?' Dr Dizzy asks as I pay for a chocolate ice cream.

'I run the small business here, which is used to generate income for the community to make them self-sufficient, and my husband helps run the cattle station. Originally, ATSIC paid our salaries, but now we are paid out of the profits from the business.'

'ATSIC?' Dr Dizzy queries.

'The Aboriginal and Torres Strait Islander Commission in Canberra.' She sees the blank look on Dr Dizzy's face. 'ATSIC was set up in 1990 combining two previous bodies, the Department of Aboriginal Affairs and the Aboriginal Development Commission. I guess cutting ourselves off from

Government funding is part of the community's process of self-determination.'

A noble thought, but I suspect there is more to cutting themselves off from easy funding than she admits.

'Have you tried to train someone to take your job?' I ask, suspicious that this is a nice sinecure for white folks even if they are paying their own way through profits generated by the business.

'I've trained members from the community to work and run the place but they don't always come to work, and you can't run a business like that.' She deflects the apparent criticism of her constituents by adding, 'It's not part of their culture to have regular hours and a set routine, or to provide a service. Attending ceremonies and funerals is an important function to them but it means it's impossible to have regular full-time employment. It's also difficult if they're working as a cashier when one of their community or family wants something and doesn't have the money. It puts a lot of pressure on someone from the community to work behind this counter. In their culture if you have, you share.'

Spice Girl walks in from doing her business in the water-driven toilets and lurks in the background eavesdropping on the conversation. A group of kids have followed her in, barefoot, some naked, all totally unselfconscious. They greet the woman behind the counter as they run around choosing things to buy, looking conspicuously happy. She continues, 'The communal sharing aspect of traditional Aboriginal life helped them survive in the past but in our competitive Western society, it's hard for a traditional Aboriginal to succeed as an individual in this materialistic world. Their timescales are different too. Whether something happened yesterday, or 5,000 years ago in the Dreaming, it's all compressed into the past. The same applies for the future.'

I watch as one of the children places a banknote on the counter, with a pile of chocolates, sweets and sodas. He keeps piling up the goodies until the cashier tells him that's all the confectionery the money will buy. When he leaves she tells us, 'They don't have the concept of coming in here and buying what they want, and then taking the change. He'll buy stuff until all the money he has been given is spent, and then he'll share what he bought with his friends.' Another child comes up to the counter and does exactly the same thing. The cashier patiently adds up the value of the sweets and chocolates until she has accumulated five dollars' worth. 'We've got a goddaughter, an Aboriginal from this community, who we have sent down to Perth for school. She's doing really well and we hope she'll come back and run the business enterprises.' She gives me my change for the ice cream as she talks.

'So there is hope?' Dr Dizzy asks, presenting a chocolate bar across the counter to be paid for.

My guess is their goddaughter won't want to return to an isolated community like this after being in the big city.

'One of our senior elders feels that for anyone over eighteen, they are a lost generation. Those who are younger have a chance of putting it all together. But that will take another thirty years.'

Taking a bite of the ice-cream, I ask her, repeating what the Coach Captain out of Alice Springs had said, 'What about stories of pastoral leases being given back to Aboriginal people and then they sit in their communities doing nothing with it?'

'Maybe we're the silly ones, running around working so hard,' the cashier replies, avoiding the thrust of the question. 'Besides, it's probably better for the environment if nothing was done with it. But if it's community-controlled and it's part of the Aboriginal movement towards self-determination, maybe that's enough.'

I have so many questions to ask the woman. She is well educated and well versed in Aboriginal affairs. It's an ideal opportunity to learn more about the communities, but Big

Face enters the shop and overhearing our discussion spouts off about the Navahos back home and soon monopolises the conversation to lecture us about North American Natives. It might be interesting if she weren't negating the chance of learning more about the country we are actually travelling in, rather than expounding on her own society half a world away.

Dr Dizzy walks out in a huff, fed up with her companion's incessant need to talk about herself and her inability to listen to others. As soon as Dr Dizzy has gone out, Crock opens the door to the shop and yells, 'Time to go!' We obediently go outside, but in fact the Oka hasn't even been re-fuelled yet.

Big Face talks with a bunch of boys and young men. They are dressed in jeans, stetson hats and cowboy boots. Realising she is American, they want to know which basketball team she follows and what the latest scores are. Gemma plays with a bunch of small children with Neat!Wow! Spice Girl disappears back to the real flush 'water-driven' toilet, suddenly panic-stricken at the thought of keeping it all in for another 400 kilometres. Sleeping Beauty is on the phone to her voice mailbox, picking up messages from her pining boyfriend in Germany.

'Know why Crock whisked us out of the community-owned service station?' Gemma asks me. 'He's jealous. He knows the flora and fauna of the bush all right but anything about the Aboriginals, beyond the clichéd Dreamtime stories, which only serve to enhance his own bush image, and his knowledge and interest in Aboriginal affairs are minimal. He's driven through this community plenty of times yet he hasn't the vaguest idea of what it is all about. Nor does he want to know.'

'How do you know?' I ask.

'Because I just asked him a few questions and he didn't have a clue and he didn't want to be bothered with a discussion on the matter.'

We climb into the Oka to drive to our camping spot for the night. Sitting next to me in the bouncing vehicle, Spice

Girl lectures, 'You know your problem Andrew? You're trying too hard to understand Aborigines and you're getting a biased view of them. I listened to you in the store back there. You look at Aborigines simply as disadvantaged natives. I've seen plenty of Aborigines getting on with their life in Melbourne. I've socialised with them, met them in bars, restaurants. It's not all just a question of dispossession you know. There are a lot of Aborigines who don't fit the stereotype image you seem to have of them.'

She's probably right.

'At least I am trying to understand the situation. That's a hell of a lot better than pretending a problem doesn't exist,' I retort.

'The problem's made worse by people like you who distinguish Aborigines from other Australians. The whole concept of victimisation is the only asset some Aborigines have and isn't it ironic that the one source of power rewards them for seeing themselves as victims rather than using their initiative?'

I couldn't agree with her more on that count.

'Have you ever thought about what happened in your part of the world?'

I don't reply and no one says anything, not even Big Face who is listening intently.

Spice Girl continues, 'As far as I'm concerned, you're a bunch of hypocrites. At the time our horrible settlers were busy poisoning and shooting and causing untold misery and basically wiping out the Aborigines, you Americans were kidnapping Africans, shipping them across the Atlantic, and those that survived you classified as property. I reckon that was worse than what we did here, so don't go waving the moral finger at us.'

Again, no one says anything although I can see in Crock's rear view mirror that he has a smile spreading across his face.

Spice Girl adds in frustration, 'Ah look, it's bloody impossible in this country to make any criticism of Aborigines without being called a bloody racist.' No one says anything; no one wants to get involved in a verbal fistfight with Spice Girl. She continues her diatribe anyway. 'They had a *Royal* Commission into Aboriginal deaths in custody and know what the results were?' she asks rhetorically. 'The bloody research showed that Aborigines were *no* more likely to die in custody than non-Aborigines. But the preconception that Aborigines are the victims of police brutality is so bloody ingrained their conclusion was seen as indicative of racism. It's a load of bullshit. The report showed that Aborigines in custody had *less* risk of death than if they *weren't* incarcerated. It's true more Aborigines die in police cells than whites but that's because there's more Aborigines in there.'

'That's the whole point,' I reply. 'Why are there more Aborigines in jail?' I ask. She doesn't answer. 'Because of the historical legacy of dispossession and racism and dis-advantage Aboriginal people suffer in nearly all aspects of their lives,' I retort using lingo I spent years studying at university, and honed working for the United Nations and other aid donors in Third World countries.

'Aborigine men end up in custody because they deliberately break the law, like throwing stones through a police station window, just so they can be put in prison and escape their responsibilities to their families,' Spice Girl throws back. 'Until they accept responsibility for their own lives, and their families, they'll always be disadvantaged. You can't blame history and racism forever. Besides, I don't think most Australians are racist, especially the younger generation.'

Spice Girl lives in Melbourne and she might accurately reflect that community's attitudes, but travelling around Queensland and the rest of the Outback, those liberal attitudes didn't strike me as being the norm.

I remain quiet and so does everyone else. We drive in absolute silence until we stop at a dry sandy riverbed where we unpack the vehicle while Crock prepares dinner. Gemma and I go in search of firewood. Returning to the Oka, we discover Neat!Wow! hurt his foot jumping on a branch trying to break it for kindling. He thinks it is broken. Crock tells him not to be such a wuss.

'What's a woose?' Neat!Wow! asks me in a whisper.

'A suck,' Big Face advises him, ever alert to conversations going on around her. Maybe we should have called her Big Ears.

The bad mood is mitigated when Gemma opens a cask of wine before dinner, and on an Irish roll she opens a second carton when the first is quickly finished. Wine with lots of sulphides gives me a raging headache, so I abstain. Neat!Wow! is in too much pain with his broken foot, and takes a box full of painkillers and passes out. Sleeping Beauty is already resting in her swag, fast sleep. Dr Dizzy and Big Face conspire together in their swags under their fly nets somewhere out in the bush. Crock, Gemma and Spice Girl get stuck into the wine good and proper. I am in my swag, dozing by the fire, half-listening to the conversation when Spice Girl lights into me again.

Fed up that my plans to be an observer and watch the group dynamics from the sidelines have backfired badly, I drag my swag into the bushes, out of sight and out of hearing.

The last words I hear in the ensuing silence are Gemma's, presumably directed at Spice Girl: 'Are you always such a bitch or is it just when you drink?'

In the morning, at precisely the time Crock Dundee had said we would depart, I diligently collect dry branches and noisily split them into smaller pieces by the bonfire. The loud cracks of breaking wood soon have the others awake. I use the three empty cardboard boxes of wine to get the fire blazing.

The peaceful sounds of the Australian outback, of doves, magpies, larks and mynah birds, are disrupted by Crock as he switches the Oka battery on and cranks up the vehicle's stereo with *Toyota's Country and Music Awards Selection* blasting the silence. When the Toyota selection is finished, we listen to Crock's favourite song, Ted Egan's *Our Coach Captain*.

Most clients who have booked to come on a tour like this through the desolate Kimberley, come to get away from civilisation and noise and stress, to find a corner of the world relatively untouched and unspoilt. It's a chance to commune with nature, get some peace and solitude. For Crock Dundee, it is another day at the office. We have no choice but to listen to his music played on what amounts to his vehicle, on his tour.

Three hours behind our scheduled departure time, we leave the campsite. I sit at the back of the Oka with Gemma. Neat!Wow! reckons he has definitely got a broken foot.

'Sometimes you have to wonder who paid to come on this trip, and who is paid to do it,' Gemma says to me, nursing her hangover and popping a couple of painkillers. We listen to Crock's selection of music turned up to full volume for the rest of the day.

In the evening Crock cooks up a stir-fry in a large wok. After dinner, having filled the wok with cold water and while lowering the wok on the glowing embers for the water to boil for washing the dishes, I spill the water onto the hot coals and I drop the wok, dumping the rest of the water into the red-hot embers. Billowing steam envelops my hands and a cloud of white ash layers my face and I scream like a stuck pig.

'Are you all right?' Gemma asks immediately.

'I've burnt my hands.'

Crock seems to find my predicament something of a joke, along with Neat!Wow!'s broken foot. 'You've got ashes all over your face and beard mate,' Crock laughs. 'Makes you look like an old man.'

I bite my tongue and dump my hands into a bucket of cold water and keep them there, waiting for the pain to subside. Neat!Wow! limps over to me. 'Keep your hands soaked in there until I find some ointment,' he advises, commiserating. The pain is excruciating and it's a frightening prospect being out here in the middle of nowhere so far from medical attention. I've burnt my fingers badly and already they are becoming stiff with the scalded skin tightening up. The compassionate Neat!Wow! hobbles over with his comprehensive First Aid Kit and wraps each of my fingers in gauze after putting a salve on. He hobbles lamely around me in his teddy-bear pyjamas, making sure I am OK and unravelling my swag for me. Before he goes to bed he somehow manages to place two bowls of water on either side of the swag.

'Keep your hands in the bowls as long as you can and keep the gauze wet all night, it'll help prevent the burn from getting worse.'

'Thanks,' I say, lying helplessly in my swag, each hand soaking in bowls of water on either side of me.

I'll never make fun of his teddy-bear pyjamas again, or all his high-tech equipment.

Promise.

In the morning Neat!Wow! limps over to see if I am all right. He takes the gauze off to let the dry air harden the skin. Bubble blisters full of liquid run the length of my fingers. I can't bend any of my digits.

The dirt road has the quality of a giant washboard and Crock reckons the faster we go the more easily the Oka's wheels will fly over the bumps. The tail of the vehicle fishtails alarmingly, raising swirls of fine dust. The pigpen at the back resembles a garbage tip with sedimentary layers of red talcum powder coating the whole mess. The only ones smiling are Spice Girl and Crock. You can tell they have been grinning because their exposed teeth are ochre coloured. When we reach the end of the Gibb River Road and are mercifully on the relatively smooth sealed road, Crock stops and gets out to inspect the undercarriage. 'Shit!' he says from under the Oka. 'Anyone know how to weld?'

'What's the problem?' Dr Dizzy asks keenly.

'One of the leaf springs is broken on the front right.' Hardly surprising, Crock, the way we were flying over bumpy ground there. 'And we've got a cracked steering joint.' Crock told us his previous career was a furniture removal van driver in Adelaide. He probably destroyed so much furniture with his wild driving they banished him to the bush where he could work on dismantling tourists.

The broken spring we can live with. The broken steering joint means that we could lose our steering at any time.

'OK guys, we're going to have to do our safety belts up,' Crock says, as if he were the pilot of a crippled aircraft preparing for a crash landing.

'For how long?' Sleeping Beauty asks.

'See how she goes, mate,' Crock replies, striking a pose, foot up on the bumper of the Oka. 'Try to get to Diggers Rest, our destination. It's a cattle station.' He stares at the far horizon as we all look at his blue eyes and wait for him to decide our future. 'They'll have some mechanics there. See if we can't get it all welded back together. We've got to fix it otherwise we've got Buckley's chance of going very far with it broken like that.'

I'm in half a mind to walk, except I know if I suggested that option, Crock would take me up on the offer. Dying of thirst in the Kimberley is a fate worse than the relatively quick death of crashing in an out-of-control Oka. I keep my mouth shut. Dr Dizzy expands on her mental list of screw-ups, which she diligently transcribes to the notebook. She frets we will be so delayed that she and Big Face won't make their flight out of Darwin. Under their matching anti-fly bush hats, they agitate each other into a frenzy of disgruntlement.

The Oka hobbles along and despite the odds, the steering joint holds until Crock pulls up in front of the cattle station, Diggers Rest. We spill out of the vehicle in a sorry state: two middle-aged American women on the point of a nervous breakdown; a Canadian with a broken foot. I have eight digits that are about as useful as overcooked bratwurst about to burst their skins. Spice Girl is severely constipated and Gemma is still so badly hung over from yesterday she looks like a walking zombie. Sleeping Beauty, the beautiful German, seems to suffer from sleeping sickness even if the disease isn't endemic here. We wake her to tell her we have arrived. Two emu hover around us with big hungry eyes, sharp beaks and fluttering eyelashes.

If we thought we were in bad shape, we're nothing compared to the crew here at this isolated cattle station. They seem to have been anaesthetised, which in a way they are. The farmhands, including the boss, are so badly hung over they are barely moving. Gemma in her zombie-like state looks like a hyperactive gymnast by comparison. The only one on two feet is Brownie, a half-caste with light green eyes. Empty bottles of alcohol litter the place.

'Don't expect to see a city-paced life out here,' Crock understates as we unload the Oka.

Big Face inflicts herself on the numbed jackeroos, jillaroos, cowboys and cowgirls and recounts to the new captive audience intricate circumstances of her life, details we have all endured already.

The farmhouse is a simple square stone building surrounded by a porch, which appears to be the general living area. Several semi-comotose stockmen and women occupy sofas and armchairs of various descriptions, bare sponge showing through worn fabric. Despite a bandage around his head, the Aboriginal farmhand is the most active of them all. There are a couple of young women who don't have Aussie accents when they speak. Crock whispers to us, 'The Dutch girl there arrived on an adventure trip like this and never left. She's a real pushover, like a one-legged girl in a desert.' One-legged or not, she gets up slowly to remove two beers from the fridge and hands one to another woman. 'And the mongrel Abo's got a family tree the size of a shrub,' Crock adds.

The more operative jillaroo feeds a bottle of milk to a calf with one hand and sips a beer in the other. 'Beautiful dog you've got. What kind is it?' I ask with a southern Texan drawl.

She looks at me incredulously. Even if I am a city slicker, thinking a baby steer is a dog is beyond belief. She adjusts her bush hat and replies with a more authentic accent, 'It's a calf, mate.'

'A Calf?' I repeat, studying it carefully as I kneel down to get a closer look. 'Never heard of them. What kind of dog is that?' I ask, patting the calf on the head. 'Looks a bit like a St. Bernard.'

The musterers are a laconic mob. A long question is answered with a short one-word answer. Even Big Face has trouble getting much response from them, although a few minutes with her and those who don't manage to get up and stagger out of range look totally sedated.

We lay out our swags outside the house, within the walled-in compound so that the emu don't mistake our ground-level eyeballs for edible grubs. Gemma unravels her swag next to mine. For the first time, Crock doesn't sleep on the roof of the Oka. Not only that, when he tosses down his swag we notice he's got the luxury of a double-bed swag twice the width of ours, with baby-blue liner-sheets inside.

The flies are something awful. No wonder the Aboriginals covered themselves in an evil smelling salve even the flies couldn't stand. Gemma, propped up on her elbow in her swag, says, 'Em, Andrew, is that a snake?' Basking in the morning sun is a long black snake, not a swag length from us.

'Yep,' I reply.

Gemma is up and out of her swag in seconds to drag back a reluctant musterer.

'What's that?' Gemma asks, pointing out the offending reptile.

'That's a black whip snake,' the Outback stockman replies.

'But do you not see? It's a couple of metres long at least!'

'And fast, too.'

'Is it poisonous?' she cross-examines.

'Only if it bites you.'

Spice Girl takes advantage of the water-driven toilet facilities, keeping several of us waiting. A pile of cheap pornographic magazines lies on the floor, distracting me temporarily with stained photographs of body parts displayed at unnatural angles. Most of the vivid images of female genitalia would be more appropriate in a gynaecologist's handbook.

The cattle station crew is looking a little sharper today, but not much. One of the musterers manages to weld the leaf spring and the steering joint. Shouldering the vehicle to protect my fingers, and Neat!Wow! on a pair of borrowed crutches, and Spice Girl in platform shoes, we push-start the Oka. Just as the engine starts one of Spice Girl's platform shoes loses its platform. You'd think she'd burnt her fingers to a crisp, or broken her foot, the way she carries on.

You win a few; you lose a few. This is one group Crock has lost. He wants to get the trip over and done with. He cranks up Spice Girl's Led Zeppelin tape and Van Morrison belts out 'G-L-O-R-I-A' as we bounce our way through the Bungle Bungles in our own little cocoon of noise. Gemma has resorted to listening to Andrew Lloyd Weber on her Walkman at full volume. I use wax earplugs.

Sleeping Beauty asks loudly in my left ear, 'Did you climb Ayers Rock?'

I remove the earplug. 'No,' I shout back. Did you?'

'No, it didn't seem fair.'

She falls asleep after that, but it was a good attempt at conversation.

In the middle of the Bungle Bungles we exit our mobile discotheque and walk into yet another series of gorges. Spice Girl has no other shoes besides her platform ones and with the sole missing on one shoe, one leg is, in effect, shorter than the other by a few centimetres; muttering profanities, she limps along beside Neat!Wow! who propels himself efficiently enough on borrowed crutches. I move ahead of the others to dupe myself into thinking that I am a lone explorer discovering the area for the first time a century ago. With not a lot of imagination, I 'discover' Cathedral Gorge, a narrow cleft in the red rock as high as a twenty-storey building. At the end of the cleft is a tunnel. I walk in as far as the light from the entrance penetrates. The interior of the tunnel is as lofty as a cathedral.

To scare myself, I walk into the cleft of rock until I can no longer see. I stop and wait for my eyes to adjust. After several minutes I continue walking, placing one foot carefully in front of the other, shielding my head with an outstretched hand as protection from potential protuberances. I sense the cave is contracting, as if it were swallowing me up. I slither along the wall of rock, around a corner, feeling my way with my hands until another rock wall meets it. There are no terms of reference. The second wall of rock doesn't quite meet the one I have been sliding along, so I force myself into the narrowing gap, totally sightless, turning sideways and pressing my body flat against the rocks so that I can squeeze into the space. When I can force myself into the crevice no further I stop, let the air out of my lungs and jam myself in a little more, perhaps another metre, until I am really stuck. I'd have to work hard to extricate myself. I stay there listening to water dripping into a pool. I remain so tightly wedged between the two rock walls I am almost unable to breathe. It's a macabre sense of contentment, pushing the limits just to scare myself.

'Agghhh!' A slimy thing the size and weight of a beanbag lands on my nose. I shake my head and slam my face into the rock. 'Ouch!' THE Thing, whatever it is, drops onto my shoulder. 'Ughhh!' Jammed in tight, it's impossible to escape. The weight on my shoulder moves. Can't be a rat, rats aren't slimy. Bats aren't either. It was slick, like a reptile, a rotund snake, maybe a toad. It jumps and lands on my head. I shake my head and it hops off, leaving me in peace. Before it changes its mind I disengage myself from the vice-grip of the rocks and retreat blindly to the wider area where I eventually hear the echoes of voices and then see the beams of torches.

By the time they reach me I have recomposed myself. Crock says, 'I knew we'd find you hiding in here.' He leads us into the cleft in the rock I have just evacuated. I couldn't have gone any further. Crock's torchlight shines on huge green frogs clinging to the rock walls. Not only are they perfectly harmless, they are rather beautiful.

From a distance, with lights shining on them.

We walk back out to the Oka and I notice Crock has taken to wearing a huge Crocodile Dundee knife hanging from his belt. I don't know if this is par for the course towards the end of a trip, but it sure looks to me like he's carrying it in case the natives, meaning us, get any more rebellious.

Dr Dizzy and Big Face abruptly decide to cut their trip short and fly out of the Bungle Bungles to Darwin on the regular mail flight. Behind Crock's back they claim they don't have any faith in the Oka making it to Darwin ever, never mind in time for their flight out. Crock takes their decision in his stride.

We watch as the two Americans, still wearing their fly net hats, load their bags into the pod underneath the fuselage of the single-engine Cessna Caravan at an airstrip scraped out of the bush. We wave goodbye as the aircraft takes off from the dusty strip. Without Big Face talking non-stop, our group is noticeably quiet.

'I guess they just got gorged, chasmed, and creeked out,' Gemma concludes, breaking the silence.

'We listened to Big Face 24-hours a day. Even when she was asleep, we had to put up with her snoring,' Spice Girl says. 'It's nice to have some peace and quiet.'

At the beginning of the trip we had competed to take our turn sitting in the front of the Oka with Crock. None of us can be bothered any more. Not even Spice Girl. Crock drives by himself up front while we all sit in the pigpen at the back, reclining seats lowered as far as they will go. The excitement we had in Broome, anticipating heading out into one of the wildest, least populated areas in the world, has collapsed into a rectangular space the dimension of the Oka. This is what it must be like to be on small group tours anywhere in the world. I could be in Africa or Arizona or Australia and although I've come to this desolate corner to experience the authentic Australia, all I've done is move within a bubble of tourists with little chance of escape, apart from getting on the mail plane.

Heading out through the Bungle Bungles on a dusty and winding track, we encounter half-a-dozen musterers on horseback herding hundreds of lowing cattle amongst big boulders. The cattle stir up the dry ground, covering us in yet another layer of red-brown dust. The horses dance at the back and sides of the cattle herd. The cracking of whips and yells of the stockmen add to this clichéd image of Australia. Not so far from here, through the Great Sandy Desert, the epic Canning Stock Route crossed 1,600 kilometres of one of the most arid regions in Australia.

Turkey Creek is an isolated outpost community of 250, comprised of a store, petrol pump, an airstrip, a couple of helicopter companies, a school and a phone booth. There's nothing around for hundreds of kilometres. A cattle road train bounces by, engulfing Turkey Creek and us in another cloud of red dust. Waiting to phone my father in Toronto on his birthday, I overhear Crock in the phone booth. 'But babe, I couldn't phone you earlier, the satellite phone isn't working . . . Yeah, don't worry, I'll be there tomorrow, when you knock off work.'

There is so much dust in the back of the Oka that touching anything releases a red puff like bloodstained talcum powder. Crock keeps the engine going; the starter motor is almost kaput. But there is good news. The tape deck won't work at all, not even slowly.

In the settlement of Kununurra, Crock picks up a couple of slabs of beer at a bottle store. He tells us it's 'on the house' but we all reckon it's because he's saved so much trip money by camping beside the road rather than at designated campsites. Neat!Wow! adjusts his gold-rimmed glasses up the bridge of his tiny Oriental nose and peers through the window and reads aloud the sign beside the bar entrance next to the bottle store: *'Patrons are required to wear clean clothes and be tidy in appearance for admission.'*

Wearing her hotpants and white socks stretched above the knee in case of snakes, Spice Girl limps lopsided to the flush toilets.

I observe quietly to Gemma, 'See how long it takes before she's thrown out.'

On top of her chronic constipation, Spice Girl is upset because she broke another one of her fingernails this morning loading up the Oka. That, and the platformless shoe, are really bugging her.

Neat!Wow! wears his teddy bear motive pyjama bottoms because they are the only pants wide enough to accommodate his swollen ankle. He hobbles to the men's. I follow him after asking Gemma if she would lower my zip. I can't bend my fingers enough to get a purchase on the metal zipper.

Standing at the urinals I suggest to Neat!Wow! that he go to the hospital here but Crock walks in and overhears my advice and tells Neat!Wow! there's not enough time. He herds us back into the Oka.

Sitting at the back, alone, I alternately occupy myself by prodding the bulging blisters on the back of my fingers and studying the boabs outside. They resemble uprooted trees shoved back into the ground upside-down. Without a lot of imagination, I can visualise them as people with pot-bellied trunks and arm-like branches, thinner twiggy branches on top like scraggly hair. Often there are two big ones surrounded by smaller ones, like parents with children. Sometimes it is dead easy to interpret their body language: two adults arguing; kids playing; a kindergarten; a teacher surrounded by children; two lovers embracing.

We cross the state border between Western Australia and the Northern Territories and Crock tells us to put our clocks forward one-and-half hours and our minds back half a century. Obviously a standard joke amongst Coach Captains and adventure tour guides whenever they cross the border into the Northern Territories. It is almost midnight, Territories time, when we pull up to a clearing at the side of the road.

'We'll camp here for the night,' Crock says, brooking no argument from the recalcitrant crew.

'Why didn't we camp at the tourist campground at Lake Argyll? This place looks like a dump,' Gemma says. 'Where are we?'

'The Victoria River is just over there,' Crock replies, as if that would explain everything.

'How far away?' Spice Girl asks.

'About a kilometre,' Crock replies, throwing supplies off the roof.

'Are there salties in the river?' Gemma asks, Aussie-experienced enough to distinguish between the harmless freshwater crocs and their life-threatening saltwater cousins.

'Sure,' he replies, lobbing swags at us as if he were trying to knock us down like bowling pins.

'I'm not sleeping down here tonight,' Spice Girl announces. 'I'm sleeping on the roof of the Oka.' She picks up her swag and passes it back up to Crock. Not very subtle, but that's one way to do it. Crock doesn't argue; it's been at least ten days . . .

'Em, how long do you think it would take one to get here?' Gemma questions nervously.

'What, a saltie?' Crock has a slightly taunting tone to his voice, but you'd never prove it in a court of law.

'Yeah.'

'They move at eighteen kilometres an hour,' Crock replies, unravelling his swag next to Spice Girl's on the Oka roof, safely out of reach of salties.

'So how long would it take them to cover a kilometre?' Gemma asks plaintively from below.

'I don't know, I'm not good at maths.'

'Wouldn't that be twenty minutes?' Spice Girl says. She doesn't have to worry now, she's sleeping out of salty range on the Oka roof, although I'm not sure she's entirely safe from the Crocks up there. Maybe that's the point.

A slab of beer and a spaghetti dinner later we are all in our swags about to fall asleep when Gemma says, 'By Jesus, that's only tree and a turd minutes.'

'What's only three and a third minutes?' I ask.

'For a salty to get here,' she says, sitting bolt upright.

Whatever plans Crock and Spice Girl might have had shacking up together on the roof of the Oka, the consumption of twenty-four beers amongst five of us has pre-empted all that. Spice Girl's fast asleep and snoring as contentedly as Big Face did.

Crock wakes us a couple of hours later, at four in the morning. 'We don't want to be late getting into Darwin,' he cajoles, chivvying us to get moving, eager to pick up his babe straight from work.

At dawn we pass through bush fires, some so close and fierce we have to drive at a snail's pace to feel our way through the dense smoke. Crock is in such a hurry to get home, though, that he drives through these flaming areas regardless. We feel like stars in a circus act. Inside the vehicle we sense the heat from the flames. It wouldn't surprise me if the Oka's paint was blistered as badly as my fingers. In a wild feeding frenzy, hundreds of kites swirl and dive at the escaping insects like seagulls feeding off a school of fry in the ocean. It's not an outrageous comparison. Half a year ago the Katherine River rose twenty metres higher than normal and flooded this whole area, although that's hard to believe looking at it now.

We continue on to Adelaide River where we stop to see Charlie the buffalo, the star in the film *Crocodile Dundee*, but none of us is in the mood to be stargazed by a two-bit extra in a Hollywood film. We sit around, dead-tired, while Crock makes another phone call to his 'babe'. Some five minutes later he returns with his face as long as Charlie's horns are wide.

'You'll be having dinner on your own tonight, folks. Bloody ex-sheila's dumped my daughter at my place and my flatmate has had to look after her. Five year-old daughter's been at my flat for two days because my ex took off with her new boyfriend to Bali.' We didn't know he had a daughter. There go his romantic plans for an evening with his current babe.

Crock is suddenly no longer in a rush to get back. Driving towards Darwin, the bush gets thicker and more tropical and then it becomes agricultural, with either an expanse of fields littered with bales of hay or groves of green mango trees. It is rush-hour traffic by the time we reach town.

Neat!Wow! insists we drop him off at the hospital in his pyjamas while the rest of us continue on to check in at a backpacker's lodge. The woman behind the counter sprays the air with air freshener when we lean over the counter. Sleeping Beauty, Gemma and I share a room. Listing at a 45° angle, Spice Girl hobbles across the road to another backpacker's. She's had enough of us. Hauling her heavy suitcase banging around her knees makes her list to the side even more dramatic.

Neat!Wow! returns a couple of hours later to a pub where we have all agreed to meet, with his foot in a cast. It was broken. He can't get his teddy bear pyjama bottoms off now because the cast is too big. He'll have to travel back to Canada like that. He rings home to Toronto to tell his parents how he broke his ankle on an adventure tour in remotest Australia. He doesn't tell them he broke it jumping on a branch to make kindling for a campfire. Spice Girl has no one to ring but this is compensated for when Neat!Wow! finds out there's no more room at our backpacker's and agrees to share her room.

Part of the price of our tour includes dinner and beer at a restaurant pub with our guide. Crock is busy babysitting his daughter. Besides, he's had enough of us. Without Crock the atmosphere among the group is better. We go out on our own, still dressed in our unwashed clothes layered in Kimberley dust. We look as if we've been invited to an ochre theme-party.

Sleeping Beauty and Gemma try to get me drunk on numerous jugs of beer. I don't get drunk but I do get very sleepy. Sleeping Beauty in the meantime wakes up for the first time. Neat!Wow! and Spice Girl decide to embark on an adventure tour to Kakadu. Another three days together! You'd never guess it, they seem totally opposites, but there's definitely romance in the air and Gemma and I missed all the signs.

I have this theory that how people dance is a good indication of how they make love. Now that she is awake, watching Sleeping Beauty dance is a sight for sore eyes. She's comfortable with her body, fluid, sensuous, uninhibited, innovative and fun, even if her eyes are closed. Spice Girl is a poser, more conscious of how she looks than enjoying the dancing for the sake of dancing. She goes through the motions, but she's not into it, her mind on whether anyone has noticed the platform off one of her shoes is missing. She has a peculiar dancing flutter as she falters across the dance floor. With every other step it looks as if she is ducking something thrown at her. Neat!Wow! thumps around diligently enough in his teddy bear motif pyjama bottoms, but he's got a broken leg in a cast, so he's got a good excuse for being a little stiff. Gemma is an enthusiastic little bumblebee, busily getting on with the job at hand. I undulate my hips and try to keep time to the music, but my sense of rhythm is awful. Depending on the beat of the music, I resemble either a frog in a blender or a puppet on strings.

Gemma's alarm sounds. It is the early hours of the morning, still dark outside. She gets out of bed, dresses quickly, sits on my bed and gives me a hug, baseball cap backwards.

'I enjoyed travelling with you Andrew. I'm going to miss you.' It's still dark; she hasn't switched on the lights.

I sit up in my sleeping bag. 'Enjoyed travelling with you too Gemma.'

'It's strange, I feel like I'm leaving a lover.'

'Better than being lovers.' I reply, propping myself against the wall. 'No demands and no expectations.'

'I feel so sad. I had a good time travelling up the West Coast with you.'

'Yeah, and the Kimberley. Thanks for sticking up for me when Spice Girl lit into me.'

'That's OK.' I can't really see her face clearly. I wonder if she is crying. 'Why do I feel so sad?' she asks.

'That's what happens when you travel, I guess. You talk a lot, share new experiences, get close to one another.'

'I've told you more about myself than even my boyfriend knows.'

'You mean like the worst thing you ever did; stealing sweets from the corner shop?'

'I told you a lot more than that.'

'I know. I'm just kidding.'

The dawn light peeks through the windows. She wipes her eyes with a tissue. 'I've written my address down for you. If you're ever in Ireland . . .'

'Yeah . . .'

She blows her nose. 'Say goodbye to Sleeping Beauty if she ever wakes up.' Sleeping Beauty is dead to the world on the third mattress on the floor. 'I'll miss talking with you.' She gives me a hug and then she hefts her pack onto her back and is off to Darwin airport to catch her flight to Sydney.

She was right; it feels lonely without Gemma. She was good fun. Times like this I don't feel like I'm really cut out to travel on my own. Mind you, I wouldn't have become so close to her if I hadn't been travelling on my own. While waiting for my free backpacker's breakfast pancake, and Sleeping Beauty to wake up, I study the notice board for inspiration:

2 spaces available in car for trip to Adelaide with two guys.
No ladies with hairy armpits need apply.

Would I have to shave mine?

Digging into my complimentary pancake, backpackers around me talk about where they have been in Australia or Asia, the foibles of their parents, what they plan to study when they get back home: general bonding stuff. For many, this is their first chance to break away from old paradigms: from home life, old friends and familiar surroundings. It's a chance to try on a different persona. After all, it's cool just being here in Darwin eating pancakes.

I love travelling and meeting people in an international setting; you avoid gossip, local petty politics and the comfortable routine of daily life. Travelling, I feel alive. My senses are alert to the new experiences around me. I relish meeting young people. They are full of life; they still have dreams, ideals and ideas. Because they haven't accomplished so much in their short lifetimes, it's easier for them to avoid the pitfall of bragging about what they have done. Or maybe that's just a guy thing and I should be more gender specific.

I talk to an older Australian couple, she a nurse and he a teacher, sitting at a table, isolated from the foreign backpackers around them. 'We just spent a year living on an Aboriginal community.' They are both disillusioned with the experience. 'We were thrown off the reserve two days ago by the town clerk, a white, for fraternising too much with members in the community. Can you believe that?'

'That's all you did wrong?' I ask sceptically.

She answers, 'The Northern Territories education curriculum is thirty years behind the times and doesn't take into account Aboriginal history.' She looks at her husband for confirmation but he's still too pissed off to talk. She continues, 'Australian children are taught about Australian history in romantic terms of explorers and settlers taming the bush, but rarely of the massacres of Aboriginals.'

'Isn't there more awareness now of these events?' I ask.

'Not by the Government; but by the Aboriginals themselves, who are taking more of the initiative in improving their position in Australian society, yes. Ninety per cent of white Australians have never met an Aboriginal face-to-face, but somehow everyone, especially those who live in the cities, knows what they are like.' She replies angrily. 'I wish white Australians in the cities could meet Aboriginals, not just the urban fringe dwellers, and get to know them and understand them, not as a race but as individuals. My husband tried to incorporate an Aboriginal curriculum in his teachings and was sacked for the effort.' She turns to look at him, as if waiting for him to interject. 'The town clerk said we were preoccupied with discrediting Australia. As far as we are concerned, the town clerk, the headmaster of the school, and a lot of the other whites, are there simply to make money. They come into an Aboriginal community hating them. They hate each other. A lot of them are bitter, twisted people. No wonder they say those who work with Aboriginal communities are mercenaries, missionaries or misfits.'

As if he just woke up, the husband adds, 'There's stories of town clerks, advisors, whatever you want to call them, siphoning off funds meant for the community they work for. They get caught feathering their nest, get fired and then work for another community elsewhere. They keep circulating around, ripping off the government and the Aboriginal people.'

The couple are taking the Greyhound back to Melbourne, bitter and twisted themselves about this whole community experience, which they had undertaken with so much enthusiasm and idealism.

I have so few days left in Australia before heading home, and I still have the Greyhound journey all the way back to Sydney. I gravitate into an art shop on Darwin's main drag where I bought a few pieces of art yesterday. The person working here looks as if he might have some Aboriginal blood in him. I interrupt his paperwork to explain, 'I'd like to be able to see what Aboriginals are doing for themselves on their communities and I don't have time to go through the normal process of applying for permission through the Northern Land Council. That takes a minimum of six weeks, if I get approval, and I'm leaving the country in a couple of weeks. Do you have any suggestions how I might get first-hand experience of what's going on?'

Although he remembers me, he regards me with a critical eye, then without saying anything, reaches for a piece of paper and writes down a name and a phone number. 'Miriam Rose Ungunmeer. She received the Order of Australia some months back for the work she has done for her community. She'd be the one to talk to.'

I phone Miriam Rose; she invites me to visit the Daly River Community and arranges for their community bus to pick me up at the backpacker's in three days.

Later in the evening I telephone Gemma at her apartment in Sydney. 'How's it?'

'Horrible. I tried phoning you at the backpacker's, but you weren't there. I miss the Outback already, the big spaces, my swag, the campfire, the stars and moons.' She sounds as if she is crying. 'Where are you going now?'

'Got an invite to a community in Daly River.'

'Where's that?'

'Down the Track to Adelaide River, then west some hours to the Daly River. But I'm going to do the three-day Greyhound tour around Kakadu National Park first. Comes with the price of my around-Australia ticket, so I might as well.'

'You might see Neat!Wow! and Spice Girl.'

'Yeah, I might.'

'Tried telling my flatmates about our trip up the coast of Western Australia and through the Kimberley, but how can you explain an experience like that?' Gemma with a 'G' tells me.

'Yeah, how can you tell people about that,' I commiserate.

# 5    The Top End

Waiting for the Greyhound bus to take me back to Darwin at the end of the three-day tour to Kakadu National Park, I had bumped into Neat!Wow! and Spice Girl sitting in the back of a Toyota in Jabiru. The Toyota looked like a troop carrier, and about as uncomfortable. She was wearing torn black bellbottoms and silver electrical tape holding the sole to one platform shoe while the other remained soleless. He was sporting grubby-looking teddy bear motif pyjama bottoms and an ochre-coloured cast. They both resembled battle-weary, wounded soldiers coming back from the front, the numerous swollen, red mosquito bites the equivalent of bullet wounds. There certainly wasn't any indication that a romance had taken place. Far from it, they seemed shell-shocked and neither had much to say.

My excursion, following the same trail, scrambling among huge boulders to Jim Jim Falls, paddling upstream on air mattresses to witness the spectacular Twin Falls, have left me in a daze as well; this rush of tourists swimming, diving and jumping around the falls has been an anticlimax. Spectacular places, which must have held so much sacred significance to the Aboriginals, seem diminished by the influx of tourists and their generic Crock Dundee guides. There was no sense of solitude or magic of the places.

At the Jabiru courthouse across the road, demonstrators chant, 'No more uranium, leave it in the ground,' waving banners, *'This is all about greed,'* or *'Respect the Planet,'* or *'No more uranium for your cranium.'*

The Greyhound bus stops and the Coach Captain, immaculate in blue shorts, white shirt and gold epaulettes, checks my name off the computerised list. The only one to board here, I join a dozen others on the full-sized coach and sit at the front.

'For those of you who have just boarded the bus,' meaning me, 'my name is Rob.' Our Coach Captain looks out his side window at the demonstrators. 'You will have noticed the protesters in front of the courthouse protesting the proposed new uranium mine. I don't mind people protesting for what they believe in, but I don't agree when outsiders disrupt people's lives. Those people are hippies come up here to winter because it's too cold down in Byron Bay and Nimbin on the East Coast. Look at them. Rastas, hippies and a token couple from the purple-rinse set in Melbourne to give them credibility. These ferals are unwashed, barefoot, unkempt and worst of all they're meddling in local affairs. I'm not saying this uranium mine is right, I'm just saying the locals should decide. There are three clans affected by it, and only one that doesn't want it. These long-grasses are being manipulated by environmentalists to use Aboriginal issues to stop projects, which otherwise cannot be prevented legally under existing environmental legislation.'

I had slept out last night at the Jabiluka blockade against the proposed new uranium mine. The local clan invited demonstrators from all over Australia to uphold and protect the cultural and environmental values of Kakadu and to this end donated an open piece of bush. We had watched a video on the Jabiluka mines as a three-quarters moon shone overhead. Demonstrators who had already seen the video chatted around a big open-air bonfire. When the video was finished the portable generator was switched off and it became deathly quiet in the camp. Those who had not yet been arrested and therefore liable to a considerable fine for being apprehended twice, volunteered themselves to trespass in the morning on the proposed uranium mining property, and get detained.

I recognise these individuals now as they chant and wait for Yvonne Margarula, the Mirrar senior traditional owner who is to appear in court for trespassing on land that was traditionally theirs. The demonstration is in objection to the land being taken from the Aboriginal people, land which they formally gained title to under the Land Rights Act in 1976. But it is also a protest march against uranium mining. If anything is fraught with political fallout, a uranium mine on Aboriginal land adjacent to a pristine national park prone to flooding should just about do it.

We leave Jabiru behind and our driver continues on a different bent. 'It may be hard for you to appreciate the traditional people, and their lifestyles, when you see the Aboriginal drunks around town.' I'm beginning to think, 'Oh no, not another.' He adds, 'But there's also a lot of white drunks around town too, and they don't reflect white society as a whole any more than the Aboriginal drunks do. The drunken Aboriginals you see are often outcasts from their own society. But there are plenty of others getting on with their lives, living on their communities, trying to bridge the gap between their traditional worlds and modern society. You don't see them. It's the drunks, the fringe dwellers, who have the highest profile.' He slows the bus and inexplicably drives onto the shoulder, opens the bus door, jumps out, and lifts a long-necked turtle off the road and places it safely in the bush.

When he climbs back into his seat he continues, 'It's unfortunate that the Aboriginal people, who were so spiritual, are in the minority now. A lot of them have lost everything except their dark skins, like those living in ghettos in Redfern, Sydney. And yet there are some communities still living completely wild, in a magical, spiritual world, hundreds of kilometres from any road.' He pulls the shade down the windscreen to block out the rays of the late afternoon sun.

We stop at Ubirr, an area of overhanging rocks with an astounding array of Aboriginal art. Rob walks us around the rocks explaining the artwork. He is an encyclopaedia of information. 'This rock face is a sacred place. It's like a blackboard, and the drawings were created to teach lessons because the Aboriginal people did not have a written language, as we know it. The origins of settlement in Australia came from the north when the sea levels were lower. Initial occupation of the Australian continent probably took place about 60,000 years ago.'

I ask Rob, 'How come you know so much about the Aboriginal people? You must have read every book that was ever written about them.'

He laughs, 'Yeah, but my wife was one too.'

'Was?'

'She died.'

We climb back on board the bus. I ask him, 'Do you know any Aboriginal people in Darwin?'

'Not as many as I knew in Alice where my wife's family came from. Used to work as a city bus driver in Darwin and I'd see them at the bus depot. They'd ask me for money, for food. I'd tell them if they wanted a feed, they could come home to my place and I'd give them a feed. Sure enough, two of them were waiting for me when I came home one day. Now they know better than to ask me for money, but they'll come over for tucker now and then. Terrific blokes when you get to know them, but most people would just see a couple of drunks.'

We stop briefly at the museum where I read how the Aboriginal people in this area tried to resist mining operations in their land; the giant uranium Ranger Mine in particular was opposed by a local clan. A map of Kakadu and Arnhem Land includes the caption:

> Look at the map for places with high uranium levels.
> Notice that these are mostly contained
> within *buladjang* (sickness country).

For tens of thousands of years the Aboriginals knew this uranium-rich area was bad for their health and avoided the place. Now the 'civilised' world digs it up to make nuclear weapons or nuclear power plants and yet there is still no realistic plan for the permanent storage of spent uranium fuel.

Instead of returning on the Arnhem Highway, we head southwest on the Kakadu Highway, a different route out of the park.

Tonight I will be in Darwin. Tomorrow, I'll visit the Daly River community for some days. From Adelaide River, I'll take the Greyhound 5,500 kilometres to Sydney, riding a tarmac strip penetrating back through the centre of this empty land, before circumnavigating its beautiful south-east coastline. I look forward to spending some days in Melbourne, the cultural centre of Australia. With a sleeping bag to protect me from the cold air-conditioning, my head supported on an inflatable pillow, I will be carried effortlessly through a landscape that just over 100 years ago took the determination, and lives, of daring if overconfident explorers. Only the occasional rumble of bus tires rattling over cattle grids will disturb the hum as we hurtle at 100 kilometres an hour through the day and night.

Bush fires contribute to a fiery sunset. Brown smoke hangs on the horizon. Several times we drive blindly through dense fumes from the burning grassland. This is the start of the *wurrgeng,* the cold weather season when Aboriginals traditionally travelled to different parts of the country to light fires before the hot dry weather of the *gurrung* started. The low-intensity fires set just after the wet season limit the spread of natural fires, as the damp areas remain unburned while the dry areas burn, creating a deliberate patchwork pattern allowing the wildlife to survive.

Our last stop on the tour is the Window over the Wetlands Visitor Centre. The passengers disembark. One Aboriginal is on the bus. I go out of my way to introduce myself. His name is Samson. Tall and well built, he fits the name. I buy him a coffee at the kiosk.

'Do you come from here?' I ask.

'From the bush near Humpty Doo. It's the next stop. I went to mission school there.' He turns to the woman behind the counter, 'Wendy, my mob told me there were photos of us. Where are they?'

'Try the computer upstairs.'

While the other passengers hang around the coffee shop, Samson and I climb the stairs to a room dominated by full pane glass windows providing a window onto the wetlands. The lights are off in the room, rendering the view outside more impressive. The sun sets on one side and on the other the full moon rises. Samson says, 'There's supposed to be pictures of my mob in here, but I don't see any.' There are a couple of computers with attached headphones for visitors to use. 'How's this work?' he asks me, pointing at a monitor with a screen displaying several icons.

I select 'The People of Kakadu' and touch the appropriate keyboard. The first images to appear on the screen are black and white photographs of Aboriginal people taken last century. Samson laughs and says, 'Those are my people!'

'How can you tell?' I ask.

He points at the screen, 'Look! The tribal scars on their arms and chests.'

I tap the keyboard to activate the next image. Colour photographs depict more recent images of Aboriginal people.

'That's my uncle!' Samson exclaims. 'How'd you do that?'

'You mean how to make the images change?'

'Yeah.'

I show him and he reaches out a long finger and touches the keyboard. The image changes again and he quickly withdraws his hand as if scalded. 'That's my sister!' He laughs, and stretches out, crossing the spectrum of time, pointing out his family. We ignore the crackling headphones and the indecipherable recorded message. It is a bizarre scene: this bush-born Aboriginal named Samson showing images of his relatives captured on a modern computer monitor. I look out the window. The sun sets into a heavy cloud of brown smoke hanging over a blazing cauldron of bush fires. We are alone in the increasingly dark room.

I select 'Bush Tucker'.

'That's a good one,' Samson says with enthusiasm as successive images of bush tucker flicker onto the screen each time he touches the keyboard with his finger. 'You can find that one right here.'

He ignores the computer and looks out the window just beyond where the coach is parked, and points at a bush. He broadly indicates the burning horizon and tells me, 'When I was a boy, we hunted goanna, long-necked turtle, kangaroo.' Standing side by side in front of the computer screens, our faces illuminated by the artificial light of the monitors, we stare through our ghostlike reflections to the fiery primeval wilderness outside.

'Now I drive a truck for the community in Jabiru. I have a green uniform. Tourists ask me about things. They think I am a ranger or something. I want to start a tourist business, buy a four-wheel drive. I could take tourists out there, take them Walkabout in the bush, tell them about our Dreaming, and teach them how to hunt. I still have my spear and *woomera* and *boomerang*.'

Miriam Rose has arranged for a driver to pick me up in front of the backpacker's in Darwin. He drives the community minibus to Darwin on a weekly run to pick up supplies for the community and passengers, a mix of outpatients with appointments at the Darwin hospital, high-school students attending private schools, and community members on shopping sorties. We stop at the hospital where nine adults and children board the bus. They smile, greet me, ask my name, where I am from. They are happy and uninhibited.

From Darwin we head south towards Adelaide River where we stop to refuel at a roadhouse. It is dark already. The driver supervises filling up with diesel. I go inside to buy him a coffee. One of our Aboriginal passengers asks, 'Brother, is it OK if I have a beer?'

I shrug my shoulders. 'I don't know.'

He stands in front of the cooler containing beers. 'The driver says no drinking beers, Brother.'

'Well, I guess you better not have a beer then.'

The driver enters the roadhouse, tells us he is ready to move. We board the minibus and he discovers two women passengers are missing. Exasperated, he gets out to look for them.

'How long are we waiting?' one of the Aboriginal men in the back asks.

'I don't know,' I reply. Surely he understands the situation better than I do.

The two missing women are located. 'They met some friends at another roadhouse 100 metres down the road,' the driver explains, 'and decided to spend the night in Adelaide River instead of heading back to their community. They could have told me,' he adds, confiscating beers someone has brought on board. Three more men board and to make more room for them, I lift a small girl with a broken arm in a cast from the back to sit next to me in the front. We divert west, on a smaller road, the head beams lighting a narrow tunnel of Australian bush.

The girl next to me is such a frail little thing. Her wide-open eyes shine brightly against her dark skin as she focuses on the road ahead, taking in every little detail. Although it is not crowded in the front seat, she leans against me. Later she falls asleep, her head resting against my arm. I wonder what it is that she dreams about, this child. I imagine her dreams are more vivid than mine, more intuitive, more spectacular, with animals and spirits haunting her thoughts. These people whose lives were until recently so intimately linked to their natural environment, must have a whole dimension of insights that we have lost over hundreds of years of 'civilisation'.

We stop at Five Mile Camp where some of the women and children get off and disappear into a pool of darkness.

'This the Daly River Community?' I ask, confused that we are not all getting off.

'No, this is the alcoholics rehabilitation camp. Members of the community who have a drinking problem come here to be rehabilitated, to become more aware of their alcohol problem. Their families come along too; there is a school here for the children so their education shouldn't be disrupted.'

The headlights illuminate a sign beside a cattle grid advising that no alcohol is permitted within the boundaries of the community. We drive alongside an airstrip and then among the houses; some houses are substantial, others are smaller. A host of children rush out of their homes and run over to meet us, screaming happily alongside the minibus. When we stop, they reach their hands through the front window for the little girl beside me and I pass her to them and they make a fuss, examining her cast. Then they all run off to their homes laughing.

None of the passengers thanks the driver or says goodbye. When I mention this curious observation he replies, 'Many tribes don't have words for please or thank you. Giving is the norm.' He shrugs his shoulders as we drive off. 'You get used to it.'

In the morning, the driver's wife walks me through the Daly River Community, or as the people here call it, the Nauiya Community. This is about as far removed from Sydney as you can get in both a literal and metaphorical sense. It is a Saturday and out-of-school curious kids come up to me and unabashedly ask my name. Although it would be difficult to find a community more remote than this, there is a suburban weekend feel to the place. The old mission houses, now inhabited by Aboriginals, have manicured lawns around each property. There is a well-maintained footy field, a huge community hall, school, health clinic, kitchens, church, general store, swimming pool, diesel generator plant and mechanics' workshop. For a place so isolated, it is surprising to find this enclave of infrastructure carved out of the Australian Outback. I am surprised, too, at the number of non-Aboriginals working here. Besides the white driver and his wife, a white couple runs the general store. Whites tend to the maintenance of the heavy machinery, vehicles and generator and the groundskeeper, accountant, town clerk and medical staff are also whites. At the general store I am introduced to a Maori, the physical sports programme co-ordinator. He is about to go hunting for wild pig and wallabies.

There are plenty of Aboriginals working around the community, cutting grass, working in the mechanics workshop. 'Who employs these people?' I ask.

'ATSIC, the Aboriginal and Torres Strait Islander Commission, pays the non-indigenous staff and the Community Development Employment Program, CDEP, pays the salaries for most of the indigenous employees.'

'How much does the community get for the CDEP programme?'

'They work out the number of people who qualify for the dole, which is 130 here. They multiply that by what they would get if they were on the dole, and that's the sum of money the community can operate with. Instead of paying out dole, it's up to the community to figure out how much to pay for work and how many people can be employed.'

It's not exactly the million dollars a year per Aboriginal suggested by my fellow coach passenger on the West Coast.

At the community's art gallery where my guide is employed, a visiting artist from another mission shows me her child's latest report card.

Richelle im gudgel langaskul im sumtain lisin la titja. Wen im wandim help im aldei askim langa im tija blanga help.

Richelle im gin recognise sumbala kala wen im titja shoim la im. Richelle sabi nomo sabi da sheip neim blanga len mo en bla wek langa skul.

I cannot understand it but when the mother reads it out loud for me, I realise it is Aboriginal Creole. 'What's that mean?' I ask.

'Richelle, she is a good girl at school and sometimes listens to her teacher. When she wants help she always asks her teacher for help. Richelle can recognise some colours when her teacher shows her. Richelle knows all her numbers and shapes a little bit. Richelle is coming to school every day to learn more and more work.'

During dinner with the art co-ordinator and her husband that evening, there's a hesitant knock on the front door of their home. Although flustered at being interrupted during the meal, she opens the door and I am introduced to Bridget, an artist who has come to ask if she would like two of her paintings to sell in the art centre. She tells Bridget we are in the middle of eating and that we'll come over after we have finished. An hour later, we walk to Bridget's simply furnished but clean and tidy house. She shows us her paintings.

'How much are they?' I ask, after complimenting her on the artistic qualities of the two works.

She replies hesitantly, 'I reckon they're worth 600 dollars. Took me three weeks to do each one.' She is soft spoken. Unlike so many other Aboriginals of her age, she shows no sign of alcohol abuse. She exudes an intrinsic strength to her character, despite her bashfulness.

'Are you an artist full time?' I ask.

'No,' she pronounces it 'now'. 'I'm a teacher at Five Mile camp, the rehabilitation centre.'

'And that is your daughter?' I ask, indicating the young girl in the room with us.

'Now, it's my granddaughter.' She giggles.

I hear something else, a scratching noise. 'What's that?'

Bridget listens, and then says something to her granddaughter, in her own dialect. The little girl reaches behind the fridge and pulls a long-necked turtle from the concrete floor, holding it by the long neck as if the head and neck was a convenient handle to a heavy pot.

Bridgit admires it. 'We got im today. Good bush tucker that one. Can you come eat im?' she offers generously.

Returning to my host's house we pass the Nauiyu Nambiyu Club. The rules of dress are more accommodating than any other clubs or bars I have seen in Australia.

Minimum standard of dress
will be
shorts and singlet.

Tacked to the wall beside this notice is a 'banned list': the names of members who have been banned from the bar for a number of weeks, depending on the offence. 'What kind of offences?' I ask.

'Usually being abusive of the bartender, or more seriously, elders. You can get banned for all kinds of reasons, but you cross an elder and the punishment is worse; it's the elders who decide the length of banishment,' she replies.

'I thought this was a dry community?' There are numerous empty bottles of beer sitting on tables.

'Yeah, it is. But you can drink light beers here up to a maximum of six. It's not a bad idea, it gives people a place to meet and socialise and it's hard to get drunk on half-a-dozen light beers. Having a few drinks like this takes some of the pressure off them leaving the community just to get drunk.'

It's a Saturday night and there are a couple of dozen men playing pool inside, or sitting outside drinking light beers, chatting to women. It's a pleasant atmosphere and there's certainly no evidence of anyone being drunk.

The bartender, a white woman, tells me, 'You should go fishing while you're here.' She brags, 'Lots of huge barramundi in that river but you got to watch out for the crocs, eh? Some really big ones in there and they aren't scared either. Last time we went out a croc much bigger than our tinny came alongside. Must have been five metres at least. His head was as big as I can stretch my arms. Wouldn't go away. Swished his tail back and forth and escorted us out of his territory. They seem to know they're protected now.'

'Salties?

'Yeah.'

'We must be almost 100 kilometres from the sea.'

'Yeah, well, the salties come up here. Freshies too. Only place in Australia where they both live side by side, eh? See dozens of them sunning themselves right here. Down the river a little way you'll see hundreds on the sandbanks but the really big smart ones hide in the bushes. Borrow someone's tinny if you want, but make sure you ask permission; last month, bloke got fourteen days in jail for borrowing someone's tinny without telling him. Serious crime, that. Same man only had to do community service for stabbing his wife in the stomach.'

'Her? Yeah, but she's always complaining,' the art co-ordinator says, dismissing the offence as if being stabbed for being a nag was acceptable.

'Ah yeah, but she had to pull the knife out, eh?' the barmaid emphasises.

They point out a man with wild, white, unkempt hair, chatting up two women who could almost fit the same description. 'See the dent in his forehead?' the bartender asks. The dent is obvious, more like a hole, as if someone had stuck a finger deep into a lump of black wax. 'He'd gone down to the water to freshen up after too many drinks at the pub. Croc grabbed him, punctured the front of his skull. Got away with only a hole in his head because he was full as a doctor's wallet and poked the croc in the eye and the croc let go of him. True. Last Christmas another got taken by a croc as he was trying to swim across the river to the same pub. Wasn't so lucky that one. Never saw him again.'

Nope. I'll leave the fishing in a tinny to the others, I think to myself as I subconsciously scratch my relatively dent-free head.

On Monday morning, I meet Miriam Rose in her office at the school. She is a tall woman, with a commanding presence. She invites me in to her office full of athletic trophies she won when she was attending the same school, as a student. She asks me to sit down in a chair opposite her. At first it is not easy to get her to talk about herself. She is reticent, almost cautious. She responds to my questions warily, unsure where my genuine sympathies lie. I ask her how the Daly River community came about.

With the palm of her hand, she wipes the coffee table separating us. 'At the time this mission was established, ten mobs with different languages and traditions from all around, settled here. We still have ten separate language groups in this community,' she explains, 'although we have one dialect that we use so that we can understand each other.'

Her secretary comes in to ask us if we want tea or coffee.

'I attended this school when the Catholics were still running Daly River as a mission. When I arrived I wasn't allowed to speak my own language. We were forced to assimilate, speak English, and integrate into the white ways.' She indicates with her eyes a map of Australia on the wall. 'There were at least 250 different languages in Australia when the whites arrived, and at least five to six hundred different dialects.'

Her comment is a reminder of how ignorant I had been when I arrived in Australia, thinking the Australian Aboriginals were one people and not a diverse group of separate tribes.

'Our languages are being forgotten, but what is left is important to us, and powerful. Language is an essential part of our being,' she adds emphatically. 'It is going back to the old ways when our language and dialect identified our tribal group, who we are in this land. At this school, in the afternoons, we teach in four dialects, taught by teachers who come from those language groups.'

Miriam is forthright in her opinions. 'That is what this school is about. I want our children to retain what we have left of our Aboriginality to preserve our culture, language and identity. After school and on weekends, elders take the boys out to hunt. The girls learn crafts, music, how to get bush tucker.' She wipes the table again thoughtfully. 'But it's a struggle to keep the academic standards high. When you were a child, you had a home environment that encouraged you to read or study; quiet areas, tables and lots of books. These children don't have that, and their parents have to create that environment. Most of the parents, like myself, were born in the bush. We have had to come a long way since then.' I don't prod, letting any silences run their course.

She stops wiping the table with her hand and looks at me. 'You know what I tell the children here? I tell them, "Look, if I can do it, so can you". It's important for them to have a role model. I left school when I was sixteen, but now I'm finishing my Masters, and soon I would like to do my doctorate.' She looks out the window. It is easy to discern the look of pride on her face as she watches the children enter their classrooms.

'Students when they finish school here don't want to leave this community. It is a safe environment where they flourish and they're not ashamed of being an Aboriginal. But there are so few opportunities for them here. It's mostly tourism, art and farm work.' I catch up with her, scribbling notes as quickly as I can.

She asks me about my trip around Australia.

I tell Miriam what I have seen, what my observations are. I am honest with her about my feelings. Without blame, I express shock at witnessing the condition of her people, and how it was in such stark contrast to what I had naïvely expected before arriving here. The result of my own frankness is that she, too, becomes candid. By honestly expressing my feelings, it is almost as if I have discovered a secret door, which she opens to allow me to enter her world.

She speaks to me, looking at me now rather than the table or out the window. Her hands are still. 'I was born under a tree. My mother showed me the place, where I used to play, where I would hunt for wild honey. The feeling I have for this place is very special. The place where I was born, it's me. I never get tired of going back. My relations tell about the origin of these places. Their stories and songs sink quietly into my mind and I hold them deep inside.' She speaks as if in a trance, as if reciting a poem or a speech, thoughts she has had so often she is intimately acquainted with them.

'This history of my ancestors has real meaning: tracks we used and our ceremonial grounds, they are a part of me, of who I am. In our ceremonies we celebrate the awareness of our lives as sacred. I love to see the painted bodies and to watch the dancers and listen to the *digeridoo* and the clapsticks. I never feel alone during the ceremonies. Sometimes at a *corroboree*, before the dancing has started, we sit and listen as the song-men or song-women begin the story. Everyone is relaxed. We feel secure and happy. We are all together and it is good.' She stares out the window of her office and is thoughtful for some time before she continues wistfully. 'We have our Dreaming and our Dreaming is our roots. To the extent that we have been moved from our traditional areas, we have lost our Dreaming and therefore our roots. I want to strengthen our Dreaming and part of that process is maintaining our language. It tells us that we belong to this land, that we have a connection with it that goes right back to the beginning of this country. It tells us that we haven't been wiped out.'

It's an emotional comment but Miriam does not seem intimidated by the frequent long silences. I continue writing in my notebook, a convenient excuse for keeping quiet.

Eventually she adds, 'I have deepest sympathy for peoples who have lost their ceremonies, their songs and dances, their culture and language. All they have is their materialism. But we have this other spiritual world we can relate to and we are richer for that.' She gazes out of the window into the manicured gardens in the courtyard of the school. 'The bush is part of my life, it is me.' She stares out the window for so long I almost wonder if she has forgotten I am there and then she continues. 'I hang around *billabongs* to heal myself, to renew my spirit. We need that even more than others.' She turns to look at me, directly in the eye. 'We have this beautiful gift, this appreciation of nature. When I am out hunting, among the trees, on a hill or by a *billabong*, these are the times when I am in God's presence. It is not just me. My people are bound from before birth to after death into an intimate personal identification with the land and its specific features.'

She turns to look outside again. Eventually she says, 'We were always very spiritual people.'

'What do you mean exactly?' I look up from my notepad. 'What do you mean by spiritual?'

She doesn't hesitate to answer. 'Spirituality is about the awareness and responsibility for knowing your place and role in the world. It's about being aware of the inter-relatedness of all that was, and is, and will be. It's about knowing your responsibilities for the past, present and future. Many of us have lost this awareness, this sense of responsibility. We have become lost. That's what we have to find again. This is what I am trying to teach my people here.'

She either lets me catch up, or is thoughtful for her own sake. I wish I had brought a tape-recorder.

'Our first contact with whites in this area was not until fifty years ago. Many of our people hadn't even seen a white person until the second half of this century. It hasn't been enough time for us to cope with this new society. It's a consumer world, and we don't fit in. Our people are spiritually and physically dying.' She stares out at the empty playground.

I don't want to interrupt her.

Her voice is subdued. 'Our culture has taught us to be still and wait; we do not try to hurry things up, we let them follow their natural course, like the seasons. We watch the moon in each of its phases and wait for the rain to fill our rivers and water the thirsty earth. When twilight comes, we prepare for the night and at dawn we rise with the sun. We watch the bush foods and wait for them to ripen before we gather them. We wait for our young people as they grow, stage by stage, through initiation ceremonies. When a relation dies, we wait a long time with the sorrow. We own our grief and allow it to heal slowly. We wait for the right time for our ceremonies and our meetings. The right people must be present; everything must be done in the proper way. Careful preparations must be made. We don't mind waiting, because we want things to be done with care. Sometimes many hours will be spent in painting a body before an important ceremony. We don't like to hurry. There is nothing more important than what we are attending to. There is nothing more urgent that we must hurry away for.' She looks at me, then back out the window, beyond the children's playground to the dense bush on the banks of the Daly River.

She speaks again, a stream of connected and unconnected thoughts. Although there are long silences, it is not as if she is at a loss for words. She is both eloquent and selective in what she says. 'Here we are river people. We cannot hurry the river. We need to move with its current and understand its ways.' She sighs and turns to face me. 'But the world out there moves too quickly. It's all been too fast. We ask people outside our community to wait for us, to give us time to catch up, to be patient. We have learned to speak the white man's language. We have listened to what he had to say. This learning and listening should go both ways. We would like people in Australia to take time to listen to us. We are hoping people will come closer. We keep on longing for the things that we have always hoped for: respect and understanding. Only a handful of us have found our goals but more of us need to say we are proud of being who we are, and still cope in your modern society. I'm 100 per cent Aboriginal, and fifty per cent white. That is what we have to be to survive. '

'That doesn't add up to 100 per cent,' I say, taking her literally.

'That's the point. But me, even if I think I'm fifty per cent white, I'd be scared to go to England, so far away from home.' She laughs, but the laugh is an ironic one. 'I was invited to a conference in Tasmania. I was really scared because of all the stories I had heard about what happened to my people there, how they were hunted down until there were no Aboriginal people left alive . . .' She stops and I can see even the thought of the genocide that took place is appalling to her.

I redirect our conversation to a more positive note. 'What did receiving the Order of Australia mean for you?'

She is careful in choosing her words. 'For me, it's simply a scale, a formal measurement of success. I've worked so hard for that to happen. Because that's what it's all about: to stand out. People are afraid to stand out. I wanted to prove that this mob can be better, and to show that women can play a part in leading our people. Sometimes I think it is harder as a woman to be in this position. Because I am working with my immediate clan, I'm vulnerable to pressure, to accept responsibility for my extended family.'

Her secretary brings in two cups of tea. One is almost the size of a bucket. Miriam sees my look of astonishment. She shrugs, a twinkle in her eye. 'I like my tea.' She offers me biscuits; we both sip the hot drink.

She continues, 'Every time I'm in town and I see another one of my people in the street, there is this feeling of connection between us. Can you imagine that?' She laughs. 'But it's true. There *is* a connection, like telepathy.' Her eyes are mischievous as she nurses the tea at her lips. 'I don't know how we can do it, but we *can* communicate in special ways. For us, this is normal.' She looks at me to see what my reaction is. 'That's probably something you find hard to understand. For us, we have other hurdles.' She puts her cup on the table.

'For example, sometimes I take children from here into Darwin. The children often say to me, "How can you do that?" I ask them, "Do what?" And they reply, "Go up to the counter, go to the market, go into a restaurant. How do you make those white people talk to you, serve you?" For us, that's a bigger challenge than communicating amongst ourselves without using words.'

'What do you tell the children?' I ask.

'I reply to the children very simply: "You have to look the whites in the eye, and be yourself."'

She amplifies, 'When I go into town, people talk to my husband instead of me. He's white.' She blows into the cup cradled in the palms of her hands. 'Maybe they think I can't speak English, but I think, well, there's nothing particularly good about being white, or male,' and she giggles, puts down her cup and claps her hands at her own joke. Her laughter is infectious. She has a laugh so genuine you can't help but join her.

Taken with the gravity of our conversation, though, she carries through with her original line of thought. 'We have to move into the future, but we have to be strong in our past. For the last 200 years people have been telling us what to do. Now we have to do what is good for us. People have to listen to us too. We're entitled to make our own mistakes.' She gets up to look through papers, trying to find something. 'The mission wanted to give this land back to us, with all the buildings and infrastructure, but the community here decided to lease it for a period, to go through our own process of deciding which mob owns this land.' She rifles through some files as she talks.

I watch her and wonder how the Aboriginal inhabitants of Daly River can achieve the contradictory goals of meeting the modern world while maintaining a traditional foundation. Self-determination, in the sense of making decisions affecting their lives over political status, economic, social and cultural development, and the capacity to control the future of their own communities seems on the surface, to be a reality here in this community. But I can imagine the process is and has been extraordinarily difficult. While such a daunting task would seem impossible for most, Miriam has the strength and power to tackle the goal. She has chosen how to lead her community, the kind of life experience they will have, at least in this protected enclave.

While she is searching for her papers I tell her, 'People everywhere tell me you are a powerful woman.' There's no doubt about it, she has a magnetism and strength that instils confidence and trust.

Miriam's secretary enters to tell her someone is waiting. 'Tell them I'll see them later.' She smiles at me and I guess that this message from her secretary is standard procedure so that Miriam can cut short a visitor's meeting. For whatever reason, I recognise Miriam feels comfortable with me. She answers my question.

'Yes, I want to be powerful, powerful in the sense of empowering people. I don't want power so people fear me. I want non-Aboriginal people to empower us to believe we can be the best we can be, but the easiest way to break an Aboriginal person is for non-Aboriginals to push us too quickly, especially in the remote areas. How do I get this reputation for being so powerful?' she asks me rhetorically. 'I don't beat people. I am kind and gentle. But I tell people to their face what I think. I've asked non-Aboriginal teachers here to leave if I didn't agree with what they were doing. I used to be frightened, but not now. You have to be straight with people. Have to be consistent, especially with kids;

whether it is with praise or punishment, you have to follow up. If a child doesn't come to school, I go to his home and ask him why he isn't at school. They know I will do that.'

She finds what she was looking for. It is a newspaper clipping with a photo of her receiving the Order of Australia. I had been told that this small article was the only press coverage of her investiture. It seems a shame that this success story should receive so little publicity and yet the negative stories about the Aboriginal people are repeated endlessly. 'The others went to Canberra to receive their awards,' I comment. 'You received yours here.'

'The award isn't for me; it's for the whole community. It was appropriate that it was given here, so that my mob could partake in the ceremony and share in the sense of achievement.'

I scribble notes as rapidly as I can. After wandering around Australia for three months I've finally found what I was looking for all along. It will be hard leaving tomorrow to catch the coach at Adelaide River back down through Katherine, the Alice, Adelaide, Melbourne and then to Sydney.

'Stay with us for a year,' Miriam suggests as if she has just read my mind. 'You can write about us.'

'It's a big commitment.' Ten years ago I would have jumped at the chance to live here for a year.

Miriam leaves the seed of the idea with me and doesn't say anything more. Instead, she leads me into a classroom. The children, sitting on the floor, stand up and clamour around me, stretching out their hands for me to shake. They ask me my name. Miriam introduces me to the teacher and the class and then leaves. Standing at the blackboard, I assess the children's basic reading and arithmetic skills. There is no doubt that they are not as advanced as white children in a city environment would be. But this is not a city environment, and these children have to learn both the white ways and their own ways. They have double the workload. Even if they cope with double the workload, their future is uncertain.

During this impromptu class, when I ask them a question, they eagerly raise their hands and call out, 'Andrew! Andrew!' as if saying my name were a significant process in bridging the gap in our lives, which it is.

When I leave an hour later, each of the children without any prompting gets off the floor and gives me a hug. With each hug, there is a connection.

The following morning Miriam's mother Mary and two of her friends, Molly and Maureen, invite me to join them to find bush tucker. It's too good an invitation to turn down. I follow them. All are silver-haired, although Molly and Maureen are a generation younger than Mary, with the tell-tale flaccid faces from alcohol abuse. Dressed simply in cotton dresses, they zigzag barefoot through the dry bush searching for tucker. They stop to remove the centre of mirripin palms with which to weave dilly bags and fishnets and show me how they strip the palm frond and roll it on their thighs with their hands to make the rope-like string. They also pull from the earth brightly coloured orange and red tubers to use for dying the frond strips.

Further into the dense dry brush, Maureen abruptly stops in her tracks and looks fixedly at the horizon and says excitedly, 'Molly! Molly!' When Molly turns around Maureen glances quickly at the ground where a bee exits a hole in the ground. ''Im sugar bag bees,' she tells me without looking at them, as if by doing so the bees would know they've been discovered. 'We come back later and get sugar bag honey,' and they all laugh as we walk away from their storeroom.

Mary runs her hand along the branches of a tree, stripping it of its foliage. She rubs the bundle of leaves between two hands then opens them palm up and says, ''Im green ants. 'Im good bush tucker, like lemon.' She extracts a crippled ant from the bundle of crushed leaves and bites the rear of the abdomen off. I do the same thing. They taste like concentrated lemon juice.

They point out the file wood tree, which they use for making *woomera*, spears, and *boomerangs*, and the leaves for smoking out evil spirits. They show me the finger bark tree which they use to cook kangaroo meat to enhance its flavour and for bark paintings. 'This tree, 'im good for poisoning fish.' Further, another tree, ''Im good for mosquitoes.' Another is good for headaches. They walk delicately, almost soundlessly, alert to the smallest bush signs, although I have no idea what they are looking for. Occasionally they stop and gently prod the ground with sticks.

At the billabong they pick lily roots and search the mud for long-necked turtles. When Mary finds a goanna hole, the others seem to know telepathically and help her dig even before she has done or said anything to alert them. Within a short time they stop, knowing the goanna has already gone.

At their favourite fishing spot we squat by the stagnant riverbank and cut up fresh wallaby meat they have brought with them in their dilly bags. They thread the flesh onto hooks, and then swing the hooks expertly through the air, tossing the bait into the placid waters. Molly hands me fishing line with the bait already attached to a simple hook. Motionless, they sit on their haunches and wait, arms resting on their knees, thin arms and skinny legs protruding from flimsy cotton dresses. Two doves sing in a tree overhead. A kite whistles.

'Im prawn,' Molly responds after watching my line jerk. I retrieve the bait with a sizeable pale-blue prawn clawing at the meat. The prawn lets go, and I chuck the bait back into the middle of the *billabong* near two bits of floating vegetation resembling debris. The bits of vegetation move parallel through the water. 'Im croc,' Molly tells me nonchalantly. Another whistling kite alights on a dead tree branch stretched across the *billabong*.

'Im hot one,' Molly says a half-hour later. There's not a breath of wind. It is absolutely quiet, and primeval. Another croc surfaces and so do two long-necked turtles.

We spend the afternoon like that: ostensibly fishing, not saying much, perched on the bank of the *billabong*. The women don't move, or talk, as if meditating. In a sense they are. They are centred in their surroundings, filling themselves with who they are. I too feel at peace. This slice of Australian life is what I came for. One afternoon sitting beside a scraggly old *billabong* with three Aboriginal women is better than all the hyped-up tourist activities of Alternative Coach Networks, scuba diving, 4WD adventure tours, scenic flights. I could have happily spent my entire three months right here in Daly River. I don't want to leave, not yet.

The stagnant *billabong* does not make much sound, but the few sounds it makes, we hear. An occasional bubble surfaces from the muddy bottom. A plop, as something jumps out of the water. Ripples from a swirling fishtail. The three women are absolutely still. There is a silent awareness and understanding of their surroundings: the anthills, the turtles, the kites, the crocodiles, the water lilies and the prawns. There is no need for words. They listen to the stillness. Listening as their people have done for tens of thousands of years: to the sound of the land, the water, animals, birds, fishes, reptiles and spirits.

Neither the silence nor the waiting threatens them. Listening to the quiet makes them whole.

They are completely at home.